THE THEOLOGY OF JOSEP

THE THEOLOGY OF JOSEPH RATZINGER

An Introductory Study

by

AIDAN NICHOLS, O.P.

T. & T. CLARK
EDINBURGH

Copyright © T. & T. Clark Ltd, 1988

Typeset by C. R. Barber & Partners (Highlands) Ltd,
Printed and bound in Great Britain
by Billing & Sons Limited, Worcester.

for

T. & T. CLARK LTD,
59 George Street, Edinburgh EH2 2LQ

First printed 1988

British Library Cataloguing in Publication Data

Nichols, Aidan
The theology of Joseph Ratzinger: an
introductory study.
1. Ratzinger, Joseph
I. Title
209'.2'4   BX4705.R34/

ISBN 0-567-29148-0

To the memory of my parents

CONTENTS

FOREWORD

Cardinal Joseph Ratzinger, writing in the preface to a work by a Dominican author, remarks: *c'est le Tout qui est la verité*.[1] 'Truth is *the whole.*' And referring back to Irenaeus of Lyons – the first great theologian in the Church's history – he reminds his readers that theology needs to express unity: the unity of the covenants, the unity of the Creator with the Redeemer, the unity of philosophy and faith.[2] For this reason, theological specialisation, despite its undoubted merits, carries occupational hazards for the wider spiritual and intellectual culture of the Church at large. Moreover, still thinking of the example offered by Irenaeus, he pleads for a recognition of the ecclesial or churchly character of theology, the way in which it should feed on the Church's sources and feel with the Church's mind. The setting of theology in the midst of the Church ought not, he says, to deprive it of its vigour or close off its openness to new styles of thought. Whether that is so in his own case, the reader may be in a position to judge from the material to be found in this book.

This study has a modest purpose: to introduce, with a good deal of both paraphrase and direct citation, the principal writings of a German Catholic theologian who has been additionally entrusted with the presidency of the doctrinal organ of the Roman primacy. His occupation of that post has not lacked its attendant controversies. This book will not enter upon an evaluation of the disciplinary actions of the Congregation for the Doctrine of the Faith under Ratzinger's prefecture. Such a project would necessitate consideration of a

---

[1] J. Ratzinger, 'Préface', in J. H. Nicolas O.P., *Synthèse dogmatique. De la Trinité à la Trinité* (Fribourg 1985), p. 5.
[2] Irenaeus, *Adversus Haereses* IV. 33. 8.

host of factors relevant to governmental prudence in the Church, taking it too far from its subject which is Ratzinger's theology. However, since the cardinal's actions can hardly be separated from his ideas, perusal of these pages may make those who are concerned with such issues better informed.

My own interest in Cardinal Ratzinger's theology arose fortuitously. When, at the suggestion of Father Fergus Kerr, then of Blackfriars, Oxford, I was invited by the Press Officer of the Apostolic Pro-Nuncio to Great Britain, Archbishop Bruno Heim, to present to the media the documents of the Congregation for the Doctrine of the Faith on liberation theology (curiously disjoined into a negative and a positive statement as these were), I naturally began to enquire into the thinking of the Prefect of the Congregation whose seal they bore. This interest was stimulated by the appearance of *Rapporto sulla fede*, Englished as *The Ratzinger Report*.[3] That 'report' made it clear that Ratzinger's criticisms of liberation theology (in some of its forms) belonged with a far wider vision of faith and the Church. On the impressive coherence of that vision, and the confidence with which it is entertained, Professor J. K. S. Reid of the Church of Scotland, a seasoned ecumenist, has lately written more sympathetically – though, of course, from a different confessional standpoint – than many Catholic commentators on the now celebrated little dark-red book which has sold world-wide some hundreds of thousands of copies.[4]

An attempt by the present writer, in the pages of the London *Tablet*, to highlight the positive challenge behind Ratzinger's

---

[3]V. Messori, *A colloquio con il cardinale Joseph Ratzinger. Rapporto sulla fede* (Milan 1985). The book was anticipated in idem., 'A colloquio con il cardinale Joseph Ratzinger: Ecco perché la fede è in crisi', *Jesus* VI. 11 (11 November 1984). The English translation is *The Ratzinger Report* (San Francisco 1985).

[4]J. K. S. Reid, 'The Ratzinger Report', *Scottish Journal of Theology* 40. 1 (1987), pp. 125–133.

negative criticisms of the present state of Church and theology met with a mixed response. Letters to the Editor remained wholly sceptical. Most of the private correspondence I received struck a different note, perhaps summed up in the elderly priest from Shropshire who wrote to share his gratified surprise that the Lord had raised up 'a new Athanasius – and from Germany, of all places!' Such disparity of judgment has its humorous aspect. Yet on a matter of such importance, a dialogue of the deaf is surely dangerous for the Church. I have written this book partly in the hope of broadening the terms of this discussion, partly for my own education, and partly in the belief that the exposition of the thinking of any notable Christian mind will be of some value to someone. For theology, which issues from preaching and returns to it, has no higher task than the edification of the Church. Like St Paul, it wishes that

> your love may abound more and more, with knowledge and all discernment, so that you may approve what is excellent, and may be pure and blameless for the day of Christ, filled with the fruits of righteousness which come through Jesus Christ, to the glory and praise of God.[5]

I must thank Pauline Stuart of Edinburgh for suggesting that I should write this book; and Elisabeth Heister of Freiburg, the Reverend Michael Sharkey of the Roman Congregation for Catholic Education, and the Reverend John Berry of Fisher House, Cambridge, for their help in procuring the materials with which to do so.

My gratitude is also due to my former Christ Church tutor, Dr. P. G. J. Pulzer, now Gladstone Professor of Politics in the University of Oxford, for his bibliographical assistance with the 'Bavarian background', and to my Prior, Father Robert

[5]Philippians 1, 9–11.

Ombres, for taking responsibility for the reading of the proofs during my unavoidable absence in the Levant.

Aidan Nichols, OP,
Blackfriars, Cambridge.
Feast of St Gregory the Great, 1987.

Chapter One

THE BAVARIAN BACKGROUND

Joseph Ratzinger is very much a Bavarian theologian. To begin with, he is of course Bavarian by birth.[1] He was born at Marktl am Inn on 16 April 1927, one of three children of a police commissioner. His home village is situated on the north side of the river Inn, as it flows eastwards towards Braunau on the Austrian border, prior to merging its waters with those of the Danube at Passau. The region is one of wooded hills, small lakes and waterways. A mile to the west, the Alz, a tributary of the Inn, finishes a short journey from the Chiemsee with its royal palace, a miniature replica of Versailles, the work of Wagner's patron, Ludwig II. Upstream, but some few miles to the south of the Inn, lies Altötting, a Marian pilgrimage shrine. In this setting, almost impossibly picture-book as it is, the young Ratzinger became aware of a possible vocation to the Catholic priesthood while still a boy. No doubt this sense was mediated by the fervent piety of the region, evoked by the mature Ratzinger in an essay on the meaning of the feast of Corpus Christi. It opens with a phrase from a eucharistic hymn of St Thomas Aquinas: *Quantum potes, tantum aude*, 'Dare to do as much as you are able'.

> I can still smell those carpets of flowers and the freshness of the birch trees; I can see all the houses decorated, the banners, the singing; I can still hear the village band, which indeed sometimes dared *more*, on this occasion, than it was able! I remember the *joie*

[1] For biographical information, see R. Tura, 'Joseph Ratzinger', in P. Vanzan and H. J. Schultz (eds.), *Lessico dei teologi del secolo XX* (Brescia 1978), pp. 747–9; see also D. O'Grady, 'The Ratzinger Round'. *The Month* CCXXXIV. 1276 (December 1973), pp. 409–412.

de vivre of the local lads, firing their gun salutes – which was their way of welcoming Christ as a head of state, *the* Head of State, the Lord of the world, present on their streets and in their village. On this day people celebrated the perpetual presence of Christ as if it were a state visit in which not even the smallest village was neglected.[2]

However, the guns would shortly be needed for another purpose. In 1943, at the age of sixteen, Ratzinger was called up for military service. He spent the last two years of the war in various military capacities: manning an anti-aircraft battery near Munich where Allied air attack was pulverising much of the historic centre and its inhabitants; as an infantryman on the Hungarian border in the line of fire of the Soviet advance; and, finally, doubtless with relief, in an American prisoner-of-war camp near Ulm.

The *Land Bayern*

An historically oriented account of this Bavarian background seems inescapable, since, were one to single out a defining characteristic of the Bavaria into which Ratzinger was born, one might well select its emphasis on cultural and institutional continuity. When on 19 September 1945 the United States proclaimed a military government in the *Land Bayern*, they were careful to restore Bavaria to its pre-1933 borders. As the leading historian of modern Bavarian political life has written, Bavarians were unique among Germans in the stress they laid upon territorial and institutional (*staatlich*) continuity.[3] And yet Bavaria was by no means as culturally homogeneous as this judgment might suggest. Modern Bavaria is a synthesis of three

[2] J. Ratzinger, *Das Fest des Glaubens* (Einsiedeln 1981); ET *The Feast of Faith. Approaches to a Theology of the Liturgy* (San Francisco 1986), p. 127.
[3] A. Mintzel, *Geschichte der CSU. Ein Überblick* (Opladen 1977), p. 22.

historic traditions: Swabia in the south-west, Old Bavaria (Altbayern) in the centre and south-east, Franconia in the north. The Franconian element contributed a significant strip of territory which was historically Protestant in religion. As always, history is the great illuminator.

Bavaria entered documented history in the sixth century.[4] Ruled as she was from 555 to 788 by a family of Frankish descent, the duchy was nevertheless effectively independent of the feeble Frankish kings. Under the Carolingians, however, the country was in practice absorbed, but in 911, at a time when, owing to Hungarian invasion, Carolingian successor government in the East Frankish kingdom had collapsed, Arnulf of Scheyern was chosen duke of the Bavarians. The duchy enjoyed a continuous existence from that time, though its boundaries were subject to notable fluctuation. In the Ottonian period, the Bavarian duchy was engaged in frequent conflict, or at any rate, tension, with the German crown. With the election of its duke as German king in 1002, it passed into the hands of the House of Luxemburg. A confused period from 1061 to 1180 was ended by the conferment of the duchy on Otto of Wittelsbach, a descendant of the original ducal family, the counts of Scheyern, by the Hohenstaufen emperor Frederick I. This family governed Bavaria until the night of 7–8 November 1918.[5]

The efforts of the Wittelsbach dukes to consolidate their authority were fairly successful in the first few generations of their rule, but the gains in terms of settled government were squandered as a result of partitions of the country among various members of the family. The compensating advantage was that, in a power vacuum, representative institutions, notably the *Landtag* or *Landschaft*, first organised in 1392, and a

[4] A. Kraus, *Geschichte Bayerns. Von den Anfängen bis zur Gegenwart* (Munich 1983), pp. 23–33.
[5] R. Reiser, *Die Wittelsbacher in Bayern* (Regensburg 1978).

strong civic spirit, notably in Munich and Regensburg, grew up. Not till 1505 was Bavaria – defined as the region lying between the Bohemian forest, the Inn, the Alps, and the Lech – re-united under duke Albert IV who, in the following year, decreed that in future the duchy should pass undivided according to the laws of primogeniture. His successor, William IV, was responsible for the firm adhesion of Bavaria to the Catholic Reformation. At first, the reformed doctrines made considerable progress in Bavaria. But the duke, who had been sympathetic to Luther's original protests, objected to doctrinal innovations. While obtaining from the pope powers to reform the morals of the clergy, he staunchly resisted the advance of Protestant teaching. His son, Albert V, a great patron of the arts, and his grandson, William V, a pupil of the Jesuits, continued on the same track. The administrative genius of Maximilian I, who succeeded on William's withdrawal to monastic life in 1579, enabled Bavaria to play an important part in the Thirty Years War, gaining an electoral vote for her ruler which greatly enhanced her place in the German world, while at the same time, as later events proved, encouraging the expansionist ambitions of her rulers.[6]

Bavarian involvement in the wars of both the Spanish and the Austrian Successions was largely dictated by competition with the Hapsburgs. But in 1778, the extinction of the direct Wittelsbach line, and the passing of the electoral dignity to a cadet branch in the person of the Elector Palatine, Charles Theodore, himself childless, gave Austria an opening for the settling of old scores. Hardly more than a decade separated the consequent War of the Bavarian Succession from the overrunning of first the Palatinate and then Bavaria itself by the French revolutionary armies. Forced to choose, the sympathies of the new elector Maximilian IV Joseph, and his minister M. J.

[6]A. Kraus, *Geschichte Bayerns* op. cit. pp. 211–269.

8

von Montgelas, proved to be French rather than Austrian. A treaty of peace and alliance with France, signed in August 1801, was followed by major acquisitions of population in the subsequent territorial re-structuring of Germany in 1803, carried out as this was under French direction. It was at this time that largely Protestant Franconia came under the rule of Maximilian as newly proclaimed first king of Bavaria. The succeeding constitution of 1808 was the result of Napoleon's direct influence, and bears the marks of his swingeing authoritarian rationalisation of State and society. What remained of the mediaeval polity in the form of local diets and corporations was swept away. (Ratzinger will point to this as an illustration of the ambiguity of the history of freedom.) A host of customary privileges and exemptions was replaced by equality before the law, universal liability to taxation, abolition of serfdom, security of person and property, liberty of conscience and of the Press. In 1813, the astute Montgelas, aware that Napoleon's sun was setting, threw in Bavaria's lot with the Allies.[7]

Although at the Congress of Vienna Bavaria agreed with the utmost reluctance to the cession to Austria of her southern gains from the French alliance, especially the Vorarlberg, Tirol and the region around Salzburg, as the nineteenth century proceeded it became clear that her chief enemy must be not Austria but Prussia. At first, her difficulties were internal. The Constitution of 1818, though guaranteeing religious equality, offended against radical sentiment by establishing a bicameral legislature, with the lower house elected on a somewhat narrow franchise. Maximilian I, after a stormy beginning with the more doctrinaire liberals in his Parliament, proved a model constitutional ruler, but the Paris revolution of 1830, with its echoes elsewhere in Europe, frightened his son Ludwig I into a

[7]Ibid. pp. 353–423.

policy of repression, directly chiefly at the Press. His position undermined by an absurd infatuation with the Irish adventuress Lola Montez, the king was unable to deal with the crisis caused by the 1848 Paris revolution, with its grave repercussions throughout the German states, and abdicated in favour of his heir Maximilian II. Though a devout supporter of the movement for pan-German unity, Maximilian opposed the rise of Prussia to outright hegemony within the German confederation, in this obtaining the full support of his Parliaments. The victory of Prussia over the combined forces of Austria and Bavaria at the battle of Königgratz in 1866, combined with the diplomatic moderation of Bismarck in not pressing home Prussia's victory, led to a reversal of this policy under the advisers of the twenty year old Ludwig II. On 24 November 1870, in the wake of the defeat of France in the Franco-Prussian war, a treaty was signed between Bavaria and the North German Confederation. By this instrument, although Bavaria became a constituent part of the new German empire, she retained a larger measure of autonomy than any other of the contracting powers. These *Reservatrechte* included a distinct diplomatic service, as well as military organisation. However, the treaty was consistently opposed by the Patriot party, who were able to draw on reserves of Catholic sympathy. Such dissent grew more bitter during the *Kulturkampf* between the imperial government and the Catholic Church, the effects of which were fully felt in Bavaria with, for example, the expulsion of the Jesuits. Only the support of the king for successive Liberal ministries prevented this opposition from gaining control of the parliamentary process.[8]

In 1886, both Ludwig II and his brother Otto being declared insane, the heir presumptive, Prince Luitpold, became regent of

[8]Ibid. pp. 436–576. For the role of the Church in society, see W. K. Blessing, *Staat und Kirche in der Gesellschaft. Institutionelle Autorität und mentaler Wandel in Bayern während des 19. Jahrhunderts* (Göttingen 1982).

Bavaria. During his regency, which lasted until 1913, Bavaria shared in the general prosperity of the Second Reich. She did not, however, forget her particularism. In late 1913, his son, who had succeeded him as regent a year earlier, was made king as Ludwig III. (His wife also claimed a throne. As the senior member of the d'Este family, dukes of Modena, she was the Legitimist pretender to the Crown of Great Britain and Ireland, under the title Mary IV and III.)[9] On the eve of the Great War, Bavaria's capital was not the worst place in the world to live in. It attracted Vassily Kandinsky from Moscow, Paul Klee from Zürich, Rainer Maria Rilke from Prague. Its tolerance did not extend to frontal attacks on Court or Church, yet in other respects it served as a safety-valve to the pressures of Wilhelmine Germany, being 'the seat of a German counter-government, endowed with a jester's licence instead of power'.[10] However, the death-toll and deprivations inflicted by the War deeply affected popular feeling in its closing months. Inspired by a breakaway group of the *Sozialdemokratische Partei*, the SDP, revolution broke out on the night of 7–8 November, before the fall of the Berlin government itself. The Wittelsbach dynasty, in the person of its septuagenarian, skittle-playing king, was deposed and a Socialist Republic inaugurated under Kurt Eisner. In the spring of the following year, in the chaos occasioned by Eisner's murder, a Bolshevik inspired Soviet Republic, the *Räterepublik*, was declared, but collapsed within a month, not without fierce fighting.[11]

The constitution of 14 August 1919 ratified by a final meeting of the old Bavarian diet, was based on the assumption that

[9]Information provided by Michael Ingram O.P., of Blackfriars, Cambridge.

[10]R. Grunberger, *Red Rising in Bavaria* (London 1973), p. 26.

[11]In fact, *two* short-lived 'Soviet Republics' followed each other in quick succession, ibid. pp. 96–138; H. Beyer, *Die Revolution in Bayern 1918–1919* (Berlin 1982), pp. 47–136.

Bavaria was still a sovereign state, although by the terms of the Weimar Constitution of 11 August, foreign policy and military affairs were now the concern of the central government. The form of the State was prescribed by the Weimar authorities. Its government was to consist of a single chamber, under a minister-president, the deputies being elected by universal suffrage on the basis of proportional representation. The dominant parties in Bavaria itself held from this point on that the Weimar constitution was excessively centralising, and wished to return to the federal constitution of the old empire. Indeed, opposition to Weimar betrayed the monarchically-inclined Bavarian cabinet of 1923 into a temporising leniency over the abortive 'Beer Hall Putsch' of the Austrian demagogue Adolf Hitler and his newly formed NSDAP, the *Nationalsozialistische Deutsche Arbeiterpartei*. It was a mistake that native political organisations would not repeat.[12]

From the middle 1920s to the present day, the public voice of Bavaria has been remarkably unitary. Yet any political organisation that claims to represent the entire Bavarian order is obliged to incorporate within itself a considerable variety of different constituencies. These include the bureaucracy, with its tradition-conscious, federalist, liberal-Conservative stance; the old established *Bürgertum* of the small towns; the farmers, and the industrial craftsmen. Above all, any body purporting to speak for the *Land Bayern* as a whole must reflect the Christian confession of faith.[13] At the time of Ratzinger's birth, during the increasingly enfeebled declining phase of the Weimar Republic, Bavaria was governed by a Catholic party, the BVP or Bavarian People's Party. The leadership which this organisation offered, until the abolition of political parties by

[12]J. Dornberg, *Munich 1923. The story of Hitler's First Grab for Power* (New York 1982).
[13]A. Mintzel, *Geschichte der CSU. Ein Überblick* op. cit. p. 24.

the National Socialist government in 1933, bore a remarkable resemblance to that provided by its post-war successor, the CSU or Christian Social Union. This is all the more surprising given the changes that have transformed Bavaria from the largely rural economy of 1946 to the mainly industrial one of today. However, the challenges which the two parties were called on to face could hardly have been more different.

The secular framework of Ratzinger's growth to adult manhood was formed by Hitler's attempted revolution in German society. Shortly after becoming Chancellor, the *Führer* had remarked that ideological movements, in contrast to 'ordinary parties', see in the achievement of political power only a prerequisite for the fulfilment of their true mission.[14] That mission was the permanent recreation of the experience of 1914.[15] It was

> the moulding of a people in the image of an army – disciplined, fanatically single-minded, obedient to death for a cause.[16]

In Bavaria, the political climate at the time of Hitler's coming to power was fervently anti-Marxist and particularist. This combination of qualities is adequately accounted for by two factors. First, there was the traditional Catholicism of an area where, by an almost exact inversion of the general pattern in Germany, nearly seventy per cent of the population had retained the old religion. Secondly, numerous unhealed scars had been left by the post-1914 history of the country: growth of anti-Prussian resentment; anxiety and alarm in the face of the Revolution of November 1918 which toppled the

[14]Cited in J. Noakes and G. Pridham (ed.), *Documents on Nazism* (London 1974), p. 333.
[15]T. W. Mason, *Sozialpolitik im Dritten Reich* (Opladen 1977), p. 26.
[16]I. Kershaw, *Popular Opinion and Political Dissent in the Third Reich. Bavaria 1933–1945.* (Oxford 1983), p. 2.

constitutional monarchy of the house of Wittelsbach; panic produced by the short-lived Communist *Räterepublik* of 1919. All of this might have seemed to make the Bavarians easy picking for the Nazis, but in fact the BVP resisted the inroads of National Socialism with remarkable success until 1933. Only in the Protestant areas of Franconia was its influence negligible, and there resentment at the control of Bavarian politics by a Catholic party constituted one of the potential strengths of Nazism – along with the very natural appeal of a new political and economic start, as well as the hope for a moral renaissance in a Germany that appeared to many to be sliding into a morass of moral decadence, secularism and atheism.[17]

Although in the Reichstag election of November 1932, all the Catholic constituencies in Bavaria registered a lower vote for the National Socialists than the Reich average, Catholic resistance to Nazi blandishments did not long survive Hitler's acceptance of office as Chancellor on 30 January 1933. By the Reichstag elections of 5 March of the same year, an astonishing swing to National Socialism had taken place. The shift can be ascribed mainly to the votes of the small farmers and petty bourgeoisie, alarmed at the failure of Weimar politics to solve their economic problems. The farms, essentially medium-sized peasant holdings, were weighed down by excessive tax burdens, as well as a labour shortage. But the honeymoon of the Catholic peasantry with the Nazis soon went sour as the National Socialist *Zwangwirtschaft*, 'coercive economy', gained momentum. Soon the struggle with the Church would add massively to their alienation. Among the petty bourgeoisie, support for Hitler derived from the fear of being snuffed out financially by large-scale capitalist enterprise, and the consequent dread of proletarianisation. But, once again, the favour which the Catholic lower middle class bestowed on the

[17]Ibid. p. 26.

Nazis in early 1933 soon drained away. The causes were the hooliganish manifestations of the social-radical element in National Socialism, and – above all – the accusation that the party was anti-Christian.[18]

The common factor in the withering away of public support for the Nazis in Bavaria was, therefore, the *Kirchenkampf*, the 'Church struggle'. National Socialist pressure on the churches was first directed to Protestants, leading to the open conflict which blazed up as early as autumn 1934. Bavaria had first acquired sizeable Protestant districts with the post-Napoleonic re-structuring of Germany in 1815. To these areas, Franconia and the former imperial cities of Augsburg and Nürnberg, there was added in 1920 the former principality of Coburg. Bavarian Protestantism was a highly self-conscious version of Lutheran orthodoxy. As a result, liberal rationalist theology, whose weak hold on doctrine made it a more likely partner for a newly dominant ideology, made few inroads. However, a synthesis of evangelical piety and *völkisch* nationalism was fairly common: a halfway house to the 'German-Christian' movement assiduously fostered by the Nazis.[19] The National Socialist take-over brought swift changes to the organisation of this Bavarian Protestant church. Although a pastor sympathetic to the régime, Hans Meiser, was imposed as presiding bishop and armed with wide executive powers, his conservative Lutheranism enabled him to defend the independence of his community despite the growing party pressure for a centralised Reich Church. Under the Reich bishop Ludwig Müller, the Nazified *Deustche Christen* intensified their efforts in this direction, using the slogan 'the swastika on our breasts, the cross in our hearts', but aiming at the subordination of Evangelical theology to the needs of nationalist ideology. This provoked the

[18]Ibid. p. 115.
[19]Ibid. pp. 157–158.

formation of the 'Pastors' Emergency League' headed by Martin Niemöller and later to become the nucleus of the 'Confessing Church'. The collapse of liberal theology before the advance of Nazi ideology would later be cited by Ratzinger as one of the more instructive lessons provided by the history of his homeland. The enforced deposition of bishop Meiser in 1934 ensured that this controversy would spill over into Bavarian Protestantism. Opposition to the deposition in Franconia reached such a pitch that the government speedily climbed down, an incident which Dr Ian Kershaw describes as

> a spectacular display of what popular protest could achieve even in the restrictive conditions of a repressive police state.[20]

In 1936, an attempt to save Protestant schools, necessarily more diffused in its defensive character, was much less successful. In the wider context of the inroads made into the attachment of youth to the Church, the forced abolition of denominational schools 'transformed attitudes of defiant opposition into despondency and resignation'.[21]

If the experiences of the Protestant church under Hitler would in retrospect profoundly impress Ratzinger, the story of Catholicism in the same period was, naturally, even more formative. Catholic institutions and religious life on the eve of this period have been described as marked by

> an extraordinary degree of inner strength, cohesion, unity, and vitality ... Student organisations flourished as never before, Parents' associations and Mothers' Unions furthered the vital emphasis laid upon Catholic education and youth work. The 'Catholic Press Association for Bavaria' supplied 660 public libraries in Bavaria with over half a million volumes on Catholic

[20]Ibid. p. 174.
[21]Ibid. p. 184.

matters, distributed brochures and pamphlets, laid on films and lectures, and shared in the publication of thirteen daily newspapers. Catholic values were also reinforced through an upsurge of popular missionary activity, much of it carried out by the still expanding religious orders.[22]

The practice of the Catholic religion was, indeed, more consistent in Bavaria than in any other part of Germany.[23] The Concordat signed between the Bavarian Government and the Papacy in 1924 had expressed outright the Christian character of the State – a unique example among the German *Länder* of the period. Of this condition of things the *Bekenntnisschule* or denominational school, as the basic unit of primary education, was the outward and visible sign.

In February 1931 the Catholic bishops of Bavaria sought to clarify the Catholic position on the Nazi movement by issuing joint pastoral instructions to their clergy. They warned against Nazism 'as long and so far as it proclaims politico-cultural views which are irreconcilable with Catholic teaching', forbade priests any involvement with the movement, banned the presence of Nazi banners at the Liturgy, and left the question of the admission of National Socialist party members to the sacraments to the judgment of individual parish priests.[24] But towards the end of March 1933, after the Party had come to power at the level of the Reich government, and in view of Hitler's promises to uphold the rights of the Churches and the

[22]Ibid. pp. 185–186; c.f. M. Spindler (ed.), *Handbuch der bayerischen Geschichte. Band IV, das neue Bayern 1800–1970* (Munich 1974–1975), pp. 933–940.
[23]L. Volk, *Der bayerische Episkopat und der Nationalsozialismus 1930–1934* (Mainz 1965), p. 43.
[24]I. Kershaw, *Popular Opinion and Political Dissent in the Third Reich. Bavaria 1933–1945*, op. cit. p. 190; see also on the Munich archdiocese in the Nazi period the massive essay collection in two volumes: G. Schwaiger (ed.), *Das Erzbistum München und Freising in der Zeit der nationalsozialistischen Herrschaft* (Zürich 1984).

17

continuance of confessional schooling, the bishops modified their stance. Though acts of injustice and violence were to be criticised, the new *Land* government was to be accorded obedience and respect. But the attempt at a *modus vivendi* lasted no longer than the summer of 1933. In the face of violent attacks on Catholic organisations, youth groups and the clergy, and the temporary internment of some two thousand members of the BVP, as well as rapid erosion of confidence in the Reich Concordat with the Holy See signed on 20 July of that year, the bishops returned to their earlier position of hostility. This was memorably symbolised by the Advent sermons delivered by cardinal Faulhaber of Munich in his cathedral towards the end of the year, when, despite repeated attempts at intimidation, he delivered a ringing defence of the Old Testament against Nazi anti-Christians and anti-Semites.[25] This was an event which Ratzinger would later recall in commenting on the comfortless account of the episcopal institution offered by Hans Küng in his *Christ sein*.[26] The sequel was a

> relentless but essentially piecemeal series of attacks on Catholic traditions and customs. On institutions, on the educational structure, and on the Catholic faith as a *Weltanschauung* . . . a war of attrition with a period of high tension between 1935 and 1938 and a final flare-up to dramatic confrontation in 1941.[27]

If the continued existence of Church schools was the burning issue of the years between 1935 and 1938, the unparalleled

[25]M. Faulhaber, *Judentum, Christentum, Germanentum* (Munich 1934).

[26]J. Ratzinger, 'On Hans Küng's *Being a Christian*', *Doctrine and Life* 27. 5 (May 1977), pp. 14–15.

[27]I. Kershaw, *Popular Opinion and Political Dissent in the Third Reich. Bavaria 1933–1945*), op. cit. p. 192. See also the anonymous *The Persecution of the Catholic Church in the Third Reigh, Facts and Documents translated from the German* (London 1940); G. Lewy, *The Catholic Church and Nazi Germany* (London 1964); J. S. Conway, *The Nazi Persecution of the Churches, 1933–1945* (London 1968).

tension of 1941, initiated by Martin Bormann's circular to all *Gauleiter*, insisting that Christianity and National Socialism being incompatible, the Party must struggle to break the power of the Church once and for all, was felt at a variety of conflict-points.[28] Ranging from the enforced closure of monasteries to the removal of crucifixes from schools, its gravest crisis concerned a Nazi attack at the heart of Christian teaching on the sanctity of innocent life: the 'euthanasia action' which accounted for the deaths of more than 70,000 mentally and physically handicapped persons. Its denunciation by bishop Galen of Münster in his sermon of 3 August 1941 was perhaps the German Church's finest hour. Although the opposition which the Catholic Church of Bavaria mounted to the Nazi régime was distinctly limited, it was by no means a collaborating Church. It awaited the downfall of the National Socialist State with impatience, accepted the military defeat of Germany by the Allies with composure, and participated in the post-war reconstruction, under the aegis of the BVP's successor party, the CSU, with enthusiasm. Ratzinger would later speak of the well-nigh religious fervour with which the return to parliamentary democracy was hailed after these years of darkness.

The Academy

Ratzinger is also a Bavarian by intellectual formation. After the war, he entered the seminary of Freising, the ancient ecclesiastical capital of the country. In 1947, he began studies at Munich University, with which he maintained a connexion, either as student or teacher, until 1959. His two first major writings, on, respectively, the African church father Augustine

[28]Ibid. pp. 259–260; 383–386.

of Hippo and the thirteenth century Italian Franciscan
Bonaventure, were produced under the supervision of older
scholars from the theology faculty of this *Ludwig Maximilian
Universität*. It was an institution of mediaeval origin.[29]
Originally founded at Ingolstadt, with a bull of approbation
from Pope Pius II, it had possessed a faculty of theology since its
inception. In the pre-Reformation period, it proved a generous
home to humanist scholarship. One of its professors, Johannes
Turmair, composed a history of Bavaria, the *Annales Boiorum*,
which, on translation into German, became the first important
history in the language.[30] During the Counter-Reformation,
Ingolstadt became the Catholic Wittenberg of southern
Germany, thanks not least to the activities of Johann Maier,
better known from his birthplace as Eck. His *Obelisci*,
'Annotations', a reply to Luther's 1517 theses on indulgences,
although intended merely for the private use of the bishop of
Eichstätt, drew Eck into controversy with Luther and Luther's
disciple Philipp Melanchthon which would endure for the rest
of his life.[31] In 1549 duke William IV of Bavaria introduced
members of the Society of Jesus to the faculties of both theology
and philosophy, notable among them the Dutchman Peter
Canisius and the Spaniard Gregory of Valencia. Jesuit influence
was considerable until the Society's suppression in 1773.[32]

During the latter part of the eighteenth century, a more
rationalist spirit invaded the University. Owing to financial
troubles, it was transferred to a new site at Landshut in 1800, by
order of the elector Joseph Maximilian, later first king of
Bavaria. Two years later it received its modern name, the

[29]For its history, see C. Prantl, *Die Geschichte der Ludwig-Maximilians-Universität in Ingolstadt, Landshut, München* (Munich 1872).
[30]See G. Bauch, *Die Anfänge des Humanismus in Ingolstadt* (Munich 1901).
[31]E. Iserloh, 'Eck, Johannes', *Lexikon für Theologie und Kirche* (cited henceforth as LexThK) (Freiburg im Breisgau 1957–1965) 3, cols. 642–644.
[32]F. Zoepfl, 'Ingolstadt, Universität', ibid. 5, col. 671–672.

'Ludwig Maximilian University'. In 1826 king Ludwig I moved it into the Bavarian capital where, from 1840 onwards, it found a permanent home in a neo-classical edifice by Andreas Gärtner in the Ludwig- and Amalienstrassen.[33] The nineteenth century was a time of renaissance for the University in more than an architectural sense. Munich played its part in the wonderful flowering of Catholic theology in the Germany of the Romantic movement. Ludwig I had himself been a pupil of Johann Michael Sailer who used the fathers, Fénelon and the philosophers of the seventeenth and eighteenth centuries in the literary service of a post-Enlightenment Catholic revival.[34] As professor at Landshut, and subsequently bishop of Regensburg, Sailer turned his philosophical and theological gifts to the practical service of Church life, in an attempt to combat various contemporary ills catalogued by one historian as:

> externalism, contempt for Christian mysticism, worldliness of the clergy, degradation of the pulpit by the treatment of secular topics, relaxation of ecclesiastical discipline, denial of the primacy of papal jurisdiction, efforts of the State to gain control of the Church, turbulent reforms within the Church, and a one-sided training of the mind in education.[35]

He enjoyed excellent relations with orthodox Protestants. Among those Sailer influenced was Franz Xaver von Baader, a lay theologian and social philosopher.[36] Baader continued

[33] M. Huber, *Ludwig I von Bayern und die Ludwig-Maximilians-Universitat* (Würzburg 1939).

[34] R. Adamski, 'Sailer, Michael', LexThK 9, cols. 214–215; and, much more fully, H. Schiel, *Johann Michael Sailer, Leben und Briefe* (Regensburg 1948–1952).

[35] R. Stöltze, 'Sailer, Johann Michael', *Catholic Encyclopaedia* XIII (London 1912), p. 328.

[36] S. J. Tonsor, 'Baader, Franz Xaver von', *New Catholic Encyclopaedia* I. p. 1; D. Baumgardt, *Franz von Baader und die philosophische Romantik* (Heidelberg 1927).

Sailer's ecumenical efforts, advocating a union of Catholics, orthodox Protestants and the Eastern churches. His own thought, Neoplatonic in character, was aimed at a reconciliation of the principles of reason and authority, while his social philosophy, deeply critical of the liberal theory of the State and the economy, laid the foundation for later corporative ideas. Baader's influence was strengthened by that of his academic colleague Johann Joseph von Görres who moved from an initial hostility to religion, and enthusiastic support for the French Revolution to a mystical Catholicism allied with a moderate conservatism in matters political.[37] The centenary of his birth would be marked by the foundation of the Görres Gesellschaft by count Georg von Hertling, professor of philosophy at Munich from 1882 to 1912, and subsequently minister president of Bavaria from 1912 to 1917. A bulwark of scholarly resistance to the Bismarckian *Kulturkampf*, it was suppressed by the Nazis in 1941 but revived after the Second World War.

In the later nineteenth century, the Munich school turned from questions of metaphysics, mysticism and society to historical scholarship. Perhaps the crucial figure in this shift of interest was Johannes Joseph von Döllinger.[38] On obtaining his doctorate from Landshut, a study of the Eucharist in the first three centuries, he was recommended by Sailer for the chair of Church history at Munich which he occupied, with a short intermission, until his removal from the post, following on his excommunication by the archbishop of Munich, in 1872. Collaborating in the *Historisch-politische Blätter* of Baader and Görres, Döllinger used his gigantic historical erudition to argue that Protestantism, liberalism and rationalism entailed

---

[37] L. Just, 'Görres, Johann Joseph', LexThK 4, cols. 1058–1060; G. Bürke, *Vom Mythos zur Mystik. Johann von Görres' mystische Lehre und die romantische Naturphilosophie* (Einsiedeln 1958).

[38] A. Schwarz, 'Döllinger, Johann Joseph Ignaz von', LexThK 3, col. 475; J. Friedrich, *Ignaz von Döllinger* (Munich 1899–1901).

destructive breaks with the historic past. His key-words were 'organic growth' and 'consistent development', while the concept of tradition, not surprisingly, played as vital a part in his work as it did in the more systematic theological constructions of the Catholic Tübingen school, and notably in the thought of Johann Adam Möhler who had himself taught at Munich from 1835 to 1838, the last three years of his life.[39] From the middle of the century, Döllinger's writings began to show a certain anti-Romanism and German nationalism. Rather like the eighteenth century German 'Febronians', he called for effective autonomy from Rome, with a German church under a German metropolitan, the education of future priests in universities, not seminaries, and an end to the interference of Church authority in matters of historical and theological research. An active, not to say intemperate, campaigner against the definition of papal primacy and infallibility at the First Vatican Council, of whose proceedings he wrote under the pseudonym 'Janus', he found himself unable to accept the Council's teaching and was excommunicated. Nevertheless, he did much to encourage Catholics to pursue the scholarly pursuit of history, especially ecclesiastical. The continuance at Munich of his heritage, within Catholic communion, was soon demonstrated in the career of Otto Bardenhewer, a student of the Fathers whose monumental *Geschichte der altkirchlichen Literatur* (1912–1932) is still used by scholars.[40] The primarily patristic interests of Döllinger and Bardenhewer were complemented by the concern with mediaeval theology of the historian of Scholasticism Martin Grabmann, professor of dogma at Munich from 1918 to 1939, and then from 1945 to 1948.[41] Grabmann's highly productive research work led his successor Michael Schmaus, one of

[39]See J. R. Geiselmann, *Lebendiger Glaube aus geheiligter Uberlieferung. J. A. Möhler und die katholische Tübinger Schule* (Mainz 1972).
[40]H. Rahner, 'Bardenhewer, Otto', LexThK 1, col. 1242.
[41]R. Bäumer, 'Grabmann, Martin', LexThK 4, col. 1156.

Ratzinger's teachers, to found the Grabmann-Institut at the University of Munich in 1954 for the study of mediaeval philosophy and theology.

Ratzinger's theological work constitutes a microcosm of the Munich inheritance. His insistence on the context of theology in ecclesial life is reminiscent of Sailer. The interest in metaphysics, mysticism and social philosophy reflects the peculiar combination of concerns of the 'Munich circle' of Baader and Görres. His belief that systematic theology must be nourished at all times by historical theology, not least for the sake of the organic continuity of Church tradition, echoes Döllinger. Detailed investigation of the patristic corpus (chiefly Augustine) continues the efforts of Bardenhewer. Enquiry into the thought of the mediaevals builds on the achievement of Grabmann and Schmaus.

Nor did Ratzinger by any means abandon this richly Catholic Bavarian scene in later life. Although successive academic appointments took him to various parts of Germany: Bonn in 1959, Münster in 1963, Tübingen in 1966, he returned to the Bavarian city of Regensburg, once the see of Sailer, in 1969, to teach dogmatic theology and the history of dogma in the newly founded divinity school there.

The Archdiocese

In March 1977 Ratzinger was made archbishop of Munich and Freising, thus becoming the senior hierarch of the Bavarian church. Once again, he took on a wealth of historical inheritance which could not but have its effect on a mind alert to the cumulative nature of the human enterprise. The archdiocesan see of Munich and Freising is the successor to the bishopric of Freising established by St Boniface in 739.[42]

[42]R. Brandlmeier, 'Munich', *New Catholic Encyclopaedia* 10, pp. 73–74; O. Breiter, *Das kirchliche München* (Munich 1951).

Originally a monastic see, it had a chapter of secular canons by 842. In the Ottonian period of German history, Freising played an important part in the building of a Christian civilisation in the south. In the Hohenstaufen age, Freising was imperialist rather than papalist, and a somewhat uneasy relation with the Wittelsbach dynasty of Bavaria itself was temporarily ended with the accession of the first prince-bishop in the wake of the Thirty Years War. The combination of spiritual and civil roles lasted until 1802. In 1818, following on the conclusion of a concordat between the Holy See and the Bavarian kingdom, a new archdiocese was created, under the title 'Munich and Freising', and incorporating both the ancient see and the short-lived 'court bishopric' of Munich itself (1789–1805). A series of distinguished archbishops were obliged to contend with a sequence of difficult problems, ranging from repairing the spiritual damage after secularisation and the vacancy of the see, under Lothar Anselm von Gebsattel (1821–1846), to resisting State interventionism under Karl August von Reisach (1846–1855); from coping with the Old Catholic schism, which fell to Gregor von Scherr (1856–1877), to maintaining the integrity of the Catholic position in the face of the Kulturkampf, under Antonius von Steichele (1878–1889). Succeeding bishops had a somewhat less tumultuous time, with Antonius von Thoma (1889–1897), Franz Joseph von Stein (1897–1909), and Franziskus von Bettinger (1909–1917) able to devote the lion's share of their attention to pastoral matters, notably in the formation of a Catholic press, Catholic schools and charitable associations. The long-serving cardinal-archbishop Michael von Faulhaber (1917–1952) was confronted with a more egregious evil than any of his predecessors, in the shape of National Socialism. As a priest of the archdiocese Ratzinger himself served under Joseph Wendel (1952–1960), and Julius Döpfner (1960–1976), both of whom received cardinals' hats in acknowledgement of the importance of the see

25

whose various works had grown tremendously since the start of the century.

Ratzinger had inherited, then, a major metropolitan see, over four thousand square miles in area and with a population of more than two million Catholics. A thousand secular priests were assisted by some five hundred of their 'regular' *confrères*, with approximately the same number of male lay-religious in addition to some six thousand religious women. The city of Munich itself, which had only three parishes in 1800, had seen sixty more opening in the course of this century.[43] It had become, in fact, the largest centre for industry and commerce in southern Federal Germany, a hub for the manufacture of cars, locomotives, machine tools, electrical appliances, optical and precision instruments; for printing and publishing; and, not least, for brewing. The round of archiepiscopal administration, and visitations began, but was informed by an unusual sophistication of theological culture which led Ratzinger to enter such controversial areas as: the execution of the liturgical reform; the debate over the foundations of moral theology; the drawing-up of a balance sheet of the virtues and vices of the post-conciliar age.[44] How the theological culture thus deployed had been acquired we shall now consider by looking, in broadly chronological terms, at the making of Ratzinger's thought.[45]

[43]R. Brandlmeier, 'Munich', art. cit. p. 74.

[44]I am indebted for this brief indication of Ratzinger's archiepiscopal tenure to conversation with Mgr Richard Malone of the John Paul II Institute of Christian Anthropology at Boston.

[45]The only general essay on Ratzinger's theology I have encountered is R. Tura, 'La teologia di J. Ratzinger. Saggio introduttivo', *Studia Patavina* 21 (1974), pp. 145–182.

Chapter Two

AUGUSTINE AND THE CHURCH

Ratzinger's earliest intellectual exploration took the form of a study of Augustine, a writer whom he has not ceased to quote. Indeed, it would not be excessive to place Ratzinger in the succession of those philosophers and theologians, or philosopher-theologians, who, in the course of the intellectual history of Europe, have drawn life from the continuing vitality of Augustinian thought. As he himself has put it, writing in 1969:

> Augustine has kept me company for more than twenty years. I have developed my theology in a dialogue with Augustine, though naturally I have tried to conduct this dialogue as a man of today.[1]

The modalities of such a relationship with Augustine are themselves very various. Henry Chadwick suggests at least seven types of Augustinian influence.[2] The theology and philosophy of the mediaeval schoolmen were rooted in Augustinian ideas of the relation between faith and reason. The Western mystics never escaped his influence, notably because of the centrality of the love of God in his thinking. Both the Reformation and the Counter-Reformation appealed to Augustine on a massive scale in their differing attempts to establish the sovereignty of divine grace vis-à-vis human works. Kant returned to Augustine, undermining the optimism of the Enlightenment by insisting that human nature was distorted by radical evil. The Romantics rediscovered the importance of the

---

[1] J. Ratzinger, 'Glaube, Geschichte und Philosophie. Zum Echo auf *Einführung in das Christentum*', *Hochland* 61 (1969), p. 543.
[2] H. Chadwick, *Augustine* (Oxford 1986), pp. 1–2.

feelings, of what Augustine had called the 'heart'. Christian Platonists (and their critics) are indebted to him for his synthesis of Christianity and Neoplatonsim, as for his judicious comments thereon in the *Retractationes*. Finally, Augustine saw with exemplary lucidity that issues of supreme importance are raised by the problem of the relation of words to the reality they attempt to describe.

A survey of the possibilities of Augustine's thought which have attracted later thinkers was also offered by a writer rather closer to Ratzinger, since belonging to the same German-speaking world. The Silesian Jesuit Erich Przywara in his *Augustinus, Die Gestalt als Gefüge* looks at the fate of Augustinianism in the mediaeval, early modern and contemporary worlds. For Przywara, Augustine is the 'concourse' where the two powers whose confluence has determined the European spirit, namely, antiquity and the Gospel, have their meeting. For, in the first place, Augustine conjoins the two 'fundamental motifs' of ancient thought: the movement from what is changing to the Changeless in Parmenides (and Plato), and the syncopated rhythm of finite being in Heraclitus (and Aristotle). These, in the second place, Augustine raises to the level of super-nature, of Christian grace. Once baptised, the unitive Parmenidean-Platonic current becomes the Johannine movement of faith through understanding into vision. Similarly, the dispersive Heraclitean-Aristotelean current becomes the Pauline movement of pastorally motivated love, becoming all things to all men in the midst of the flux of time. And in Augustine these two movements are one. According to Przywara, Augustine's writing is a banquet of fertile antitheses on which European thought has never ceased to feed: from Scotus to Nicholas of Cusa; from Descartes to Hegel; from Baader to Kierkegaard.[3]

[3]E. Przywara, *Augustin. Passions et destins de l'Occident* (Paris 1987), pp. 11–13. A key notion of Przywara's own theology is entering into this

What, then, does Ratzinger draw from this richness by way of a theological offering of his own? Believing with Romano Guardini that the twentieth century was proving, theologically, the 'century of the Church', when the idea of the Church was re-awakening in all its breadth and depth, Ratzinger chose to scour the Augustinian corpus for insight into the nature of the Christian community of faith. Conceived as one of a series of soundings in New Testament and patristic ecclesiology master-minded by Ratzinger's teacher Gottlieb Söhngen, he would investigate two inter-related themes of Augustine's ecclesiology.[4] For Augustine, the Church is at once the 'people and the house of God'.

In a revealing preface, Ratzinger indicates just what he thinks the value of historical theology to be. In what it had newly become fashionable to call a 'hermeneutical circle', systematic understanding of the Christian faith generates questions to be put to the theology of the past. The answers which ancient texts offer back then broaden the systematic theologian's field of vision. Looking at Augustine's ecclesiology from the Munich of 1951, Ratzinger acknowledged two giants among his German predecessors. The first was Hermann Reuter whose collected essays, *Augustinische Studien*, are a fund of sparkling insight and hypothesis, though written as long ago as 1883, at the highpoint of Wilhelmine Germany.[5] The second was Fritz Hofmann, whose magisterial study of Augustine's concept of the Church was produced in the year of Hitler's coming to power, mandated to lead a *Volk* whose definition brought him, as we have seen, into open conflict with the inherently multi-ethnic

---

analysis: see his *Polarity. A German Catholic's Interpretation of Religion* (London 1935).

[4] J. Ratzinger, *Volk und Haus Gottes in Augustine Lehre von der Kirche* (Munich 1954), p. vii. Cited below as VHG.

[5] H. Reuter, *Augustinische Studien* (Gotha 1887²).

Volk of the *populus Dei*.[6] Since Hofmann was as Bavarian and Catholic as Reuter was Prussian and Protestant, these two authors between them spanned the spectrum of German scholarship on their subject.

It follows from Ratzinger's preface that he received the theme of the 'people and house of God' from contemporary ecclesiology, and proposed to enquire what, if anything, might correspond to it in the work of the bishop of Hippo. If this seems to the mind of Anglo-Saxon patristic scholarship a somewhat curious procedure, Ratzinger reports that the effort has proved very worthwhile. The theme turns out to bind together a number of vital issues for the patristic West: the status of the Old Testament in relation to the New; the relation of law to sacrament; the attitude of Christians to the pagan State, and to paganism at large. At the same time, the enquiry helps to locate Augustine in terms of the history of religion in his age. His wrestling with philosophical questions was complemented by the sense of the Church, *Kirchlichkeit*, which he found in the North African Catholicism of his day. In the resultant controversies with pagan 'theologians', Augustine gained new insight into the Church's nature, over and above that available to his predecessors. Fundamentally, Ratzinger sees Augustine's concept of the Church as dependent upon a double *a priori* or set of presuppositions. On the one hand, these stem from his own philosophy; on the other, from the theology of Roman North Africa. Yet even more important than the question of whence Augustine took his ecclesiology is that of what he did with it. Basically, he set it to use in two ways: dogmatically, vis-à-vis the Catholic sect of the Donatists, and apologetically, vis-à-vis the last autonomous representatives of pagan culture in the Roman West.

[6]F. Hofmann, *Der Kirchenbegriff des hl. Augustines in seinen Grundlagen und seiner Entwicklung* (Munich 1933).

The early Augustine

Ratzinger's analysis of the idea of the Church in Augustine's *early writings* is nuanced and complex. He points out that the debate as to whether Augustine's 386 conversion to the Gospel was simply a conversion to 'spirituality' or to the historic Christian faith is essentially a discussion of his concept of the Church. Did he at this point genuinely embrace the earthly Church 'with all its so often painful littleness of humanity' which hides away so deeply 'the precious treasure of God's glory'?[7] The question of Augustine's experience of the Church at the time of his conversion is no other than a question about the meaning and content of the conversion itself. Was it acceptance of the concrete Christian Church community, or merely a change in philosophical standpoint? From the surface of the text of the *Confessions* Augustine's way seems to have been a road between God and his soul 'and no further'.

In one sense, Augustine's conversion *was* the attaining of a complete, and completely pure, philosophy: a vision of the truth of eternal Being, conferring wisdom and blessedness, the *patria pacis* glimpsed already with the aid of the Neo-platonist philosophers. Yet the relation of philosophy to religion in the ancient world differed *toto caelo* from that with which we are familiar. The ultimate *archē* of things sought by the philosopher was precisely that which is worthy of religious adoration in a human community. This pervasive assumption of the classical world shaped the expectations of Neoplatonists. The purgation of mind they sought was to lead to the depths of the Divinity itself. By analogy with this royal way of the philosophical few, they also recognised a 'purgation of spirit' with which the mass of men must content themselves on the 'universal way' offered by religious cultus, a kind of *Ersatzform der Philosophie*.[8] Thus a

[7]VHG, pp. 1–2.
[8]Ibid. p. 8.

philosophical conversion in the ancient world at least opened a door to religion.

But there was more than this. Augustine was deeply impressed by the Christian claim to be at once *via regia*, the 'royal highway', the unconditionally best, and *salus populi*, 'popular salvation', the universally accessible. The Church proposed to mediate to the many what was to the philosophically-minded a completeness of salvation attainable only by the few. Augustine's acceptance of this way of the common life of the Church, a way of faith, rather than the way of the individual's metaphysical search, a way of insight, was made possible by his realisation how many truths of human living come from 'faith': most notably, through our parents. 'A mother's authority brought him a deeper understanding of authority in the realm of Wisdom'.[9] Man is an immature child, not yet able to stand on his own feet in matters of the spirit. Ratzinger places great weight on a text of the *Confessions* where Augustine laments that a momentary vision of God which once came to him could not be sustained or re-created in memory, owing to human 'infirmity'.[10] Because of such weakness some means of help beyond the self must be sought. 'He snatches up the Bible again – and understands it anew'.[11] Since he cannot bear the divine 'food' in its pure form, the divine Word has mingled itself with flesh so that man may be able to enjoy it. In the Church, the divine humility has provided a medicine by its own example for the sickness from which none is immune.

None the less, the culture which Augustine brought to the exploration of the Christian faith in his early writings was largely philosophical, and so it is, naturally, from a philosophical perspective that Augustine first considered the mystery of the Church. Here Ratzinger identifies two main

[9]Ibid.
[10]*Confessiones* VII. 10, 16.
[11]VHG p. 9.

elements that form the *Ansätze*, 'starting-points' of Augustinian ecclesiology. Augustine's reflections on the concept of faith will be vital for his understanding of the Church as *people* of God. By contrast, his concept of love is more important for his portrait of the Church as the *house* of God: the other wing of the diptych which the title of Ratzinger's thesis evokes.[12] It is not difficult to see how the young Augustine, desirous of finding truth both for himself and for others, and struggling with the notions of scepticism and authority, could light upon an idea of faith which included an essential reference to the *Catholica*: the 'universal' Church, the people of God. This Church is the place where God gives us the Invisible to feed upon in visible form, thus leading us ever more towards the Invisible until we are become adults in his presence. Because of man's wounding through sin, the Church now becomes a necessary stage in the ascent of the soul to Wisdom. *All* must pass through the triad of *credere, auctoritas, humilitas,* 'have faith, accept authority, practise humility', if they are to see the divine Wisdom in its beauty.[13]

More difficult to grasp is the relation Ratzinger claims to find between Augustine's notion of love and the theme of the Church as God's house. Ratzinger frankly admits that the phrase 'house of God' does not, in fact, occur in the early works. But what does occur, and recur, is discussion of prayer and sacrifice with their 'intimate relation to the realm of the Church as the locus of their realisation'.[14] As the *De magistro* makes clear, the temple of the spiritual God must be man's interiority.[15] But here faith, Church and sacraments are conspicuous by their absence. What gives grounds for hope that

---

[12] See also on this, J. Ratzinger, 'Der Weg der religiösen Erkenntnis nach dem heiligen Augustinus', in P. Granfield – J. A. Jungmann (eds.), *Kyriakon II. Festschrift J. Quasten* (Münster 1970), pp. 553–564.

[13] VHG p. 10.

[14] Ibid. p. 36.

[15] *De magistro* 1, 2.

this grievous omission might be rectified in the future, in a fuller, and genuinely ecclesial notion of God's 'temple', is the importance to Augustine of the ideas of love, *dilectio*, and unity, *unitas*. The divine discipline sets before us the *regula disciplinae* of the command to love our neighbour; as for unity, the Platonist conviction that all things that are must possess a form of unity was, at any rate, *entwicklungsfähig*, 'capable of development' in the direction of a doctrine of the Church when it came into contact with the North African Christian tradition.[16] That tradition Augustine would come to know with ever greater experiential fulness after his ordination, in 391, to the presbyterate of the Catholic Church.

Notable throughout this discussion is Ratzinger's own nuanced attitude to Christian Platonism. He rejoices to see Augustine move closer to the salvation-historical sensibility of the Scriptures; yet he does not regret the continuing role of Platonist themes in Augustine's work. Thus, for instance, when speaking of Augustine's Neoplatonist belief that this world is a 'reflection', *Abstrahlung*, of a more real and truly intelligible world beyond our own, Ratzinger counsels his readers not to assume too readily that this thought is incompatible with the Gospel.[17] There is a Christian dualism: that of the created and the Uncreated. What is lacking to the early Augustine is a full grasp of the intimate involvement of the Uncreated with the created in the history of salvation.

Augustine's intellectual journey will lead him increasingly from a purely metaphysical theology to a more historical understanding of Christianity, from a purely pegagogical account of the value of the historical order to a realisation of the intrinsic meaningfulness of concrete form in history. And the concrete historical form of the Christian reality is – the Church.

[16]VHG p. 43.
[17]Ibid. p. 16.

But as yet for the young Augustine:

> The historical saving activity of God and its living presence in
> the Church ... belong entirely within the provisional and
> transient sphere of *mundus hic*.[18]

Only later will Augustine see the divine world, no longer as the
world of the eternal *Urgestalten*, the primordial and timeless
Forms, but as the holy community of God's angels, a part of
which is journeying on its earthly pilgrimage, awaiting the
reunion of the entire household of God. Gradually, Augustine
will re-locate the Church, the travelling People of God, at the
very heart of the *mundus intelligibilis*, the 'intelligible world', of
ultimate reality. This shift in Augustine's thinking about the
microcosm is paralleled, as Ratzinger explains, in a similar
development in his understanding of the macrocosm, man. The
'fleshly' is no longer the sensuous, but that which lives *secundum
se ipsum*, ccording to itself, serving its own purposes, while the
'spiritual' is not just the intelligible or ideal, but whoever lives
secundum Deum, according to God, and his will. The more that,
in these ways, Augustine transposes the Neoplatonic doctrine of
the two worlds into the strictly *historical* terms of acceptance or
rejection of God's design for his creation (grace or sin?), the
closer he moves to the properly biblical understanding of
reality. While Ratzinger affirms this quite explicitly, he does
not under-estimate the claims of Platonism as a philosophical
partner to Christian revelation. Turning to the Platonic corpus
for assistance will recur in his own evolution.

Learning from Africa

The journey of thought from Neoplatonism to biblical faith in
its fulness would not have been possible for Augustine, or so

---

[18]Ibid. p. 18.

Ratzinger implies, without the stimulus he received from the great masters of North African ecclesiology; Tertullian, Cyprian and Optatus of Milevis.

> Entry into the public life of the Church signified simultaneously coming into contact with a definite ecclesial tradition, with an objective spirituality, which gave fellow-Christians a distinctive stamp as well as specifying a given direction for the understanding of Scripture.[19]

Ratzinger does not attempt to show, however, any 'literary-historical' or 'source-critical' dependence of Augustine on the North African writers. The question is, rather, one of tracing the outlines of the spiritual world which Augustine entered on his return to Africa as a Catholic Christian.

In *Tertullian* he would have found an ecclesiology hammered out in debate with Gnosticism. It is the whole man, body and soul, who puts on Christ. This baptismal clothing, a fundamental image already found in Paul, is closely associated by Tertullian with the Church's visible order or 'discipline'. *Disciplina* includes *sacramenta*, since it means not just the ethical or canon-legal aspect of the Church's life, as distinct from her sacraments and worship, but her entire pattern of life as a community carrying the grace of Christ and the power of the Spirit.

> The Lord's grace is not communicated as an idea, as *gnōsis*, or as the outcome of a cultic happening in some individualistic *thiasos* unconcerned with the personal lives of its cult-brethren. It comes to us in the concrete order of a holy community, a community that understands itself as the legal order of a common life, though 'law' is here of a holy and pneumatic kind. The inner content of this 'law' is the 'sacraments' and their Spirit-given life-forming power. If Greek theology answered

---

[19]Ibid. p. 44.

the Gnostics by opposing a Christian *gnōsis* to their heretical variety, the response of the West to the same challenge was, most profoundly, the historical form of the Church.[20]

And Ratzinger points out how apt a corrective of the early Augustine's *Deus et anima – nihil aliud, nihil* this Tertullianic vision of the historical and ecclesial nature of Christian salvation offered. Moreover, he suggests, it was 'no great distance' from Tertullian's notion of the Church as *disciplina*, in the sense outlined above, to the mature Augustine's preferred ecclesiological image of the 'People of God'.

Augustine could also have found in Tertullian a pregnant use of the metaphor of the 'House of God'. The human body is, for Tertullian, a house which becomes through baptism the temple of the Holy Spirit. But he also speaks of the desecrator of God's temple, the post-baptismal sinner, as shut out from that other corporate temple of God which is the Church. In this picture of the individual Christian who is a microcosmic image of the whole Church, *die Gesamtkirche*, we find a notion which Augustine will take further. Lastly, Tertullian charges the image of the divine temple with a third valency, this time of a cosmic nature. The world too is God's house, though it will one day fall to be replaced by a new dwelling-place in heaven.

Ratzinger finds other Tertullianic motifs which will recur in Augustine's mature doctrine of the Church, notably in the way that the lay apologist compares and contrasts the Church community with those of the Old Testament, of the pagans, and of the time of the End. But it may suffice to mention one final theme, highlighted by Ratzinger, which will take on increasing importance, not just in Augustine's ecclesiology but in that of his twentieth century Bavarian disciple. And that is the union in the Church of 'inner' and 'outer', holiness and visible – even governmental – structure, the key to which union is the

[20]Ibid. p. 56. Nb. A *thiasis* was a group of people dedicated to a particular god.

Eucharist. For Tertullian had not neglected the central importance of the Holy Eucharist in the 'community of discipline' which he described. The Christian is the *communicator*, conjoined with Christ in the unity of the body of Christ, itself at once the Church and the eucharistic sacrament. Hence the importance in Tertullian's eyes of excommunication and penance, safeguarding as these do the holy order of the *pax ecclesiae*, the 'Church's peace'. It was, Ratzinger suggests, because Tertullian took the visible Church with such seriousness that his sense of the Church's vocation to be the community of the holy became so acute. In itself, this was nothing but gain: it was the *manner* in which Tertullian related the visible Church to the holy Church which spawned his Montanism. The Church is not only founded by the Son; it is also animated by the Holy Spirit. But these two divine economies could, alas, be treated as parallel rather than as mutually entailing, just as, in his doctrine of the sacraments, Tertullian is inclined to find two parallel realities – a water baptism, continuing the baptism of repentance of John, alongside the sacrament of faith which restores the divine likeness in the Spirit, or a two-fold Eucharist where the Bread of Christ's body, the creative agent of the Church, is less important than the inner, life-giving power of Christ's Spirit. We shall later find the mature Ratzinger seizing on an ecclesiology of communion as the best way to avoid all dualism of the kind which eventually led Tertullian to contrast the 'Church of the Spirit', *ecclesia spiritus*, the charismatic community, with the 'episcopal Church', *ecclesia numerus episcoporum*, the community of the sacraments and the everyday Christian life.

If *Cyprian* is a less theologically creative figure than Tertullian, his somewhat restricted handling of beliefs and values gives us, by way of compensation, a more faithful picture of what the African Christian of the third century had grasped of the Gospel. What governs Cyprian's picture of the Church is the simple and fundamental structure of the *ordines*, the threefold ordained ministry of bishop, presbyter and deacon (assisted by other ministers), and the *plebs*, the layfolk, who are truly God's people only insofar as they are united with the bishop, the head of the *ordo*, who incorporates the Church in himself. Cyprian draws out the significance of this bipartite unity in two 'conceptual images': *mater ecclesia*, associated especially with the bishop's baptism, and *fraternitas christianorum*, related more particularly to the Eucharistic assembly of all believers. Whereas Tertullian's chief foe, in his Catholic period, was Gnosis, the enemy which Cyprian found himself obliged to confront was splinter-groups. His great preoccupation is the unity of the Church. This he expressed in two chief ways, so Ratzinger reports: the *house* of the Lord and the *body* of Christ. If the former is evoked by way of a rich variety of biblical illustration, the latter is understood in a fashion more sociological than eucharistic, so that Ratzinger terms it, by contrast with the earlier tradition, *der neue Leibbegriff*. As Ratzinger sees it, Cyprian bequeathed a somewhat ambiguous legacy: though the Carthaginian bishop preserved the nucleus of a eucharistic ecclesiology, in which the Church finds her unity in the sacramental body of the Redeemer, he also initiated, by his more secular and sociological use of the term 'body', that train of thought which would lead to the non-eucharistic, corporatist ecclesiology of the later Middle Ages. Similarly, whilst he finds the fulfilment of Melchisedek's blessing of Abraham in the Sacrifice of Christ, wherein the pagans are blessed and come to be a new spiritual people, the Church, Cyprian also speaks of the 'people' in contra-distinction to the clergy, something Ratzinger evidently considers a deviant and misleading use of the term. This will be a point of some substance in the post-conciliar era.

Ratzinger's last ecclesiological master in the African trio of Augustine's predecessors is *Optatus* of Milevis, a lesser known figure but who, importantly, anticipated Augustine in combatting the schism of the Donatists. In this grave situation, where the Catholic Church faced an episcopally ordered *pars Donatista* whose devout followers where no less numerous than her own, the Cyprianic prescription for curing lay or, at worst, presbyteral schism – 'Where the bishop is, there is the Church' – was wholly impotent. A new criterion had to be found. Optatus met this need in part by stressing the importance of communion with the *cathedra Petri* at Rome. The Donatists were sufficiently impressed by the argument to institute a Roman bishop of their own whose status as an interloper however, might easily be ascertained from the local succession-lists. In this they had, in point of fact, failed to grasp the significance of Optatus' move. Whoever communicates with Rome, communicates with the world. But no-one can communicate with the world, no matter how he strive to set up his own ecclesiastical representative at the tombs of the apostles, if he reduce the Church of Jesus Christ to the 'little plot of African land in which he lives'. For Optatus:

> The true Church is the world-Church, and the Church of the peoples.[21]

The Donatists, in insisting that they possessed the bridal gift of baptism, had forgotten the bride herself, the living body of their Mother.

Although, for Optatus, *fraternitas*, Christian 'brotherhood', extends beyond the visible boundaries of the Church's unity to embrace all those who have undergone the re-birth of baptism, there is a dividing-wall between *communio nostra* and *communio vestra*. The peace and unity of the Church lie now only with those linked by the Catholic Eucharist: were it not so, Christ's sacramental mediation of the divine unity would be only a piece

---

[21]Ibid. p. 106.

of cult. When Optatus reproaches the Donatists with their lack of love, he means their lack of participation in the sacramental brotherhood of the Church. Ratzinger will himself develop further the implications of the notion of Christian brotherhood in his own book of that name.

The mature Augustine

So far as Augustine himself is concerned, Ratzinger deals with those of his *later writings* that are relevant to the concept of the Church in two stages. The materials which Augustine had quarried in both ancient philosophy and the North African Christian tradition he would put to use in two contexts: first, the conflict with the Donatists; secondly, the debate with the representatives of the dying pagan civilisation, carried forward in, above all, the *De civitate Dei*. Like every great theology, remarks Ratzinger briskly, Augustine's grew out of 'polemic against error', adding, in more philosophical temper, that here as elsewhere *without* error 'movement of a living, spiritual kind is hardly thinkable'.[22]

Fundamentally, as Nicholas Wiseman was to remind the still Anglican John Henry Newman to such devastating effect in the pages of the *Dublin Review*, Augustine's defence of the Catholic Church against the Donatists consisted in the claim that the true Church must be *ecclesia omnium gentium*, the 'Church of all nations'. Such 'extensive catholicity' is not simply a mere *Tatsachenwahrheit*, a 'truth of fact'. Through the truth of fact, a *Wesenswahrheit* or truth about the *essence* of the Church is given. For only such a Church can be the fulfilment of scriptural prophecy. In support of this revived, and deepened, version of Optatus' apologetic, Augustine built up a whole armoury of

[22]Ibid. p. 124.

texts: the Church of Christ must be, as the book of Daniel had prophesied, a stone that becomes a mountain and thus fills the whole earth.[23] Especially dear to Augustine in this connexion were the words of the risen Christ at the Ascension in St Luke's gospel, with their own dominical – and thus certainly veridical – interpretation of the Old Testament to this effect.

> Thus it is written, that the Christ should suffer and on the third day rise from the dead, and that repentance and forgiveness of sins should be preached in his name to all nations, beginning from Jerusalem.[24]

Also prominent in the anti-Donatist addresses is the Genesis promise to Abraham that 'by your descendants shall all the nations of the earth bless themselves', taken in conjunction with St Paul's assurance that this promise to Abraham's offspring refers to Christ. As Ratzinger sums up Augustine's exegesis of these passages:

> The multitude of nations who live within the earth's girdle now stands forth as the single people of Abraham, brought together out of their mutually separating multiplicity and bound together in an inner unity through the Seed of Abraham, Jesus Christ.[25]

It is in this light, Ratzinger suggests, that we may progress to an understanding of why, for Augustine, the one thing needful which the Donatists lack is *caritas*. Augustine's 'charity' is, in the ecclesiological context, what Ratzinger helpfully terms 'objective charity'. It does not betoken a subjective attitude, but rather belonging to the Church, and more specifically to that

[23]Daniel 2:35.
[24]Luke 24:46–47.
[25]VHG. pp. 133–134.

Church which itself lives in charity, that is, 'in eucharistic love-relationship with (other Christians in) the whole world'.[26]

This, however, is not all that Augustine means by *caritas*, and to fill in the picture here is to see why Augustine's concept of the Church must be called 'dialectical', characterised by internal tensions that can never be entirely smoothed out. The Church is Christ's Bride only as the (universal) People of God: like Hosea's wife, this spouse may be unfaithful, but she is still his only partner. Anyone who belongs to her enjoys an external and visible participation in *caritas*. But this will not suffice for salvation. The inner meaning of charity is grace and the Holy Spirit. Sinners are, in this connexion, ultimately one with schismatics. The 'holy Church', *ecclesia sancta* is found within the Catholic Church, *ecclesia catholica*, but the two are not identical. The latter is a *corpus permixtum*, a 'mixed body, tares and wheat growing together until the Kingdom, and at times is so much the 'Church of sinners' that one might wonder, Augustine bleakly observes, whether there is a just man left in her at all. On the one hand, Ratzinger points out:

> Augustine can say: The Catholic Church is the true Church of the holy. Sinners are not really in her, for their membership is only a seeming reality, like that of the *mundus sensibilis*. But on the other hand, he can stress that it is no part of the Church's business to discharge such sinners, just as it is not her affair to cast off this body of flesh. It is the Lord's task, who will awaken her (at the End) and give her the true form of her holiness.[27]

Hence the 'twilight' in which the key terms of Augustine's ecclesiology dwell, half-concealed from the later student, and a fertile source of misunderstanding to him.

Yet already the shift from the early to the mature Augustine

[26]Ibid. p. 138.
[27]Ibid. p. 146.

in this domain is clear. It is a change in emphasis – no more, but certainly no less – from the truth of God to the love of God. *Caritas* now appears as the 'power of God's inner unity of essence, become person in the Holy Spirit'. This unity is mirrored in that of the Church where through the unifying force of love, which the Holy Spirit, *vinculum amoris*, personally is, the many believers are ushered into the unity of the body of Christ. Whereas earlier, salvation was measured by intellectual insight, it now consists in that being in the Church which is simultaneously a being-in-love. The Church is now re-situated within the *mundus intelligibilis* hitherto reserved for non-sensuous realities. She has a 'revelation-character', being the 'factual appearing of the Invisible in this world'.[28] Ratzinger points out that, whereas in the Greek East, theology circled around the concepts of God, his Logos and his Spirit, with the Church tacitly omitted from an account of the inner reality of salvation, Augustine makes the Church 'an inner-dogmatic affair'. In Augustine's eyes, Donatism is not primarily a heresy because it includes a doctrinal departure from the teaching of the Great Church on the issue of re-baptism – as it was for, say, the Theodosian Code. It is heresy because it is *schisma inveteratum*: 'hard-necked persistence in separation from the Church's community', and as such, the very kernel of heresy.

How, then, does Ratzinger sum up Augustine's teaching on the Church as 'People and House of God' at the close of his anti-Donatist period? He finds that Augustine uses the term 'People of God' on three levels. In one usage, it refers to Israel, which was a *populus* in the common or garden sense of the word, yet also had the special vocation to act as a sign of the coming 'true' People of God, the spiritual Church. And this is Augustine's second usage, on whose image-character Ratzinger dilates:

The language of images is admittedly the only means of access

[28]Ibid. p. 153.

44

here to the authentic reality. But then again, that whole reality is only to be grasped *in via* by images and analogies.[29]

But, thirdly, Augustine also, though in a fashion as yet not fully clear, ascribes to the empirical Catholic Church that title which fully befits only her heavenly and eschatological counterpart.

On 'House of God', Ratzinger points out that the architecture and mosaic art of church-buildings in the North Africa of Augustine's age was itself a rich invitation to theological reflection. Indeed, one mosaic portrays a basilica with the enlightening inscription, *Ecclesia mater*. 'The church-building is here the visible form of Mother Church.' Yet the Augustinian equivalent to the reality of the pagan temples is not the basilica or martyr's memorial but 'we ourselves': *ecclesia dicit locus, quo ecclesia congregatur*. The stone and mosaics are an image of the true house, the living stones of God's people. In them, God's Holy Spirit has taken up his dwelling, just as did the divine Name in the temple of Zion of old. Or again, in Augustine's exegesis of Matthew 16, 18, the Christ whom Peter's faith accepts becomes the *petra*, the foundation stone of the community of Peter's co-believers. But, as Augustine's painful and protracted struggle with the *pars Donatista* made clear, this faith must be united with 'charity', for without universal communion in the Lord's body his house cannot be constructed.[30]

Finally, Ratzinger turns to Augustine's debate with the last representatives of pagan culture. Reflected in the sermons, the *Tractatus in Joannem* and the *Enarrationes in psalmos* as this is, it achieved its fullest form in the *De civitate Dei*, Augustine's apology for the Church *contra paganos*. When historians of theology speak of the Fathers as standing at the inter-section of antique and biblical thought they generally have in mind the

[29]Ibid. p. 167–168; cf. pp. 175–177.
[30]Ibid. p. 170.

Christian reception of Hellenistic philosophy. But Ratzinger points out that this is to give undue weight to the Greek genius over against the Roman. Roman concern with the State and its law has its own irreplaceable value for the life of the mind. Its encounter with the Church's Latin-speaking apologists made of it an 'inner factor in Christian theology' whose significance, Ratzinger complains, has scarcely as yet been noted.[31] Implicitly, he is claiming that the historical theologian, and notably the student of the Latin fathers, is well equipped to enter into debate about the relationship between Church and State, politics and the Gospel. In due course, Ratzinger will make his own contributions in this area, in the form of a theology of political ethics.

His account of the gestation of the *De civitate Dei* shows a masterly grasp of the inter-relation of Augustine's themes. When in 410 *Roma aeterna* fell into the hands of Alaric and his Goths, traumatised pagan sensibility reacted by calling for the restoration of the taditional sacrificial cultus as necessary to the welfare, the *beatitudo*, of the State. Augustine's reply was that human beatitude consists, rather, in loving union with the one God. Love, *amor* is that power of movement by which man is propelled towards blessedness; yet blessedness is only possible through self-surrender to God. In this way Augustine is able to

> oppose to the ancient Roman city of the gods and their cultus the City of God now revealed in the Church as the site of lawful and saving worship. The fundamental constitution which forms it from within is love.[32]

Moreover, the principal meaning of sacrificial worship, according to Augustine, is human life itself, as lived according to God. But in the pagan State, men do not act 'in the form of

[31]Ibid. p. 187.
[32]Ibid. pp. 190–191.

God'; their worship, therefore, can only be demonic. Through sin, man's point of spiritual contact with God has ceased to govern his being and behaviour. His relationship with God has been destroyed. Hence his need for a Mediator, who will share mortality with us, but blessedness with God, and out of his own *misericordia*, 'mercy', will assume our *miseria*, 'wretchedness', to withdraw us from subjection to demons and replace us in relationship to God.[33] In the mediatorial act, performed by the Incarnate Son in the Atonement, Christ as man gladly became the sacrifice that we should have offered, but could not, even though as God he had more properly received it than made it.

It is this sacrifice of the Mediator, which is to be, in the *polis* that no human being lives outside, the true worship, the cultus of the City of God. But how does the sacrifice of the Mediator become also the sacrifice of those whose humanity he has assumed, whose first-fruits he has become, whose voice he has made his own as the Head of the body, the Church? Ratzinger shows how, in attempting to answer this question, Augustine continued a line of Christian thought which moves from the Apologists and Irenaeus, through the anti-Arian writings of Athanasius, to Hilary and Chrysostom. We are united with Christ by faith whereby his Spirit dwells in us; yet the Spirit of Christ is not other than the grace of Christ, the *caritas* which is spread abroad in our hearts by the Holy Spirit; in referring to such *caritas* we overstep the boundaries of the individual to enter the realm of the community, the Church which is Christ's body.[34] And while that ecclesial *corpus Christi* is not directly accessible to us, it may be found in its 'holy sign', its sacrament, the *Eucharist*.

Here Ratzinger alights on what will be the central motif of his own ecclesiology: for he is, along with Henri de Lubac, one

[33]Ibid. p. 173.
[34]Ibid. pp. 209–210.

of the first Catholic thinkers to adopt a full–scale, systematically elaborated, 'eucharistic ecclesiology'. In the sacrament of the true sacrifice of Christians, lies the inner *Leib-Christi-Sein* of the holy, their existence as the body of Christ. And deepest, and most inwardly of all, then, lies the *caritas* which *is* the Spirit of Christ. Yet, as Ratzinger points out, here the most interior is also the most exterior, the most mystical the most ordinary. For charity is

> the unity of the Church; and more, it is the real, sober, working love of the Christian heart. And that means that every act of genuine Christian love, every work of mercy is in a real and authentic sense sacrifice, a celebration of the one and only *sacrificium christianorum*.[35]

There can be no moral or personal effort sundered from the cultic, the liturgical – and vice versa – for in the Eucharistic fellowship the two are one.

The contrast of the two cities, the connecting thread which runs through the *De civitate Dei*. serves only to enhance the centrality of charity as the heart of Church and Eucharist alike. The civil theology of Varro which Augustine set himself to counter contained an unwitting parody of such charity. For if a people be, as Augustine's definition proposed:

> the association of a multitude of rational beings united by a common agreement on the objects of their love[36]

then such aspects of civil religion as Roman belief in the divinity of Romulus sprang from an 'error of love': it was because she loved Romulus that Rome believed him to be a god. But the true God, conversely, must precede the *civitas*: love can be

[35] Ibid. p. 213.
[36] *De Civitate Dei* XIX. 24.

humanity's unifying force only if men recognise God as the *summum bonum* of all the world.[37] Admitting that his exegesis of Book XXII of Augustine's apologia goes beyond the text to seek its 'inner-theological principles', Ratzinger suggests that in this distinction the love which is 'responsive co-acting' with God and each other is pitted against its counterfeit: a falsely creative 'self-acting'.[38] The *civitas terrena* grounds itself, and its characteristic mark is its sense of at-homeness in the world, of satisfaction with the here and now. The *civitas Dei* on the other hand is from above. Its foundation lies in God and his angels, and *its* tell-tale sign is its sense of strangeness here, its unwillingness to tarry, its hope for something beyond. But the cause of these respective signs must be found in the contrasting loves of the cities: the *cupido* of the earthly city, the *caritas* of the heavenly. It can be no coincidence that the term which had carried so much ecclesiological significance in Augustine's anti-Donatist polemic now returns in a new context. The Church and the City of God are not, *pace* some Protestant readings of Augustine, two wholly distinct quantities. Rather, that City has its 'pilgrim colony on earth': the community which, by its self-offering in outward signs in the *communio caritatis*, comes before God in the sacrament of Christ's body.

But before leaving Ratzinger's Augustine, we may note one last point of rather wider significance than the hints for a future ecclesiology which the young Bavarian *doktor* took from the theologians of Roman North Africa. It concerns eschatology, and the implications of the Christian vision of the End for the Church's practice. Augustine's notion of charity is, as Erich Przywara pointed out, far removed from an activist concept of the same. In charity Augustine saw, beyond all the 'urgencies of

[37]Cf. Ibid. XXII. 6, 1.
[38]VHG pp. 274–275.

action', what Przywara terms 'the free festivity of love'.[39] Charity is the breath from on high of the eternal Sabbath, perceptible in all the active mission of the *civitas Dei*. From this flows, Przywara thinks, the characteristic ethos of Latin Christianity at its missionary best: humility, poverty, 'indifference', qualities which make Augustine the inspiration of so many different kinds of Christian life in the Western church, from the Benedictines to the Society of Jesus. Here we have the fulfilment of the high priestly prayer of the Messiah at the Supper to the effect that his disciples may be in the world, yet not of it. In time this will become perhaps the most insistent refrain in Ratzinger's criticism of the Catholic Church's modern self-reform.

[39]E. Pryzwara, *Augustin. Passions et destin de l'Occident op. cit. p. 14.*

CHAPTER THREE

BONAVENTURE AND SAVING HISTORY

Ratzinger opens his study of the Franciscan friar, cardinal and theologian St Bonaventure by pointing out that we tend to find people concerned with the theology and philosophy of history at times of great crisis in the historical process itself. Augustine's own *De civitate Dei* was a product of the bitter self-questioning which befell the Roman imperial state on the sack of Rome by Alaric. Ratzinger finds a second high-point of such reflection in Bonaventure's commentary on the biblical story of creation, his *Collationes in Hexaemeron.*

What led Ratzinger to turn away from the ecclesiological focus of interest manifest in *Volk und Haus Gottes* to this new concern? The foreword to the American edition of *Die Geschichtstheologie des heiligen Bonaventura* helps us to answer this question.[1] In the 1950s, when he began work on the subject, Catholic theology in the German-speaking world was worried by the relation of salvation-history to metaphysics. The idea of salvation-history, the construal of God's nature by reference to his actions in a special, supernaturalised history interwoven with history at large, was increasingly regarded as the primary theological key to understanding Christian revelation. But what relation could this have to metaphysics, an account of the divine being on the basis of general experience, and hitherto a vital part of Catholic theology to which it had traditionally contributed the important feature of philosophical realism? The relation of salvation-history to metaphysics began to seem problematic as a result of Catholic contact with Protestant

[1] J. Ratzinger, *Die Geschichtstheologie des heiligen Bonaventura* (Munich 1959); ET *The Theology of History in Saint Bonaventure* (Chicago 1971). Cited below as THB.

theology. The latter, ever since Luther, had tended to see in metaphysical thinking a deviation from the specific, biblically-based, rationality of Christian faith. That faith directed people to a God who acts in time, in history, and not just to the Eternal *tout court*. Inheritors of the Lutheran tradition were asking Catholics:

> Has not the 'Hellenisation' of Christianity, which attempted to overcome the scandal of particularity by a blending of faith and metaphysics led to a development in a false direction?

And Catholics, in their turn, were demanding of Lutherans:

> How can the unique and unrepeatable have a universal significance?[2]

For Ratzinger, conscious of the great heritage of historical theology in German Catholicism of the nineteenth and twentieth centuries, the attempt to answer these questions could not be carried out in a purely *a priori* fashion. Working out the relationship between salvation-history and an appropriate metaphysic needed to be done 'in dialogue with that very theological tradition which was being called into question'. And what better way could there be to do so than interrogating a Scholastic theologian of the high mediaeval period who was, at the same time, an upholder of the salvation-historical approach? Thus it was that Bonaventure's candidacy suggested itself.

On the basis of his research, Ratzinger became convinced that the clue to grasping Bonaventure's theology of history lay in *eschatology*, the theological label for the world's ultimate destiny. If this was true, then Bonaventure's theology of history not only permitted but actively required a positive relationship with metaphysics of some sort. By the same token, if

[2]Ibid. p. xi.

eschatology was the heart of the mediaeval Franciscan's concerns, then his work was 'anchored in the central issue of the New Testament question itself'.[3] No theme could be more all-pervasive in the New Testament than the eschatology theme – as exegetes as different as C. H. Dodd, Oscar Cullmann and Jean Daniélou were currently making clear. Some years later, in his own book on eschatology, Ratzinger would go on to consider the eschatology issue in just this light – as what gives us access to the central affirmations of the primitive Gospel.

Bonaventure's theology of history

In large measure, Bonaventure's theology of history took the form of an orthodox corrective to the speculations of the brilliant, but wayward, Calabrian abbot Joachim of Fiore. The Franciscan Order, of which Bonaventure was minister-general, was strained to breaking-point by the claims of Joachim's Franciscan sympathisers. They maintained that the Church, founded hitherto on the sacramental and ministerial pattern laid down by God the Son, made man in Jesus, was shortly to enter a new charismatic condition of unmediated access to grace – the reign of God the Spirit whose herald, they insisted, was Francis of Assisi himself. According to Ratzinger, the *Collationes in Hexaemeron* were Bonaventure's response to the Joachimite question. And this response consisted, not in a total rejection of Joachim's teaching, as with Thomas Aquinas, but in a corrective interpretation. Whereas the Joachimites were interpreting Joachim against tradition, Bonaventure would interpret him within, indeed back into, tradition. This ecclesial re-interpretation of deviant divines, rather than their outright condemnation, was evidently something Ratzinger approved of in the Franciscan thinker.

[3] Ibid. p. xiii.

Ratzinger's study is a *tour de force* of detailed exegesis applied to a difficult, not to say rebarbative, document. When Bonaventure wrote the *Collationes* in 1273, he was, in effect, expounding the problems which had led to the downfall of his predecessor as minister-general, John of Parma, in 1257. John of Parma had supported both the prophecies of abbot Joachim and the Joachimite conception of the Franciscan Order entertained by its 'Spiritualist' component. His position had, however, become untenable with the papal condemnation in 1255 of the *Evangelium aeternum*, the attempt of a certain Gerard of Borgo San Donnino to give Franciscan Spiritualism theological formulation. What Bonaventure produced was perhaps the most substantial high mediaeval synthesis of the historical and symbolist thinking characteristic of the patristic and early mediaeval eras with the conceptual and abstract style of reflection preferred by mature Scholasticism. Unfortunately, as Ratzinger points out, the inherent difficulty of Bonaventure's text deprived it of the readership it deserved. For one thing, it consists of lectures taken down by members of an audience. This can never be a fully satisfactory procedure, especially when the transmission of the text, is, as in this case, confused. For another, the book was never finished, owing to Bonaventure's elevation to the cardinalate. Lastly, parts of the work, and notably the sections containing predictions about the future, are presented in an opaque manner which the author evidently considered only proper for a continuation of biblical apocalyptic.

However, this is not to say that Bonaventure's text is formless, or rambling. Its aim is to render the reader a *sapiens* or 'wise man', and its method is to consider the six days of creation described in the first chapter of the book of Genesis. Its author finds reason to relate these six days, the *hexaemeron*, not only to six periods of salvation history but also to six degrees of knowledge. This scheme, though allegorical, is not entirely arbitrary. It is, as Ratzinger puts it:

a fitting reflection of reality, itself characterised by an historical, step-by-step, progress in knowledge.[4]

Yet Bonaventure's approach to the first of the Genesis creation stories obviously differs markedly from what might be offered by a typical historical-critical exegete of the present day. Hence Ratzinger is obliged to consider the underlying hermeneutic, or theory of biblical interpretation, which warrants Bonaventure in constructing a comprehensive theology of history from the building blocks of the stories of Scripture.

Bonaventure regarded the Bible as possessing three levels of meaning. On a first plane, the believer's 'spiritual intelligence' sifts the literal sense of the biblical text in order to identify the further senses traditionally termed, at least since the time of John Cassian in the fifth century, the allegorical (or typological), the tropological (or moral), and the anagogical (or eschatological) meanings of Scripture. So far, this is pretty well the common teaching of theologians in Bonaventure's period. But Bonaventure is more original in proposing the existence of a second plane, inhabited by what he calls *figurae sacramentales*. These are the signbearers: figures, types or images in which the entire Bible speaks of Christ – and of Anti-Christ. And then thirdly, by a deft transferral of the Stoic and patristic idea of 'seminal seeds' from its home in cosmology to the text of Scripture, Bonaventure speaks of a third dimension to the Bible's meaning. Just as the plant in flower scatters new seeds, so from Scripture too there comes forth a rich plenitude of fresh meanings. These *multiformes theoriae* are the intimations Scripture offers about future ages. As Ratzinger sums up:

Scripture points to the future. But only he who has understood the past can grasp the interpretation of the future. This is so because the whole of history develops in one unbroken line of

4Ibid. p. 7.

55

meaning whereby that which is to come may be understood in the present on the basis of the past. . . . In this way, the exegisis of Scripture becomes a theology of history; the clarification of the past leads to prophecy concerning the future.[5]

This is the charter for an eminently Augustinian project: to make the Church's present and future intelligible by relation to its past.

On this crucial third plane of the historical–theological meaning of Scripture, Bonaventure offers a complex account of the world–process. Its main structuring principle is that of typological correspondence between the Old and New Testaments. However, this correspondence can itself be construed according to a variety of schemata, based on numerical divisions from 1:1 up to 7:7. It is this latter, seven-fold, schema which is the most interesting in Bonaventure's eyes, as it had been to Augustine in the *De civitate Dei*. What emerges from Ratzinger's necessarily convoluted discussion, is that Bonaventure, just like Joachim, hopes for a new age of salvation within history. Between Jesus Christ and the final consummation of history he makes space for an 'inner-historical transformation of the Church'.[6] Before this immediately pre-eschatological 'seventh age', there lies a small section of our present sixth age which is yet to be realised. Here is where Bonaventure's attention is focussed, in a

mysterious border-line area separating the perilous time of the present from that age of Sabbath Rest which is yet to come within the framework of this world.[7]

Within the single covenant of the New Testament, the present sixth age is being brought to its climax. In this, the crucial role is

[5]Ibid. pp. 8–9.
[6]Ibid. p. 14.
[7]Ibid. p. 22.

that played by St Francis who, as we shall see, recurs in Ratzinger's own work as a central inspirational symbol for the Christian life.

The significance of Francis

How does Bonaventure present Francis as the key-figure in ushering in for the Church a new era which can only be compared to the beatitude of heaven itself? Drawing on his plan of biblical correspondences, he gave the Hohenstaufen emperors Henry IV and Frederick I an analogous place in the economy of the New Testament community to that occupied by the anti-Yahwist king Manasseh in the Old. They plunged the Church into a time of tribulation, typologically predictable. Corresponding to the intensification of prophetic activity under Manasseh in the kingdom of Judah, we have, in the time of the Church, the emergence of St Francis, the 'Angel of the Seals' foretold in the book of the Apocalypse, and the rise of the prophetic movement he started, namely, Franciscanism.

Francis is for Bonaventure not just another saint, but the sign of a new age. Francis had called himself, according to the *Legenda Major*, 'the herald of a great King'.[8] This enabled Bonaventure to see him, not just as a new John the Baptist – the herald of Christ, but also as a new Elijah. For the New Testament itself presented Jesus' own precursor as one in whom Elijah was come to life again, a herald of the Last Age, sent out 'before the great and terrible Day comes'. Bonaventure accepted Joachim's insistence that the final coming of Elijah is to become a reality in the mission of the 'two witnesses' of the Johannine Apocalypse. Elijah will come again, accompanied by that other Old Testament deathless man, Enoch. For

[8] *Legenda Major* 2, 5.

Bonaventure, this definitive sign has happened. The two witnesses have borne their testimony: Francis, attended by his spiritual companion, St Dominic.[9] But more than this, Francis is the *angelus ascendens ab ortu solis*, the 'angel arising with the dawn', marked with the seal of the living God, the *stigmata*, the very impress of Christ crucified. Consonant with Joachim's prophecy that the Angel of the Seal would receive full power to renew the Christian religion, Francis seals the elect, thus establishing the community of the Last Age.[10] This he does by drawing men and women to make profession, through the vows of the Religious life, to a contemplative form of Christianity, stamped by love as wax is in-formed by a seal. This people will enjoy here and now the peace of the seventh day, the dawn of the Lord's Parousia.

Naturally, Ratzinger has to consider here the charge that all of this is a grotesque exaggeration of the significance of Francis' career, and a wild over-estimate of the place of the Religious life in relation to the destiny of the Church at large. He points out that, in the first place, Francis did see himself as, in a sense, as eschatological figure. For, while Francis was

> far removed from any historical-theological speculation concerning the nature and timing of the End. (Yet) ... in an amazing and entirely authentic, though totally unreflective, way he was filled with that primitive eschatological mood of Christianity which is expressed in the statement: 'The Kingdom of God is at hand'.[11]

And in the second place, while Bonaventure considered the 'new people of God' that he envisaged for the future as the true fulfilment of Francis' intentions, he was not so arrogant as to suppose that this *novus ordo* was identical with the present

[9]*Collationes in Hexaemeron* 15, 28.
[10]*Concordia* 4, 31.
[11]THB p. 39, citing Mark 1, 15.

Franciscan Order. As Ratzinger stresses:

> For the present, the Dominican and Franciscan Orders stand together at the inauguration of a new period for which they are preparing. But they cannot bring this period into actuality all by themselves. When this age arrives, it will be a time of contemplation, a time of the full understanding of Scripture and, in this respect, a time of the Holy Spirit who leads us into the fulness of the truth of Jesus Christ.[12]

Nevertheless, when all the necessary caveats have been entered, Bonaventure takes Francis to anticipate in his own person that eschatological form of life which will be general in the future. Although the Religious Order he founded was merely *cherubicus*, concerned, like that of the Dominicans, with devotion and theological speculation, Francis himself more truly belonged to the *ordo seraphicus*. His life was given over to thanksgiving and praise. Had not the crucified Christ appeared to him in the form of a seraph, indicating that Francis had grasped the Gospel at its profoundest depth, the depth of love which is how the seraphim also understand God?

The final age of the world will find the Church a contemplative church, *ecclesia contemplativa*. As such, it will enjoy an unparalleled fulness of revelation. This is not to say that Bonaventure regards the objective reality of revelation as less than complete in the age of Christ and his apostles. Rather does he use the term *revelatio* for the divinely enabled (subjective) penetration of the content of God's self-communication in history, as well as for that (objective) content itself. 'Revelation' is, in not the least important of its denotations, the unveiling of the hidden meaning of the Bible.

The stages of faith are also stages of mysticism. And, in such a

[12]Ibid. p. 55.

THE THEOLOGY OF JOSEPH RATZINGER

viewpoint, they are seen quite naturally as stages of *revelatio* as well. *Revelatio* refers not to the letter of Scripture, but to the understanding of the letter. And this understanding can be increased. If we were to suppose the possibility of a period of time in which the power of genuine mystical elevation were granted to all human beings, then – in this perspective – we could refer to such a time as a time of revelation in a quite new sense.[13]

In the present epoch where, thanks to the activity of the Franciscan and Dominican Orders, there is already a considerable upsurge of biblical exegesis and preaching, 'revelation' in this sense has started to expand again. But the revelation of the seventh age will far exceed such modest advances. If will go beyond the *sapientia multiformis*, the 'multiform wisdom' of the present age, whose model is Augustine. It will transform itself into a *sapientia nulliformis*, a wisdom which is formless to the degree that it lies beyond all forms. The exemplar of this non-discursive, non-Scholastic acquaintance with the mystery of the Word of God, simple, inner, familiar, is Denys the Areopagite. Bonaventure predicts an end to rational theology. The 'gold and silver vessels' with which the Tent of Meeting between God and man was arrayed, will lose their value.[14] The Scholastic, even scientific, Franciscanism practised by Bonaventure will come to an end. In the Church of the final age, Francis' own manner of life will triumph, impracticable though it is if lived *sine glossa* here and now. The Poor Man of Assisi, the *simplex*, the *idiota*, will turn out to have more penetration into God than all the learned men of his time, because he loved God more.[15]

[13]Ibid. p. 68.
[14]Exodus 3, 22; 12, 36.
[15]THB pp. 161–162.

60

Wisdom and metaphysics

Between this multiform wisdom of sound theological speculation, summed up in Augustine, and the wisdom beyond form of Denys' loving unknowing of God, there is however a third kind of Bonaventurian wisdom which Ratzinger must deal with if his picture is to be complete. This is the *sapientia omniformis*, the omnibus wisdom, whereby created things become meaningful for us and speak to us of the glory of their Maker.[16] In his *Commentary on the Sentences* Bonaventure had early developed the view that, in the contemporary period, man's contemplative power is so reduced that only the healing and helping grace of God can revive his understanding of the 'book' of creation. Divine grace so acts upon us as to set up a ladder leading from the creation to the Creator, an idea most fully set out in Bonaventure's *Journey of the Mind towards God*.

This inevitably brings Ratzinger to the topic of Bonaventure's metaphysical views, and so into the arena of scholarly debate about the Franciscan theologian's 'Neo-Augustinianism' and supposed opposition to Aristotle's influence in theology. In Paris, Etienne Gilson, the historian of mediaeval philosophy, had described the whole of Bonaventure's work on the hypothesis of his anti-Aristoteleanism.[17] Whilst conceding that in his early years as a *magister*, Bonaventure had cited Aristotle with approval, Gilson believed that after 1273 – the year of the composition of the *Collationes in Hexaemeron* – he turned decisively away from Aristotle's naturalism. In Louvain, however, Gilson's colleague Fernand van Steenberghen produced a very different estimate.

[16]Ibid. p. 85. See further on this, J. Ratzinger, 'Der Wortgebrauch von *natura* und die beginnende Verselbständigung der Metaphysik bei Bonaventura', in P. Wilpert (ed.), *Die Metaphysik in Mittelalter. Ihr Ursprung and ihre Bedeutung* (Berlin 1964), pp. 483–498.
[17]E. Gilson, *La Philosophie de saint Bonaventure* (Paris 1924; 1943[2]).

For him, Bonaventure remained his whole life long within the Neo-Platonising Aristoteleanism developed by his Franciscan masters, Alexander of Hales and John of Rupella. According to the Louvain historian, Bonaventure's position is that of a 'Neo-Platonising, above all Augustinising, eclectic Aristo teleanism'.[18] One should not oppose the teaching of Bonaventure to that of Thomas Aquinas as though these were competing systems, the one Augustinian, the other Aristotelean. Both were forms of Neo-Platonising Aristoteleanism, though at different stages of development. Fundamentally, Ratzinger accepts van Steenberghen's case. This means that Ratzinger's sympathy for Bonaventure and the Franciscan school should not be regarded as anti-Thomist. Indeed, Ratzinger has expressed himself on the subject of Thomas with a good deal more warmth than formal ceremony requires.[19]

But on the other hand, Ratzinger does not embrace the recreated philosophical Bonaventure of van Steenberghen without reservation. Unwittingly, Bonaventure *did* assist in the shaping of an anti-Aristotelean Neo-Augustinianism, and this was because of his opposition to the developing differentiation of philosophy and theology in Thomist thought. He thought it important that Christian wisdom should be one. According to Ratzinger, the emergence of anti-Aristotelean feeling in Bonaventure's thought is bound up with his theology of history. The Church's *Heilsgeschichte* had its negative image in a philosophical *Unheilsgeschichte* among Christian Aristoteleans. The latter, in their regrettable denial of the Platonic doctrine of Ideas, were ceasing to see creatures as exemplars of God's own notions, enfolded in the divine providence which disposed

[18]F. van Steenberghen, *Histoire de la philosophie. Période chrétienne* (Louvain – Paris 1964), pp. 92–94.
[19]E.g. ' "Consecrate them in the truth": a homily for St Thomas' day', *New Blackfriars* 68. 803 (March 1987), pp. 112–115.

worldly events as its goodness suggested. In particular, the acceptance of Aristotle's evident conviction that the Prime Mover's existence was perfectly compatible with the eternity of the world had, in Bonaventure's eyes, disastrous consequences. Once applied to the realm of historical events, it reduces history to the level of an accidental infinity, disjoined from the ordered cosmos whose genuinely causal inter-connexions are of another kind.

In reality, however, time is always saving time. History is a movement of *egressus* from God, and *regressus* to him through Jesus Christ who is the 'centre that both divides and unites'. Through Bonaventure's work, Ratzinger here encountered, and appropriated, the Christocentricity which was being discovered anew by Catholic dogmaticians in the 1950s. Indeed, Bonaventure pressed Christocentrism to the point of making the Christ who is the centre of all the centre, even, of all the sciences. In each case, he urges us to press beyond the 'literal sense' of any given discipline to its ultimate meaning: thus the *De reductione artium ad theologiam*. More particularly, Christ is the *medium distantiae*, the defining centre, in his *Crucifixion*.

> With his Cross he has uncovered the lost centre of the world's circle, thus giving their true dimensions and meaning to the movement both of individual lives and of human history as a whole.[20]

This makes it intelligible why Bonaventure could regard the counter-doctrine of the eternally cyclical character of the world as the supreme philosophical error. After 1267, with the rise of Latin Averroism, he will describe it as the Sign of the Beast. It also makes it plain why Ratzinger could find himself in due course so sympathetic to the principal prophet of a renewed

[20]THB p. 146.

Christocentrism in Catholic theology: Hans Urs von Balthasar.[21]

Ratzinger's study of Bonaventure brought him to two conclusions which will be important for the future. First, though Scholastic theology, and its various subsequent offshoots, whether speculative, systematic or academic in the modern fashion, has its own value and merits our respect, the attention of the one who theologises is ultimately directed not here but to the eschatological divine peace which passes all understanding.

> With his roots in the ground of Franciscanism, Bonaventure sees the entire phenomenon of Scholasticism and of scientific thought in a new and different way. He does not cease to recognise its great value for the present time; he himself does not cease pursuing it and loving it; he does not give up his concern for its correctness. But at the same time, he sees that it is not final in itself.[22]

The mature Ratzinger likewise will speak of theology as subordinate, in the last analysis, to contemplation, charity, holiness and – not least – the attaining of poverty of spirit. As he would put it, writing in 1977, true theology is always 'ordered to the experience of the saints'.[23] Behind Athanasius, he insisted there stands Anthony of Egypt; behind Gregory the Great, Benedict of Nursia; behind Bonaventure, Francis of Assisi.

Yet, and this is the second lasting consequence of his Bonaventure studies, Ratzinger found himself unable to accept the mediaeval Franciscan's belief that, prior to history's entry

[21]For von Balthasar's attempted Christocentric revolution, see A. Nichols O.P., 'Balthasar and his Christology', *New Blackfriars* 66. 781/2 (July/August 1985), pp. 317–324.
[22]THB p. 162.
[23]J. Ratzinger, 'Preface' to C. B. del Zotto, *La teologia dell'immagine in S. Bonaventura* (Vicenza 1977), p. viii.

into God's eternity, there will be a 'last age' in which the poverty of the Church's Jerusalem beginnings will blossom again in a reign of the poor on earth. Before the name 'liberation theology' was ever heard of, Ratzinger had to arrive at some judgment about this uncanny thirteenth century anticipation of liberationist eschatology. He points out that this kind of eschatological thinking does not really reproduce the pattern of eschatology in the New Testament.

> For, in a certain sense, a new, second, 'End' is set up next to Christ. Even though Christ is the centre, the one who supports and bears all things, still he is no longer simply that *telos* in whom all things flow together and in whom the world is ended and overcome.[24]

Nevertheless, Ratzinger ends on a reconciling note. Over and above all differences about the timetable of the End, Bonaventure realised, with Augustine, that the kingdom of eternal peace is 'growing in the hearts of those who fulfil Christ's law of love in their own particular age'. Both saw themselves as subject to the word of the apostle:

> So faith, hope, love, abide, these three;
> but the greatest of these is love.[25]

[24]THB p. 114.
[25]I Corinthians 12, 13.

Chapter Four

CHRISTIAN BROTHERHOOD

Ratzinger's first widely disseminated essay treating of a
doctrinal topic *in propria persona*, rather than by way of the
exposition of some earlier father or doctor, is his study *Die
christliche Brüderlichkeit.*[1] Christian brotherhood was a theme he
had already touched on in Augustine, and Augustine's African
predecessor, Optatus. It was also, perhaps, an obvious
ecclesiological subject in a self-consciously democratic
European world, and especially so on the eve of a great Church
council which would underline the fundamental equality of all
the baptised, and their common call to uncommon holiness –
though without prejudice to the place of the threefold apostolic
ministry, created as this was by the Lord Jesus Christ for the
service of his disciples. But Ratzinger's treatment is both more
original, and more thoughtful, than one might suppose.

The paradox of brotherhood

The great problem of brotherhood, he points out, is that all
unions entail the separating off of those who are united from the
rest whom they leave behind. This is a paradox which can be
proved by everyday experience. Ratzinger confronts it, in the
hope of resolving it, by considering the witness of the biblical
revelation. For the Old Testament, a brother was someone who
belonged with you in the unity of the common people of God.
Here what was crucial was the fatherhood of God, which

---

[1] J. Ratzinger, *Die christliche Brüderlichkeit* (Munich 1960); ET. *Christian
Brotherhood* (London 1966), cited below as CB.

provided Israelite brotherhood with its essential basis. There is, however, something strange here. For prophetic Yahwism, Israel's *national* God is the *universal* God. This position is in itself inherently unstable. It might lead to the conclusion that the formation of a unified brotherhood within the Israelite nation is unthinkable; or again, it might lead to the opposite conclusion that any form of wider, international brotherhood is undesirable. Everything turns on just how people make the connexion between the non-national, universal God and the fact that there is only one people who worship him as *their* God. For Old Testament faith, this connexion is made not by Israel but by Israel's Lord. He chooses Israel for no merits of its own but by a free decision of his grace. On the same basis, he is free to reject Israel, something for which the subsequent transgressions of the Israelites would provide more than sufficient justification.

The upshot of Old Testament faith in God's covenant with Israel, notably in its Deuteronomic form, is that God is said to have a special, though not an exclusive, relationship with the Hebrew nation.

> Whereas he was the father of all the peoples of the world through the creation, he was beyond that the father of Israel through election. But this special situation was the free disposition of God, which could, therefore, be altered at any time.[2]

The effect of this is to introduce an element of uncertainty into any tendency to set apart the brotherly community of Israel too rigorously. The prophets often tried to stimulate a sense of the potential openness of the Hebrew religion, both in prophecies of woe directed to Israel and in prophecies of weal which embraced other nations or in some way opened on to a more universal *mise-en-scène*.

[2]Ibid. p. 8.

But another, darker side of the coin is shown in the emergence of Judaism as a faith in certain respects dissimilar to Old Testament religion, something which happened in the Hellenistic period. Ratzinger sees a certain process of rationalisation at work in this period, making people uneasy with the idea of gratuitous – and in that sense uncaused – divine election. So the thought arose that God had offered the Torah to all the peoples of the world, but only Israel had accepted it, thus becoming the one and only people of God. Superficially a more reasonable concept of the God–Israel relationship, it carried with it an unfortunate consequence: in the last analysis, it implied that it was not so much God who chose Israel, but Israel who chose God. Moreover, it appears to have led in practice to an even stricter sealing-off of the Jews from the *goyim* who, after all, must voluntarily have renounced the special fatherhood of God and thus were justly deprived of the brotherly comradeship of his true children. We are at this point, Ratzinger sombrely remarks, at the dividing-line which separates the Old Testament as *preparatio evangelica* from Judaism as the 'synagogue'.

The fundamental picture that Ratzinger discerned in the Old Testament doctrine of election he found confirmed in its theological anthropology. All men are united in Adam, and in Noah; yet a special covenant binds the God of all to Abraham and his seed. Israelites are, in a heightened sense, brothers – but because of the unity which characterises both humankind and its Creator, others are, in a wider sense, brothers also. The Mosaic law recognises this in its provision for the 'stranger at the gates'.

From the angle of these foundations in the Old Testament Word of God, Ratzinger goes on to review briefly the fate of the idea of brotherhood in the secular context from Hellenism to Karl Marx. The Enlightenment brought the Stoic idea of a universal human brotherhood to its apogee. Ratzinger pokes some gentle fun at its hymnic expression in J. C. F. von Schiller's 'Be embraced, ye millions', as set by Beethoven in the *Choral*

Symphony. 'A brotherhood which embraces everyone in equal manner cannot expect to be taken seriously by anyone'.[3] And the French Revolution, ostensibly the happy fulfilment of Schiller's *Ode an die Freude* of 1785, turned out to distinguish drastically between the inner fraternal circle of revolutionaries and all the rest, thus disclosing its discontinuity (as well as continuity) with Enlightenment thought. The dream of a perfect circle of brothers continued in post-Restoration liberalism, where its characteristic form was that of Freemasonry. In Marxism, the return to the idea of 'two ethical zones' of brotherhood and non-brotherhood is carried through with a radical thoroughness hitherto unheard of. Yet in all fairness, as Ratzinger points out, Marxism has its own hope for eschatological reunion of a temporal and secular kind.

And so Ratzinger comes at last to the New Testament in which, as the scriptural witness to the climax of the divine plan for humanity, he hopes with some confidence to find the resolution of the paradox of brotherhood. At first, however, the sayings of Jesus only seem to perpetuate the problem. For, on first hearing, those sayings seem to present the same ambivalence which has dogged the issue throughout its history:

> On the one hand, it is clear that all those who need help are, irrespective of any barriers, through their very plight the brothers of Jesus. On the other hand, it is also apparent that the coming community of the faithful will form a new fraternal community which will be distinct from those who do not believe.[4]

A universal idea of brotherhood, in other words, stands cheek by jowl with a particular or limited one. The inspired commentary of the New Testament writers is of some assistance

[3] Ibid. p. 16.
[4] Ibid. pp. 29–30.

here. In Paul, while the idea of fatherhood is rendered more profound by incipient Trinitarianism, of even greater significance is the doctrine of Christ as the Second Adam. For this teaches that though men are not yet brothers in Christ they can and must become so. The *philadelphia* owed to one's fellow Christian does not exclude, but rather implies, the appropriateness of the *agapē* offered to every man.[5] Meanwhile, in John, the idea of Christian brotherhood reaches a supreme intensity, but at the risk, for the unwary, of endangering the universal outreach implicit in Christ's message.

Ratzinger finds the patristic development of these motifs somewhat ambivalent. Concentrating his attention on the North African tradition which, through his study of Augustine, he knew best, he traces in Tertullian a sympathetic doctrine of a twofold brotherhood, one depending on common descent and embracing all men, the other dependent, rather, on the shared knowledge of God and the Spirit of holiness given to Christians to drink. In Cyprian, by contrast, the language of brotherhood is increasingly confined to fellow-bishops, or to ascetics. It is odd that, to offset this dubious development, Ratzinger does not invoke his other favoured witnesses, Optatus and Augustine himself.

A theology of brotherhood

The need is for a new synthesis. Ratzinger offers one of his own in four stages. First, he insists that the foundation of Christian brotherhood can only be faith. Christian brotherhood, unlike the secular brotherhood of Marxism, can only be based on the common fatherhood of God.

[5] Here Ratzinger draws on H. Schürmann's 'Gemeinde als Bruderschaft im Licht des Neuen Testaments', *Diaspora, Gabe und Aufgabe* (Paderborn 1955), pp. 21–31.

Unlike the impersonal Stoic idea of God the Father and the vague paternal idea of the Enlightenment, the fatherhood of God is a fatherhood mediated by the Son, and including brotherly union in the Son.[6]

For its realisation, it requires a 'vital knowledge of God's fatherhood' and a 'vital joining with Jesus Christ in a union of grace'.[7] To the conscious spiritual acceptance of God's fatherhood the 'our' of the *Pater noster* is as important as the 'Father': something which Cyprian *did* realise in his commentary on the Lord's Prayer.[8] This social dimension must be renewed, Ratzinger insists, in the common awareness of the faithful. For a deeper understanding of our union through the life of Christ, Ratzinger turns for inspiration to a mediaeval German source: Meister Eckhart. For the Rhineland mystic, to become one with Christ means to lose one's 'oneself', to cease to regard one's own ego as an absolute.[9] And all of this depends, in the last analysis, on acceptance of the Chalcedonian faith that Jesus Christ is both God and man. He is

the true and real Israel because he possesses the highest distinction of Israel, the sonship of God, in an infinitely more real way than was the case with the old people of God. At the same time, the fact that he as himself become a man, ... shows that he does not regard his divine sonship as something reserved only for himself: the meaning of the incarnation is, rather, to make what is his available for all.[10]

Thus the new Israel of the faithful is no longer son merely

---

[6]CB p. 44.
[7]Ibid. pp. 51–52.
[8]Cyprian, *De dominica oratione* 8.
[9]For this social character of Eckhart's mysticism, see H. Piesch, *Meister Eckharts Ethik* (Lucerne 1935), pp. 111–122; O. Karrer, *Meister Eckehart* (Munich 1926), pp. 189–193.
[10]CB pp. 48–49.

because of God's elective call, the concrete form of which is the Torah of the Jewish people. She is, as Eckhart constantly repeated, a 'son in the Son', through sharing in the life of the 'innate' Son of the Father, with whom we are one body.

Secondly, then, this divine gift of a new brotherhood carries with it a human imperative: to remove all barriers to fraternity within the Christian household. As Ratzinger puts it, with the teaching of the Letter to the Ephesians in mind, 'The mystery of Christ is the mystery of the removal of barriers'.[11] Significantly, among those barriers he lists first that of nationality, referring to the 'overcoming of nationalism' as a task which every generation must set itself anew. After this, he cites the need to remove whatever is destructive of Christian brotherhood in differences of class. Lastly, he speaks of the desirability of ecclesiastical office being, and appearing to be, a service to the Church at large.

The third constituent of Ratzinger's synthesis consists, more soberly, of a warning against too heady an optimism about the creation of the brotherly community. Jesus' own promise of a new fraternity was itself made in close connexion with prediction of the failure of all earthly brotherhood and family life together, both of which raise expectations greather than they have power to satisfy.[12] And even in the new brotherhood of grace, a colony on earth of heaven, there are pitfalls a-plenty on the way to *philadelphia*. Though the brotherhood receives its source and centre in the gift of the Eucharist, it needs to develop appropriate forms of community life outwith the Liturgy, so as to supplement its unitive effect.

Ratzinger's synthesis culminates in a vision of what he terms 'true universalism'. As he wrote:

The separating-off of the limited Christian brotherhood is not

[11] Ibid. p. 57.
[12] Cf. Mark 10, 21 with ibid. 10, 30.

the creation of some esoteric circle, but is intended to serve the whole. The Christian brotherly community does not stand against, but for the whole.[13]

In this view of the Church as elected for the sake of the non-elected, as the means to save the other brother who was *not* chosen, Ratzinger is explicitly under the influence of Karl Barth. In the *Church Dogmatics*, Barth had transformed Calvin's doctrine of double predestination, *praedestinatio gemina*, in just this fashion.[14] Thus Barth, and here Ratzinger after him, could maintain the full, gracious reality of the Church's distinctive election, while at the same time opening wide the doors of salvation to all. For though universalism, the salvation of everyman, is not part of Christian faith, it is assuredly part of Christian hope.

How, then, according to Ratzinger, does the Christian brotherhood exercise its responsibility for the whole? It does so in three ways: through mission, through charity, and through suffering. Through *mission*: in which Ratzinger recommends a 'holy discretion'.

> He best disseminates the Word who does not squander it (for what is too cheap or too easy is reckoned of little value) but proclaims it.[15]

Through *charity*: here Ratzinger maintains a high doctrine of the works of mercy.

> A true parousia of Christ takes place whenever a man recognises and affirms the claim on his love that goes on from a fellow man in need.[16]

Through *suffering*, awareness of whose redemptive value is, in

[13]CB p. 75.
[14]*Church Dogmatics* II.2.
[15]CB p. 83.
[16]Ibid. p. 84.

Ratzinger's eyes, the foundation of the only genuine Christian triumphalism, that of sharing in the Lord's paschal mystery.

> When all other ways fail, there will always remain the royal way of vicarious suffering by the side of the Lord. It is in its defeat that the Church constantly achieves its highest victory, and stands nearest to Christ.[17]

In an ecumenical postscript, Ratzinger suggests that, if Christian brotherhood may mean all of this, then the term 'separated brethren', as used by Catholics of non-Catholic Christians, can acquire 'an exact and valuable meaning'.[18] And in a remark which anticipates his mature evaluation of Martin Luther, he reflects that, whilst something once rightly condemned as heresy cannot subsequently become true, it may nonetheless gradually develop its own positive ecclesial nature, so that the individual lives from a schismatic tradition 'as a believer, not as a heretic'.[19]

Ratzinger's thesis was welcome. His theme was, as Father Fergus Kerr of Blackfriars, Oxford, remarked

> something that is central to the Church, for in saying that the people has priority over the individual, that salvation is 'communitarian', one is pointing in the end to the experience which the New Testament writings describe as *koinonia* (fellowship, communion) and *philadelphia* (fraternal affection, brotherly love).[20]

And Kerr called Ratzinger's book the 'essential' study of its subject by a Catholic author, worthy to stand alongside the Anglican Lionel Thornton's *The Common Life in the Body of*

[17]Ibid. pp. 84–5.
[18]Ibid. p. 94.
[19]Ibid. p. 90.
[20]F. Kerr, 'Church: Brotherhood and Eschatology', *New Blackfriars* 51. 598 (March 1970), pp. 144–154, and here at p. 148.

Christ.[21] The Scottish theologian took up with enthusiasm Ratzinger's conviction that specifically Christian brotherhood can have no other source or centre than the eucharistic mysteries in which the new life of the world to come is made present here and now. Brotherhood, as the Catholic Christian conceives it, is inseparable from eschatology. It was in this connexion that Kerr hoped to find a means of overcoming the rupture in sensibility which the manner of introduction of the Second Vatican Council had regrettably brought about by the time that Ratzinger's study was available to the English-speaking public.

> It seems to me (he wrote) that these two themes, brotherhood and eschatology, take up precisely what was good in the sort of Catholicism with which we were familiar, at least in this country, before the Council.[22]

Evoking the rite of Solemn Benediction in a North-country English parish, the sense of solidarity in the 'loud and draughty singing', and of the presence of the Supernatural in the hush at the blessing, Kerr pleaded that

> we must surely do what we can to retain and develop that old-fashioned sense of community and the supernatural. Because it seems to me that both are threatened, and that brotherhood and eschatology are all the terms that point to the greatest dangers in the Church today – the danger of schism and the danger of secularism.[23]

It is to the Second Vatican Council, and Ratzinger's response thereto, that we must now turn.

[21]L. S. Thornton, The Common Life in the Body of Christ (Westminster 1941; London 1963[4]).

[22]F. Kerr, art. cit. p. 153.

[23]Ibid. The description of pre-conciliar English congregational singing is from Archbishop David Mathew's preface to the *Westminster Hymnal* (London 1939), p. vi.

Chapter Five

THE EVENT OF THE COUNCIL

Ratzinger attended the Council as a theological adviser to the archbishop of Cologne, cardinal Joseph Frings. He registered his reactions to the main events of the Council in four booklets which reported on its sessions, while more extended comments on some of its major texts can be found in the contributions he made to Herbert Vorgrimler's great commentary on the texts and their background.

The first session

Ratzinger attended the opening Mass of the Council with – by his own confession – a certain unease. It quite failed to correspond to enlightened liturgical principles as these had been worked out in the 'Liturgical Movement', prominent not least in German-speaking Europe since the First World War. The separate Liturgy of the Word (was not the 'Mass of Catechumens' precisely that?); the Creed postponed till Mass was finished (for rubrical reasons, presumably); the intoning of litanies (where there should have been the ancient 'Prayer of the Faithful'); above all, the lack of active participation of the assembly – all of this he found distinctly galling. Ruefully, Ratzinger remarks in his 1963 study of the opening session of the Council that the success of the conciliar event could probably be gauged by how different its concluding Mass was from its opening one. He was heartened to find that, at the end of the first session, the Mass responses were sung in common by the bishops and all present.[1]

[1] J. Ratzinger, *Die erste Sitzungsperiode des zweiten Vatikan Konzils. Ein Rückblick* (Cologne 1963), p. 11. Cited below as ESVNT.

Whatever deficiencies the opening Liturgy might suffer from were, however, effaced by Ratzinger's delight at the tenor of pope John's address. The aim of the Council would be, not the doctrinal refinement of particular aspects of the deposit of faith, but the 'fundamental renewal of the whole' – and that in a living exchange with today's world and its needs.[2] Ratzinger was also pleased by the decision to postpone the choice of members of the various conciliar commissions until the bishops had time to get to know each other. As this decision was inspired by Ratzinger's own patron, Frings of Cologne, as well as by cardinal Achille Liénart of Liége, it may be supposed that he played some part in it. Such reciprocal understanding by the bishops would strengthen the Church's horizontal catholicity, the necessary complement of its vertical catholicity as found in their communion with and obedience to the Holy See. He was gratified to see the bishops acting as a genuinely formative power in the Church, bringing their own experience into its highest counsels. This experience also reflected, he thought, the spirituality of the Church in their own countries, and the struggle with an atheistic world, as well as ecumenical contacts with separated Christians. He looked forward to a time of 'fruitful tension' between periphery and centre. The episcopate is primarily concerned, he thought, with the 'living multiplicity' of the Church; the Roman primacy with its unity. Each element, if true to itself, will pull in rather different directions, but on the whole the resulting strain will exercise in healthy fashion the whole body.[3] Ratzinger was impressed by the spirit of freedom at the Council, something as ascribed to pope John's personality. This would lead, he predicted, to an overcoming of the 'Antimodernist neurosis', and a new brotherly openness in the Church at large.

[2] Ibid. p. 12.
[3] Ibid. p. 17.

As is well-known, the first of the Council's great debates, and major documents, concerned the Liturgy. Ratzinger noted the procedural difficulties of the discussion. A large and heterogeneous body such as the Council fathers met with problems when called upon to debate a text in parliamentary fashion. Some proposed that the assembly should split up into small groups, each responsible for a section. Ratzinger opposed this, not least on the ground that it might lead to fragmentation into national groupings. But the substance of the debate could only be welcomed. Giving priority to the Liturgy was an inspired choice: a 'confession of the true centre of the Church'. That centre is the Church's celebrations of her nuptials with her Lord in the eucharistic mystery. In that sacramental share in the sacrifice of Christ, the Church receives her deepest mission: the adoration of the triune God. The Liturgy schema, Ratzinger thought, thus had important implications for ecclesiology: A doctrine of the Church which was hardly more than a meditation on the Church's hierarchy – what Père Congar called a 'hierarchology' – would be overcome by a heightened awareness of the Liturgy as 'the true life-spring of the Church and so the authentic starting-point of all renewal'.[4]   Ratzinger greeted the dogmatic constitution on the Liturgy with enthusiasm. It was at one and the same time a return to the sources, and a return to the heart of Christian worship. Thus, for example, it rightly gave the primacy to the paschal celebration of Sunday, the weekly Easter, over against commemorations of the saints. It emphasised the objective Mystery rather than the individual's private devotions. It offered a plain and intelligible structure instead of the luxuriant foliage of forms where the wood was too easily lost to sight among the trees. The greater stress on the place of Scripture would make the Liturgy a house with two tables. Before feasting at the Table of the Supper, one

[4]Ibid. pp. 25–26.

takes the *antipasta* of the Table of the Word. Here Ratzinger looked forward with eagerness to the composition of a new Lectionary. The more marked active participation of the laity would find its chief expression, he believed, in the ever more widespread practice of communion under both kinds. The concession to episcopal Conferences of certain powers over the liturgical law of the Latin church in their regions might be more important, ecclesiologically speaking, because more practical, than exalted statements of a high doctrine of the episcopate which could remain just rhetoric. Those Conferences, Ratzinger confidently expected, would thus come to form an intermediate body of a quasi-synodal kind between the individual bishop and the Pope – a view which, in the post-conciliar period he would come to modify, alarmed at the evidence of a possible breakdown in the unity of the magisterium. On the matter of the language of the Liturgy, he went considerably further than *Sacrosanctum Concilium* itself. He cited approvingly the words of the Melchite patriarch of Antioch, Maximos IV: language is for men, not angels. Or, as Ratzinger put it in more philosophical terms, language is the incarnation of spirit, which, as human spirit 'can only think by speaking, and, in and from speech lives'.[5] And in a sharp statement, he went on to attack the long reign of the Latin language in the Church's higher schools. The sterility of much Catholic theology since the end of the Enlightenment must be explained in part by its enforced union with a language which had ceased to be the vehicle of the movement of the human spirit. Here the celebration of the various Eastern liturgies in St Peter's during the conciliar sessions was helpful: a good corrective to Latin exclusivity.

Of even greater interest to Ratzinger was the Council's discussion of the idea of revelation, eventually to issue in its

[5]Ibid. p. 34.

THE THEOLOGY OF JOSEPH RATZINGER

second dogmatic constitution, *Dei Verbum*. The great triumph of this debate, in Ratzinger's eyes, was the refusal to let the whole issue be defined by the need to combat Modernism. What he meant was plain: every orthodox attempt to confront heresy leads to a certain imbalance, as the illumination of one necessary truth places others in shadow. Having the serenity to see the Modernist crisis as an episode of the past held out the hope of adopting a more holistic vision of revelation, itself the key disputed question of Modernist and Anti-Modernist polemic. Holistic: Ratzinger's own terms were 'pastoral' and 'ecumenical', which did not, he insisted, mean 'muddled' and 'ambiguous'! Dogmatic formulations must retain their value as objective truth, the bearing of which can be gauged unambiguously from their history. 'Pastoral' must not mean wishy-washy, *substanzlos*. Rather should it signify a concern for modern people who 'want to hear what the faith has positively to teach them'. This will mean freeing preaching and confession from the language of the Schools, a language which has its own legitimacy, even necessity, in theological study, but which should elsewhere give way to that of Scripture, the Fathers and contemporary culture. Here Ratzinger showed the characteristic conviction of the neo-biblical and neo-patristic revival of the 1950's known as *la Nouvelle Théologie* that *hae tres unum sunt*. So much for the sense of 'pastoral'; but what of 'ecumenical'?

> 'Ecumenical' should not mean a silence about particular truths, for fear of being out of step with other people. What is true must be spoken openly, without dissimulation. Perfect truth is an aspect of perfect love.[6]

Ecumenism should consist, rather, in ceasing to regard the Other as the Enemy, seeing him as a brother with whom to

[6]Ibid. p. 46.

speak and from whom to learn. Moreover:

> 'Ecumenical' should mean ... to support the inner wholeness of
> faith, and thus make the separated brother aware that everything
> truly Christian finds shelter in the Catholic.[7]

After all, Ratzinger points out, 'ecumenical' and 'Catholic'
originally meant the same thing: the fulness of the Christian.

Ratzinger contributed a lengthy commentary on *Dei Verbum*
to the Vorgrimler commentary on the Council documents. For
Ratzinger, the important thing was to ensure the incorporation
into this text of the theological advances in understanding the
authority both of Tradition and of Scripture in the previous
hundred years. Tradition is the living environment which
witnesses to the meaning of Scripture. Scripture is the soul of all
Christian reflection on revelation: these were to be the *idées-
clefs*.[8]

The preface to *Dei Verbum* he considered especially happy.
Dei verbum religiose audiens et fidenter proclamans: 'devoutly
attending to the Word of God and faithfully proclaiming it',
this *incipit* of the document set the tone for what would follow.
Most importantly, it bid fair to save the Council from an
inverted, and ultimately destructive, ecclesio-centredness.

> If sometimes it might appear that the Council was tending
> towards an ecclesiological mirroring of itself, in which the
> Church moved completely within its own orbit, and made itself
> the central object of its own proclamation, instead of constantly
> pointing beyond itself, here the whole of the life of the Church
> is, as it were, opened upwards, and its whole being gathered
> together in the attitude of listening, which can be the only
> source of what it has to say.[9]

[7]Ibid. p. 47.
[8]H. Vorgrimler (ed.), *Commentary on the Documents of Vatican II. Volume
Four* (London and New York 1969), pp. 156–159; cited below as CDVT.
[9]Ibid. p. 167.

In its remarks on the subject of revelation, the Council could claim with accuracy to be 'treading in the footmarks' of Trent and Vatican I. In its simultaneous fidelity to those earlier Councils, yet surpassing of their perspectives, it provided, according to Ratzinger, a perfect example of dogmatic development, the inner *relecture* of dogma in dogmatic history.

On the body of the text, Ratzinger found much to praise, though occasional shortcomings to blame. His principal anxiety over the final document concerned the question of soteriological optimism. The mystery of iniquity – sin – and its dreadful cost to the God-man on Calvary, tended, he thought, to evaporate in the warm sunshine of an optimistic age. Thinking not least of the massive tradition of Lutheran exegesis of the opening sections of the Letter to the Romans, cited in *Dei Verbum* 1, he asked:

> When salvation is being treated should not the mystery of the anger of God also have been mentioned, weighing so heavily, as it does, upon these chapters?[10]

And he concluded that the pastoral optimism of an age concerned above all with understanding and reconciliation – perhaps he had in mind Madame de Stäel's axiom, 'Tout comprendre, c'est tout pardonner' – seems to have 'somewhat blinded the Council to a not immaterial section of the testimony of Scripture'. Divine salvation comes essentially as a justification of the sinner; grace is given through the judgment of the Cross.

But though this question of 'over-optimism' was no mere bagatelle, and would recur, it failed to spoil his pleasure at the Constitution as a whole. Some of his warmest writing is devoted to the praise of Scripture in *Dei Verbum*. In the Latin tradition from Jerome and Augustine down to the author of the *Imitation of Christ*, the Church has spoken of the Bible as the

[10]Ibid. p. 174.

'bread of life', offered to us on the table of the Word. He exults in the concreteness of Scripture:

> It breathes the 'smell of the earth' of the land of the patriarchs; it gives us the unmistakeable tone in which the prophets talked, the way in which Israel prayed in its great and in its sorrowful days; it gives us the voice of Jesus Christ – in the various and particularly striking Aramaic phrases that were handed down untranslated; we hear him speak his native language; we meet him across the gulf of centuries, as he lived, a man among men.[11]

But, recognising the danger of a literary romanticism here, Ratzinger also hailed the firm manner in which the Constitution spoke of Scripture's theological status. We treasure it because, through the divine inspiration of the sacred authors, it preserves for us the fundamental dialogue which God has established with man. In theology it must be as the foundation to the building; the life-force to the organism; the soul to the body. Piety, too, must be renewed by better acquaintance with the Scriptures whose private reading reaches its culmination in hearing the text proclaimed in the liturgical assembly. The daily enthronement of the Bible in the Council's own liturgy was, for Ratzinger, the best possible reminder of the Church's relation to the word: she is first of all a listening Church, precisely in order to become a Church that teaches.

Not that Ratzinger imagined that this passionate recommendation of the Bible was un-problematic. He pointed out the difficulty some found in relating exegesis to systematic theology; the tendency of biblical studies to go *incommunicado*, leaving their telephone receivers from other branch-lines of theology off the hook. He warned that any attempt to separate Scripture from the total of the Church will lead 'either to

[11]Ibid. p. 263.

biblicism or Modernism or both'.[12] He noted the way in which succeeding drafts of *Dei Verbum* tended to eliminate the notion of progress in exegesis: 'where one is dealing with the essentials of man, the model of progress breaks down'.[13] It would be, in any case, anathema to the Eastern Orthodox, for whom the rule of biblical interpretation was always the faith of the undivided Church of antiquity, and to orthodox Protestants whose sixteenth century Reformation was based precisely on the denial of a continuous linear progression. Nor had he failed to notice some grim words of the Lutheran scholar Ernst Käsemann on the perils of relying on exegesis to defend the kerygma, the Christian proclamation:

> It seems to me (Käsemann had written) safer to walk through a minefield blindfold. Is it possible to forget for a second that we are daily concerned with a flood of doubtful, even abstruse ideas in the fields of exegesis, history and theology, and that our scholarship has gradually degenerated into a world-wide guerilla warfare ...? Can we free ourselves from the *massa perditionis*? Can we pursue our craft in any other way than in the knowledge that those who will carry us out have long been standing outside the door?[14]

Though considering this to be a *factually* exaggerated statement, Ratzinger felt that Käsemann was right on the *principle* involved.

In an attempt to mitigate the force of these difficulties, the bishops, to Ratzinger's satisfaction, advised that the Church fathers and the venerable liturgies of East and West should be used as guides to exegesis. In this context, the Council could even preserve the Tridentine emphasis on the Vulgate text, albeit in diluted form. For the Vulgate was the Bible of the Latin

[12]Ibid. p. 267.
[13]Ibid. p. 266.
[14]Cited ibid. p. 193 from E. Käsemann, *Exegetische Versuche und Besinnungen* II (Tübingen 1964), pp. 36f.

fathers, and shows us how the ancient Church of the West understood the Scriptures. The Bible must be studied with the best modern exegetical tools, but its hermeneutical context is the 'sense of the Church', wherein the exegete must let himself be guided by her magisterium. Ratzinger was realistic enough to expect a certain 'tension' between those tools and that context, and to discourage expectations that it would ever be wholly eliminated.

The *sensus Ecclesiae* which is to be, then, the exegete's ultimate criterion is found in Tradition, which the magisterium interprets with authority, in the service of the Word of God. Such an organic and 'total' use of the term 'tradition', which thereby cries out for, and receives, an initial capital letter, is not that of the Council of Trent. Whereas Trent had been concerned with particular *traditiones* in the plural, given ways of behaving, notably liturgical, in the life of the Church, *Dei Verbum*, indebted at this point to the pen of the French Dominican Yves Congar and his favourite sources in the Catholic Tübingen school of the nineteenth century, had returned to a more ancient notion of Tradition as the entire ecclesial context for the reading of Scripture. Tradition is handed on in teaching, life and worship, and, as Ratzinger remarks in an explanatory aside which would later take on great importance in debate with 'dissenting' theologians:

> It has its place not only in the explicitly traditional statements of Church doctrine, but in the unstated – and often unstatable – elements of the whole service of the Christian worship of God and the life of the Church.[15]

However, in so describing Tradition as the perpetuation of everything the Church is and believes, the Council had failed to

[15]CDVT IV. p. 184.

make room, so Ratzinger notes, for a judicious criticism of particular elements within Tradition. He considered that, rather than dissipate their energies in what proved a fruitless attempt to resolve the dispute, inherited from the late mediaeval Church and left open at Trent, about the 'quantitative completeness of Scripture', the Council fathers would have been better advised to work out criteria for the possible – and even necessary – criticism of tradition within the Church. But this anxiety that the effect of *Dei Verbum*'s teaching on Tradition would be to induce an attitude of 'Whatever is, is right' in the Church after the Council could hardly have been wider of the mark.

Ratzinger closed his account of the first session of the Council with gratitude to God, but a certain sobriety of future expectation. On the one hand, the conciliar event, regarded so sceptically by some, had shown itself to be of irreplaceable value. The texts so far achieved were 'precious fruits' of the 'horizontal catholicity' of the world-wide episcopate, each of whose members had come with the gift of his own experience, and that of his church and situation, yet so as to join the 'school' of the conciliar assembly.[16] On the other hand, Ratzinger warned, we must be clear what the Council could *not* achieve. It cannot of itself take away the human frailty of the Church. Renewal will be needful until the world's end, and the Lord's return. Again, it cannot have as its direct consequence that reunion of Christians everywhere which was so much on the Council fathers' lips and in their hearts as the preparations for the second session began. The Council can show how much of the Christian inheritance is held in common, and encourage people to feel the 'weight of that fundamental unity'. But the realisation of full unity can only be entrusted to the patience and concern of the work-a-day future.[17]

[16]ESZVK pp. 56–57.
[17]Ibid. pp. 59–61.

The second session

In between the sessions, the death of John XXIII, *der gütige Papst*, placed a question mark over the Council's future, but the election of his Milanese friend Montini as Paul VI brought such uncertainty to a speedy end. Ratzinger gave special emphasis here to Paul VI's speech of 21 September to the members of the Roman Curia. Bearing in mind that the popes of the late mediaeval period and the age of the Catholic Reformation had jealously reserved any reform of the Curia to themselves, since it was their 'personal organ', Paul VI's decision to place Curial reform on the conciliar agenda was a milestone in conciliar history in the Western church.[18] And yet there was here no *break* with the past. The pope sought from the Council its *proposals*: not an executive decision, but a consultative participation in an eventual judgment on the concrete workings of the primacy. In this Ratzinger found the typical personal signature of Paul VI:

the readiness to go out to meet what is coming, what is new – but always in a way that is in keeping with historical continuity.[19]

Despite the contrast between the new pope's temperament and that of his predecessor, Ratzinger found this

near allied to the attitude of John XXIII, who used to say of himself that he was the pope both of those who used the accelerator and of those who used the brake.[20]

Paul VI's speech opening the second session on 29 September

[18]J. Ratzinger, *Das Konzil auf dem Weg. Rückblick auf die zweite Sitzungsperiode* (Cologne 1964), pp. 10–11. Cited below as KW.
[19]Ibid. pp. 10–11.
[20]Ibid. p. 12.

was, like John XXIII's at the first session, a programmatic pronouncement.[21] While admitting that in an account of it, someone else might place the accent differently, Ratzinger took from it, above all, its Christocentrism. Presenting Christ as the only mediator and hope of the Church, the pope declared that the Saviour was the true 'president' of the Council. And he evoked for his listeners the great apsidal mosaic at Saint Paul's outside the Walls, where Christ the Pantocrator dwarfs the tiny figure of pope Honorius III who, bowed low in *proskunēsis* before him, touches his feet with a kiss. In his address the pope, in Ratzinger's words, declared Christ the 'interpreter of the present and the measure of all that is happening'.[22] Finally, Paul VI outlined, under four heads, the agenda for the future of the Council. The building was to be supported by four pillars: the articulation of the Church's self-understanding; the Church's renewal; the restoration of the unity of all Christians; the 'conversation' of the Church with the men of our time. Closing his speech, as he did, by some words in Greek and Russian, the pope underlined his commitment to ecumenism, 'stepping out of the space of Latinity' into the pentecostal universality of the Church of all nations.[23]

Ratzinger now turns, as did the Council itself, to the making of the Dogmatic Constitution on the Church: *Lumen Gentium*. The draft text placed before the Council fathers was the work of Belgian theologians, seeking to trace a *via media* between Roman and Hispanic Scholastic treatises on the one hand and, on the other, the work of modern French and German ecclesiologists. Ratzinger felt that, though open to criticism on some points, it was basically a good piece of work: we should

---

[21] The speech is conveniently accessible in Y. Congar, *Report from Rome II. The second session of the Vatican Council* (London 1964), pp. 133–159.
[22] KW p. 19.
[23] Ibid. p. 22.

avoid 'unrealistic perfectionism' in these matters.[24] Though the most obvious feature of the text was its attempt at catholicity – seeing the Church as determined by the economies of both the Son and the Spirit, a structure at once sacramental and charismatic, Ratzinger identified, in addition, two *Leitmotive*.

The first of these was the *historicity* of the Church, not simply in the sense in which that term might be applied to any institution but in the special sense of a body that belongs to the saving history of God-with-us. The Church is as yet unfinished, and pock-marked by sin; grace has still much to do within her; yet all the time she is pressing forward to meet her Lord. In this connexion Ratzinger treats of the notion, for which the Council was indebted to the 'Romance lands', that the Church is *eine Kirche der Armen*, 'a Church of the poor'. Though the idea could lead to misunderstandings, and encourage a sentimentalism that would do no one much good, least of all the poor, it was, he thought, basically sound and indeed, 'the expression of an important historical breakthrough'.

> The Church, which for a time seemed to belong to the Baroque princes, is renewing herself on the way to that simplicity of spirit which is the seal of her origin in the 'Servant of the Lord' who wished to be on this earth a carpenter's son and chose fishermen for his first ambassadors.[25]

The second *Leitmotiv* Ratzinger drew attention to in the draft *Lumen Gentium* is the notion of the Church as *sign*. Augustine had defined *sacramentum* as 'a holy sign': so a 'sacramental' view of the Church would require her to become ever more truly a window – something which 'best fulfils its function when it permits one to look out through it onto a greater reality'.[26]

[24]Ibid. p. 25.
[25]Ibid. p. 30.
[26]Ibid. p. 31.

Church offices, in this context, would have to be understood not in a secular fashion, but as a service to 'God's holy signs', and so in a deeper and more spiritual way.

Ratzinger devoted the rest of his account of the making of *Lumen Gentium* – so far as the Council's *second* session was concerned – to five topics: the bishops and their collegiality; the deacon; layfolk; various 'practical questions' of Church government; and last but not least the matter of Mariology. Of the three-fold apostolic ministry, the presbyterate sat in the shade at the Council: bishops and deacons were of greater interest. On the bishops the hot potato was the idea of episcopal collegiality, the most passionately debated issue of the second session. The apostolic succession, it was proposed, does not take place simply via the individual linkage of one apostle to one bishop, and of that bishop to his successor. More importantly, it is the 'community', *Gemeinschaft*, or 'college', *Kollegium*, of the universal episcopate which succeeds to that of the apostles in the primitive Church. *Bischofsein*, 'being a bishop', is enjoyed only through being united with others in the same office. Though Ratzinger shows a slight hesitation about the term 'college' – perhaps because its Roman-legal connotations were somewhat out of place in a description of the archetypal New Testament community, he nevertheless endorsed the recovery of this corporate doctrine of the episcopate with some enthusiasm. It was a retrieval of the true spiritual structure of the Church. But what of the Pope, the 'Petrine' office-bearer? On the one hand, Peter's function is independent of collegiality – it is a unique position personally given him by Christ. On the other hand, this office does not remove him from the circle of the Twelve, among whose number he is still reckoned. Without saying so in as many words, Ratzinger gives the impression that there may well be a certain tension here for the future. Still, it is a great advance that 'vertical' catholicity, looking to Rome, should be complemented by its 'horizontal' counterpart, looking to one's neighbours. A communion of bishops in a communion of churches: this new, yet old, perspective should enable us to build a bridge to the churches of the East, where 'communion consciousness' has remained more vigorous than in the West.[27]

On the diaconate, Ratzinger sees its restoration as a permanent, married state, as one of the gifts of the Latin American Church to the Council. In that continent, there were sufficient priests for a basic sacramental life to be continued. What was missing was an effective presence of the ministry of the Word, the preaching and proclamation without which no thorough Christianisation is possible. The Council was mindful of the exactly analogous situation faced by the apostles in the Jerusalem church as described in the Acts of the Apostles. The Seven were ordained for the 'service of tables', that the Twelve might devote themselves more whole-heartedly to prayer and the ministry of the Word. Ratzinger was impressed by the 'hunger for the Word' which the effort to re-create this office implied, and also hopeful for the prospect of making spiritual office more 'flexible and dynamic'.[28]

He was, by contrast, rather disappointed in the speeches on the laity, which he found colourless and dull. Though the idea of lay holiness, and a call to perfection unrestricted to the monastic life was enormously valuable, the proposed text was insufficiently concrete, he felt, about the positive ecclesial possibilities of lay existence. More might be said about these, without jeopardising the *indoles saecularis* of the laity, their mission to give the Gospel roots in the world beyond the Church.[29]

On the practical, governmental questions which the doctrine of episcopal collegiality raised for the wider Church of layfolk,

[27]Ibid. p. 36.
[28]Ibid. p. 39.
[29]Ibid. pp. 42–43.

deacons and priests, Ratzinger pointed out that two distinct tendencies were at work. The first was centrifugal. It desired to scatter the papal *plenitudo potestatis* among the bishops who, united to each other in 'conferences', would thus re-create the synodal structure of the ancient Church. The other tendency was centripetal. Its most cherished value was unity, the utility of which could hardly be doubted in a world of ever-accelerating communications and international co-operation.[30] Ratzinger's account of this second tendency was distinctly lack-lustre. Père Congar was more vivid:

> It should be proclaimed from the housetops, with historians like Adolf von Harnack, how great a benefit the Papacy has been in the course of history for the independence and freedom of the Church and, therefore, for the authority of the bishops themselves.[31]

And Congar noted of episcopal Conferences, 'Any sort of particularism which endangers them must be shunned like the plague'. Ratzinger would return to this topic before the Council ended. For now, he contents himself with presenting the idea of a regular meeting of episcopal representatives in Rome, there to exchange experience with Pope and Curia, as a compromise between the competing demands of these two tendencies. So far as the Curia was concerned, it is *piquant* to note his comments on the great verbal duel between his own conciliar bishop, Frings of Cologne, and Alfredo Ottaviani, the cardinal prefect of the Holy Office.[32] He concurred in the judgment of the French Jesuit scholar Jean Daniélou that their conflict was 'institutional not theological'. That is, it concerned the *concrete form* of the 'service' which the office that Ottaviani

[30]Ibid. p. 43.
[31]Y. Congar, *Report from Rome* II, op. cit. p. 107.
[32]KW pp. 44–46.

occupied performed for the Church in guarding the purity of its faith. Ratzinger regarded Frings' intervention as a 'wholly realistic contribution to the theme of Christian freedom', underlining the importance of suitable canonical procedures that would ensure respect for individuals in the Church. He noted that the personal relationship between Frings and Ottaviani grew warmer, not cooler, after this encounter – a fact he ascribed to the Council's human and spiritual atmosphere.

Before leaving the embryonic *Lumen Gentium*, Ratzinger had a word to say about Mariology, a topic which, at the suggestion of cardinal Franz König of Vienna, was incorporated into this fundamentally ecclesiological text. The marriage of Mariology with ecclesiology emphasised that the idea of the Church necessarily includes that of the 'heavenly Church,' *ecclesia caelestis*. The Church's reality extends into the mystery of the End, which eludes all human concepts and dispositions. The figure of the Lord's Mother tells us much about the Church: how it is in lowliness that she, the Church, is made great, and how she

> comes forth from the root of Israel, and in her laborious wandering on the road of history carries the hope of the world in her heart, that hope from which, hidden though it be, all humanity lives.[33]

In such an account of the place of the Mother of God among the Christian people, Ratzinger saw, too, the possibility of a greater consensus about her significance among divided Christians.

It was to the decree on Ecumenism that the Council indeed now turned. Ratzinger saw *Unitatis redintegratio* as essentially the application of the newly minted Dogmatic Constitution on the Church to a special case. It was not a 'Union manifesto',

[33]Ibid. p. 48.

much less a direct appeal to non-Catholic Christians. Instead, it could be thought of as a pastoral appeal to Catholics to orient themselves ecumenically. *Lumen Gentium*, he suggested, was itself ecumenical in the sense that it was not directed *against* anyone, but tried to think through the mystery of the Church 'from the root of a common origin upwards'.[34] Though the decree on ecumenism could not be described as the direct product of the Ecumenical Movement, in the way in which such a relation might well be plotted between the Liturgy Constitution and the Liturgical Movement, nevertheless, it was unthinkable without that great stirring among the Protestant, Anglican and Orthodox communions to which Catholics had made a belated contribution.

Ratzinger restricted himself to the closer consideration of one aspect of the Council's thoughts on ecumenism, but that aspect was a vital one: the relation of 'the Church to the churches': *Kirchengliedschaft*, the question 'Who belongs to the Church?'. He pointed out that the customary approach to this issue in pre-conciliar ecclesiology was unsatisfactory. To speak of membership of the Church in terms of the three conditions of baptism, the confession of a common faith and adhesion to a self-identical hierarchy with the Roman bishop at its summit was to have in mind only Catholic Christians. To make room for the rest by means of the concept of the *votum Ecclesiae*, the implicit desire to be one with the Church so defined, was to adopt a 'fictitious psychology', ascribing to the separated brethren a wish of which they were wholly unconscious. Although the text of *Lumen Gentium* was not yet finalised, the direction in which the debate was flowing was towards a more generous, and less individualistic, view of the gifts of grace in non-Catholic ecclesial bodies. Divided Christians shared, after all, many common treasures: faith in Christ as Son of God and

[34]Ibid. p. 53.

Saviour; baptism; in some cases, other sacraments; Scripture; the hidden fruitfulness of the Holy Spirit, manifested in gifts of piety and understanding.

At the same time, Ratzinger was anxious to preserve the faith-insight of Catholic Christians that there is not simply a plurality of churches, which may achieve co-ordination through some organisational means. Commenting on a press-conference given by a Lutheran-Evangelical observer, Edmund Schlink of Heidelberg, Ratzinger remarked:

> In the Catholic concepton, it is essential to believe (and has been since the 'Frühkatholizismus' of the New Testament period) that there is in fact such a thing as *the* Church, however imperfect it may be. It is given in the visible, liturgy-celebrating, concretely acting Church.... (which) in the midst of all its human deficiencies, is the very tabernacle of God, pitched among men, 'the Church' itself.[35]

However, within this one Church, there is also, indeed, a multiplicity of local churches, *Ortsgemeinden*: the Church's unity does not exclude a plurality. And Ratzinger looked to an ecumenical future whereby, without absorption, separated churches might nevertheless be united to the Catholic communion as forms of the one visible community of Christ on earth. This would remain a permanent conviction.

As the second session closed, Ratzinger noted a certain chill in the air. Those who feared that after the Council, all would remain much as before, were more vocal in their scepticism. Those who feared, rather, a choppy journey on uncertain seas were more forthright in their opposition. Ratzinger's response to this shift of mood was, once again, sober. A Council had no conclusion, save in the daily faith, hope and charity of each member of the Church.

[35]Ibid. p. 63.

The third session

Ratzinger opened his account of the *third* session of the Council with an overview of its documents so far, and of the problems and questions these documents were intended to address. He identified six concrete concerns as fundamental: the problem of the Liturgy; the question of 'centralism' in the Church; relations with non-Catholic Christians and the Ecumenical Movement; a new orientation in Church-State relations; the problem of faith and science, notably *historical* science as represented by the invasion of theology by the historical-critical method; and what to make of the 'new ethical problems' that arise from an increasingly technological world.[36] Though offering brief animadversions on each of these, his portrait of the Council's penultimate meeting is concerned primarily with the issue of episcopal collegiality which he terms not simply an ecclesiological but also an ecumenical issue. If, in this way, his account of the second session seems stuck in a groove, this is because he, like the Council itself, was obliged to backtrack to the unfinished business of *Lumen Gentium* and notably the relation between the local Roman church and bishop, with their universal primacy, and the other churches that made up the single *Catholica*. As he pointed out, no question had been so quantitatively important as this, none occupied more contentious hours of conciliar time.

I think it fair to say that Ratzinger's comments on the third session represent the high point of his – as it turned out – short-lived reaction against the Church of the pre-conciliar period, – of, above all, the sixteenth century Catholic Reformation and the nineteenth century Catholic Revival. His comments on the liturgical life of the age which closed with the Council's

[36]J. Ratzinger, *Ergebnisse und Probleme der dritten Konzilsperiode* (Cologne 1965). Cited below as EPDK.

opening, the last serene procession of the Counter-Reformation Church, were particularly acerbic. He spoke of an 'archeological' Liturgy, a picture so encrusted that the original image could hardly be seen. Such a liturgy was, he implied, a closed book to the faithful, just as it had been an irrelevancy to the saints of the Catholic Reform. On his second 'concrete problem', centralism, he described the proclamation of the 1870 dogma of the Roman bishop's primacy of jurisdiction as followed by many ill consequences. Mission, for instance, was deprived of its 'breathing space', since all mankind had to be fitted somehow into the frame of Latinity. On ecumenism, he lamented the new obstacles that some of the conciliar fathers would place in the way of unity through their exaggerated Marian piety. Concern with Joseph as husband of Mary, with the Rosary, consecration to Mary, devotion to the heart of Mary, the title 'Mother of the Church' and the search for other such titles – these things said nothing for the theological enlightenment of the bishops. On the topic of religious liberty, he happily abandoned the notion that the State might be called on to help protect the faith by its own means. Under the heading 'faith and history' he spoke with confidence of the 'broad highway' which the new openness of theology to the methods of historical criticism would lay out before it. Only on his sixth and final 'concrete problem' – the relation of Church and world – does he simply record the unresolved tension between two tendencies, one which gave enthusiastic affirmation to the world in a theology of incarnation, the other presenting the much more critical posture of a theology of the Cross.

This contrast enables us to establish more closely the nature of Ratzinger's 'progressivism' at this point. It was controlled not so much by the imperative of modernisation or adaptation, *aggiornamento*, but by that of a return to the biblical, patristic and high mediaeval sources, *ressourcement*. His was what Pére

Congar termed

> a 'return-to-sources' Catholicism which is, by the same token,
> Catholicism wholly centred on Christ and also biblical,
> liturgical, paschal, community-minded, ecumenical and
> missionary ...[37]

The implicit question reserved for the future would be: can one
(logically and psychologically) uphold such a neo-patristic
Catholicism in consistent fashion while regarding much of the
intervening generations as sterile in insight for the theory and
practice of the faith. For the principle which sustains the first,
positive attitude – namely, the Spirit-guided self-identity of the
Gospel in transmission in the Church – would seem to require
the radical revision of its second, negative accompaniment.
Some of the difficulties which could attend an attempted
historical reconstruction of the life of the patristic Church were,
indeed, exemplified in Ratzinger's resumed discussion of
episcopal collegiality. It came as something of a shock when the
Orthodox observer Nikos Nissiotis declared collegiality to be
'biblically and historically ill-founded', and his Lutheran
colleague Kirsten Skydsgaard took seriously Ottaviani's
exasperated *bon mot* that; in the Garden of Gethsemane 'the
apostles *did* act collegially – they all left the Lord in the lurch'.
Without the history of failure, desertion, the Cross, protested
the representative of Danish Lutheranism, we have not grasped
the mystery of the Church.[38] Indeed, if Ratzinger is correct,
accusations that the Council was succumbing to a spirit of
Modernistic innovation had spread from the conservative
minority to the ecumenical Observers. Rumour of them
reached Paul VI who endeavoured to answer them in his speech

---

[37]Y. Congar, *Report from Rome II*, op. cit. p. 82; cf. EPDK p. 61.
[38]Ibid. pp. 63–64.

of closure of the session.[39] The pope's intervention in the debate on the Church's governance, which produced the *nota praevia* or 'explanatory remarks' to the Council's text on collegiality meant, so Ratzinger noted, that the doctrine was now biased in a 'primatialistic' direction. He felt it important to recognise, however, not least for the sake of ecumenical outreach to the separated Eastern churches, that many of the functions of the pope in the West were exercised not as universal primate, but as Western patriarch. Such matters did not touch the essence of the collegiality doctrine which was the 'inner co-penetration of the plurality of sacramental communities and the papally preserved unity of service'.[40]

The fourth session

And so to the fourth and last session of the Council whose principal work would be *Gaudium et Spes*, the Pastoral Constitution on the Church in the Modern World. As Ratzinger's commentary makes plain, it was at this point that the alliance of Francophone and Germanophone theologians and bishops so vital to the successful *démarches* of the Council in its three Dogmatic Constitutions, the Liturgy, divine Revelation and the Church, began to break down. His own mood of dis-engagement, and its cause, was unmistakeable. The draft text of *Gaudium et Spes*, in its laudable desire to address modern people from beyond the confines of a theological study-house, had gone seriously astray. Its authors had,

> unfortunately dragged beyond the protecting walls of the theology faculty building just those affirmations which

[39] J. Ratzinger, *Die letzte Sitzungsperiode des Konzils* (Cologne 1966), p. 12. Cited below as LSZ.
[40] EPDK p. 79.

theology shares anyhow with any spiritual-ethical picture of man whatsoever. Whereas what is proper to theology, discourse about Christ and his work, was left behind in a conceptual deep-freeze, and so allowed to appear, in contrast with the understandable part, even more unintelligible and antiquated.[41]

Ratzinger felt obliged to ask the architects of the – largely French – document:

> In this case, what is salvation all about? What does its totality mean for man, if he can be described perfectly well without it, and have his portrait painted in an accurate and satisfying way as a result?[42]

Either faith in Christ reaches into the heart of human existence so that whoever has that faith can only describe the human on its basis, or it belongs to some other world, and will shortly be unmasked for what it is, ideology. Ratzinger also objected to the manner in which the draft Constitution deployed its own key-concept of dialogue with the world. It fell into

> a way of speaking in which faith appears to be a kind of obscure philosophy which deals with things about which man really knows nothing, though he would like to know something, and perhaps even ought to, since after all they do concern his own destiny.[43]

But the essence of faith, Ratzinger objects, is to provide the firm ground on which people can stand and can live, precisely in those matters where other ways of knowledge lead at best to probabilities. The schema was in danger of making doubt the content of faith rather than its opposite while at the same time making demands and issuing commands on other secular issues

[41] Ibid. p. 34.
[42] Ibid.
[43] Ibid. pp. 35–36.

THE EVENT OF THE COUNCIL

where, in fact, certainty was on any reckoning hardly called for. Ratzinger also objected to the use of the term 'People of God' in this context. The impression given was that those in the Church understood human problems by empathy, rather than because they were human themselves! Moreover, it appeared that they were to comport themselves as a sociological grouping seeking out links with others like itself – a reduction of the claims of faith to a level quite inadequate to their real dimensions.[44] In other words, the underlying ecclesiology was both too 'high' and too 'low' in different respects. All that could be said in defence of the *general approach* of the document – for Ratzinger was perfectly favourable to some of its particular judgments, for example the enhanced personalism of its teaching on marriage and its concern for the limitation and, where possible, humanisation of war – was that its artisans had no models to follow. Hitherto, conciliar utterances had taken their cue from the great Creeds: they were authoritative explorations of the world of faith, not sympathetic overtures to non-believers. Ratzinger agreed that the finding of a suitable ecclesial yet 'non-authoritarian' manner of addressing the secular world of today was important, yet asked to be excused from believing that this was the right way to set about it. He particularly objected to the presence of a vulgarised *Teilhardisme* for which human progress and Christian hope, technological liberation and Christian redemption could stand in linear continuity, if not simple identity.

> In the last analysis, it is still true that the world is redeemed by love, not by apparatus.... The service that technology can render is Christianised when it is governed by that ethos which itself serves to make man more human, which itself serves love.[45]

[44]Cf. J. Ratzinger, 'The Dignity of the Human Person', in CDVT V. pp. 115–163.
[45]EPDK p. 42.

The Council's last two discussions concerned mission and priesthood. On the first, Ratzinger recorded that the 'missionary idea' had entered a phase of crisis. He noted that one relevant factor, the optimistic understanding of world religions, showed that 'not all the intellectual darlings of modern theology are biblical through and through'.[46] On the question of ordaining married men to the presbyterate, raised by some South American bishops, Ratzinger commented that the climate of sensationalism which was now enveloping the Council, as well as the disquiet overtaking many Catholics beyonds the walls of the council aula, did not constitute the 'right preconditions for a peaceful debate over so difficult a problem'.[47]

Ratzinger's 'Epilogue' strikes more than one sombre note. Here and there, he thought, and perhaps more frequently than this phrase would imply, 'renewal' would be regarded as synonymous with the 'dilution and trivialisation of the whole'. Here and there, the pleasure of liturgical experimentation would 'belittle and discredit' the reform in worship. Here and there, people would enquire after modernity, not after truth, and make what was contemporary the measure of all they did. Already, he noted, the faithful were complaining of preachers whose sermon pattern was 'It was said to you of old – but I say to you ...'[48] Amid the joy at the Council's many evangelical achievements, such warning-signs should not, he felt, be overlooked.

> Above all, we must not forget that the Church remains the Church of all ages. In all generations, the way of the Gospel could be found in her, and was found.[49]

[46]Ibid. p. 60.
[47]Ibid. p. 67.
[48]Ibid. p. 75.
[49]Ibid. p. 76. For confirmation of the crucial role of *Gaudium et Spes* in Ratzinger's attitude to the Council, one might consult his 'Der Weltdienst der

He recalled, in his closing paragraph, a book of the high church Lutheran Friedrich Heiler which, after some hard sayings about the dogmas and methods of the Church of Rome, reminded its readers how many millions of human beings saw that Church as a 'spiritual mother ... in whose bosom they were sheltered in life and in death'. Perhaps, he thought, because he himself had so little experience of the deaths of Christians, Heiler's remark struck him with great force, and could serve to put into perspective the necessarily limited significance of such a thing as a Council. In the end, the Church lives, in whatever age, in the faith of the simple-hearted: in Zechariah, Elizabeth, Joseph, Mary, in whom the Old Testament reaches its consummation and the New Testament enters on its hidden way of glory.

Kirche. Auswirkungen von *Gaudium et Spes* im letzten Jahrzehnt', in M. Seybold (ed.), *Zehn Jahre Vaticanum II* (Regensburg 1976), p. 36. Here Ratzinger asks that we decide whether *Gaudium et Spes* it so be regarded as the climax of the Council, and so the basis for interpreting everything else it had to say, or whether it should take a more modest place as an attempt to apply, at a given historical juncture, the vision of the Christian faith found in the three Dogmatic Constitutions of the earlier sessions.

Chapter Six

REFLECTIONS ON THE CREED

Not the least of the Council's *desiderata* for theology was a more holistic and unified presentation of Catholic teaching, with particular reference to the mystery of Christ which is its centre. An 'Introduction to Christianity' consisting in a series of theological raids on the deep places of the Creed, would answer well to this request. Ratzinger's reflections on the Creed began life as a series of lectures given at Tübingen in 1967.[1] These were directed, not at divinity students in particular but to allcomers. Though closely argued, they bear marks of their relatively popular origin, notably in the author's choice of illustrations from German folklore. An example occurs in the preface. Ratzinger is seeking a comparison for the contemporary theologian who, rather too often, if for the best of pastoral motives, waters down the content of the faith for the easier consumption of his hearers. The comparison he lights on is with 'Lucky Jack', a folk-character whose lump of gold was so heavy that he was prevailed on to exchange it for increasingly valueless substitutes. Eventually, finishing up with a whetstone, Lucky Jack has no hesitation about chucking it away altogether. Ratzinger evidently hoped that the same fate would not meet his own efforts. He thought they might perform for the students who listened to him something of the service which the Tübingen theologian Karl Adam had done for students in the 1930s with his *The Spirit of Catholicism*.[2]

[1] J. Ratzinger, *Einführung in das Christentum. Vorlesungen über das apostolische Glaubensbekenntnis* (Munich 1968); ET *Introduction to Christianity* (London 1969). Cited below as IC.

[2] K. Adam, *Das Wesen des Katholizismus* (Düsseldorf 1928); ET *The Spirit of Catholicism* (London 1934).

I believe ...

Ratzinger opens by considering what it is like to believe in the world of today. He calls to mind Kierkegaard's celebrated analogy for the Christian preacher: a circus clown desperately trying to deliver a deadly serious message. When he found that people took his warning about a forest fire as knock-about, he got ever more worked up – which only made his hearers laugh the more until in the end their village and they themselves were engulfed in flames.[3] And yet, Ratzinger insists, it is not enough for the preacher, or the theologian, simply to doff his antique dress in order for him to be taken *au sérieux*. We live in a world where unbelief presses upon the believer, just as belief presses upon the unbeliever, whose 'Perhaps it *is* true' mirrors the believer's 'Perhaps it is *not*'. Yet there is some comfort in the thought that transforming the ritual 'I' of the Creed's opening word, *credo*, into the personal 'I' of one's own intimate convictions has never been easy. The reason why not, according to Ratzinger, has to do with the very nature of God, and, more especially, with his transcendence of the world.

God belongs essentially, and not just contingently, beyond our field of vision. This is a fundamental affirmation of the Old Testament. To say *credo* is, therefore, to lay claim to a new mode of access to reality, and one that decisively enlarges the 'world' to which I belong. To say *credo* is to confess that what cannot be seen may still be real, in fact supremely real, the element that supports and makes possible the rest of reality. Moreover, for the Bible this element is also what enables people to lead a truly human existence. Giving them, as it does, their true selves, it can be attained only by a change of direction in their lives, by what is called 'conversion'.

It is when we come to ask after the content of this *credo* that

[3] S. Kierkegaard, cited in H. Cox, *The Secular City* (London 1968), p. 256.

the trouble starts. Current attempts at *aggiornamento* in theology only serve to make us more painfully aware of how old-fashioned what we are being offered is. They have the effect of strengthening the

> suspicion that a convulsive effort is being made to proclaim as contemporary something that is really in fact a relic of days gone by.[4]

There is a symptom of this in the modern Catholic theology of Tradition. Tradition is frequently interpreted as the future-oriented *force motrice* inherent in the sense of faith, rather than as the firm and settled legacy of the primitive Church. Alas: neither the intellectualism of the demythologisers nor the pragmatism of the up-to-daters can suppress the scandal at the heart of Christianity. This scandal Ratzinger terms the 'positivity of Christianity'. Christian belief is concerned primarily with God-in-history, God as involved with man. It claims that in Jesus the Eternal has been introduced into this world. Following the Prologue to the Fourth Gospel, Jesus is the Father's 'exegesis'. *Prima facie* such finding God in a man might seem to make things easier. But in actuality:

> today we stand baffled before this Christian 'revelation' and wonder, especially when we compare it with the religiosity of Asia, whether it would not have been much simpler to believe in the Mysterious Eternal, entrusting ourselves to it in longing thought; whether God would not have done better, so to speak, to leave us at an infinite distance; whether it would not really be easier to ascend out of the world and hear the eternally unfathomable secret in quiet contemplation than to give oneself up to the positivity of belief in one single figure and to set the salvation of man and of the world on the pin-point, so to speak, of this one chance moment in history.[5]

[4]IC p. 26.
[5]Ibid. p. 28.

And Ratzinger asks whether it is even consonant with intellectual integrity today to believe at all.

By way of answering his own question, he considers how we have come to our present picture of what is 'real' fundamentally, that phenomena are — and nothing else. Summarising interpretatively an enormous slice of intellectual history, Ratzinger selects Gianbattista Vico and Karl Marx as the crucial figures in the story. For Vico, what can be known is what man has done, his own historical action and achievement: *verum quia factum*. Unfortunately, the victory of Vico's historicism coincided in the mid-nineteenth century with Darwin's biological discoveries.

> At the very moment when radical anthropocentrism set in and man could only know his own work, he had to learn to accept himself as merely a chance occurrence, just another 'fact'.[6]

But if the significance of history was expelled with a pitchfork by Darwin it returned through the back door with Marx. In Marxism, truth is centred on action and the future. What can be known is man's revolutionary transformation of the world — when it happens. Here the axiom is *verum quia faciendum*. This turn towards sociology and future expectation wrecked the attempts of theology to come to terms with Vico and the movement he inaugurated. Now, in place of presenting faith as history, an interpretation of what people had experienced in the past, theologians, in order to keep up with the intellectual times, found themselves obliged to regard the language of faith as a rhetoric enabling future action.[7] The idea of 'salvation history'

[6]Ibid. p. 34.

[7]Here Ratzinger touches for the first time on the group of theologies that revolve around the motif of a 'political theology': theologies of revolution, represented by T. Rendtorff-H. E. Tödt, *Theologie der Revolution. Analysen und Materialen* (Frankfurt 1968); theologies of hope, as in J. Moltmann, *Theologie der Hoffnung* (Munich 1964); and theologies of 'the world', notably J. B. Metz, *Zur Theologie der Welt* (Mainz-Munich 1968). IC p. 38.

gave way to political and liberation theology. Neither of those
two approaches is valueless. Each brings to light important
facets of what faith is. Yet taken exclusively they conceal rather
than reveal the meaning of the word *credo*. For underlying this
word there is, Ratzinger insists, a specifically biblical approach
to reality which can be tied neither to Vico nor to Marx.
Ratzinger sums up this biblical approach in the pair of terms
'stand' and 'understand', with special reference to Isaiah 7,9:

> If you do not believe, then you will have no hold.

Essentially, this is a matter of:

> entrusting oneself to that which has not been made by oneself
> and never could be made, and which, for that very reason,
> supports and renders possible all our making.[8]

Through faith we acknowledge that a meaning adequate to
making sense of experience can only be received. Like Raspe's
Baron Münchausen, we cannot pull ourselves out of the bog by
getting hold of our own hair. In saying *credo*, we declare that
in this world the receiving of meaning is prior to its making by
man – though without denying the value of human creativity.
So far from being irrational, faith is therefore a movement
towards meaning and truth, towards the *logos*. Ratzinger
presents the Hellenisation of the Gospel in the Greek-speaking
world of the first Christian centuries as not merely legitimate
but providential – and finds indications of a claim to that effect
in the text of Acts.

Yet though *credo* is a word in a dialogue, a word addressed to a
Thou, the setting of the Creed is not a purely individual one,
between God and the soul, but the corporate one of the
Church's life. Turning, then, to the ecclesial form of faith,

[8]IC p. 40.

Ratzinger explains why he intends to use the Apostles' Creed (or Old Roman creed) as the basis for 'introducing Christianity'. It is the Church's own formulation of faith for the candidate entering upon the life of faith by baptism. Of course it is not the only Creed known to Church historians. As a Latin creed, it reflects to some degree the growing divergence of Western and Eastern Christendom, testifying, in this way, to the simultaneous grandeur and misery of Christian history – a reminiscence of Pascal's account of man.[9] Still, the Apostles' Creed reflects the faith of ancient Church which, in its kernel, captures the faith of the New Testament itself. Ratzinger points out that the triform, Trinitarian pattern of this creed corresponds to a threefold renunciation, of the world, the flesh and the Devil, asked of the neophyte.[10] Doctrine is inseparable from the conversion of one's whole being. Ratzinger considers that in this regard the personal singular (*credo* not *credimus*) is theologically preferable. The plural form, in Greek *pisteuomen*, came in when the baptismal creeds were turned to fresh purposes, as common statements of bishops striving for doctrinal unity. Of course this development was quite legitimate: the 'I'-'Thou' dialogue leads naturally to the 'We' of all who believe in the same way. Ratzinger, following here the lead of Karl Rahner, finds it instructive that those who formulated the Church's first dogmatic professions used the term *symbolum, symbolon*, for what they were about. Originally, in the ancient world, a 'symbol' was the two corresponding halves of a ring, staff or tablet. Possession of one half enabled the holder of the other to recognise a guest, messenger or the like. Thus the credal *symbolon* points to the unity of many persons in the single Word.[11] As with Marius Victorinus, the Neo-

[9]Ibid. p. 53.
[10]Ibid. p. 54, with reference to the baptismal liturgy of Hippolytus of Rome, *Traditio apostolica*.
[11]J. H. Emminghaus, 'Symbol III', LexThK, IX. pp. 1208ff.

platonist philosopher in Augustine's time who at first saw no need for the institutional Church until at last he grasped the Christian idea, so everyone who would claim the name of Christian must find the Logos in the community.[12]

> Christian belief is not an idea but life; it is not mind existing for itself, but incarnation, mind in the body of history and its 'We'.[13]

in God. . . .

And so we come at last to the *content* of the Creed, as distinct from the formal nature of its demands upon us. The Creed opens with a summary of biblical faith in God.

> I believe in God, the Father almighty,
> Maker of heaven and earth.

Ratzinger points out that the Bible *presupposes* the concept of God, an idea which

> has left its stamp on the whole history of humanity and right up to the present can raise such passionate argument – yes, right up to this very moment when the cry that God is dead resounds on every side and when nevertheless, in fact for this very reason, the question of God casts its shadow overpoweringly over all of us.[14]

Ratzinger indicates some of the key experiences which led people to excogitate the idea of God. He distinguishes here between experiences relative to human existence, and those

---

[12] Augustine, *Confessiones* VIII. 2, 3–5.
[13] IC p. 64.
[14] Ibid. p. 67.

more bound up with the existence of the world as such. Both negative and positive experiences of human life raise the question of God. Human impoverishment and loneliness lead us to yearn for a fulness of life and relationship. Human happiness and fulfilment prompts us to seek the meaning of such riches.[15] Following the lead of the French Catholic poet Paul Claudel in his play *Le Soulier de Satin*, Ratzinger suggests that the limitations of every human 'Thou' echoing allow us to hear the call of the absolute divine 'Thou' through them.[16] Analogously, men are led to produce the concept of God through reflection on the being of the non-human world, the cosmos: that world manifests the 'all-surpassing power' that both threatens human life and supports it. Ratzinger deals very briefly with this point: after all, he is not a Thomist!

Ratzinger considers that all serious claimants to metaphysical truth accept implicitly the unity of the Absolute whether if, as in theism, they consider it to be consciousness, or as in materialism, matter, or in polytheism as 'supporting power'. The significance of the credal, and biblical, belief in 'one God', is chiefly, then, an existential renunciation of other ways of conceiving of the Absolute and notably that of polytheism for which, characteristically, cosmic and political powers were erected into objects of worship. He offers two important examples suggested by the early Christian opposition to the emperor-cult and to patterns of sexual behaviour in the late antique world.

> The confession 'There is only one God' is, precisely because it has itself no political aims, a programme of decisive political importance, and through the relativisation to which it relegates

[15]This point, that God must be found in our strengths as well as our weaknesses is taken from D. Bonhöffer, *Widerstand und Ergebung* (Munich 1964[12]), p. 182.
[16]P. Claudel, *Le Soulier de Satin* (1921).

all political communities in comparison with the unity of the
God who embraces them all, it forms the only definitive
protection against the power of the collective and at the same
time implies the complete abolition of any idea of exclusiveness
in humanity as a whole.[17]

Similarly:

the unity, finality and indivisibility of the love between man and
woman can in the last analysis only be made a reality and
understood in the light of belief in the unity and indivisibility of
the love of God.[18]

Ratzinger then traces (highly schematically) the
development of biblical faith in this one God. He takes as central
the revelation of the divine Name to Moses in the burning bush
of *Exodus* 3. By a creative process which was simultaneously the
reception of revelation, Israel in Moses produced the name
'Yahweh' as 'the final development of their own name for God
and in it of their own image of God'. Building on the
suggestions of the Old Testament scholar Henri Cazelles,
Ratzinger proposes that this name combines two elements in its
two syllables, one denoting personal self-bestowal and the other
timeless power – itself increasingly summed up in the idea of
Being, so dear to readers of the Septuagint version of this
passage.[19] Like the God of the Fathers, Abraham, Isaac and
Jacob, Yahweh is essentially a personal God, 'to be thought of
and found on the plane of I and You, not primarily in holy
places'.[20] But this affirmation is extended by the claim that this
God is a Being-for which is also Being-in-itself. The elusive

[17]IC p. 75.
[18]Ibid. pp. 75–76.
[19]H. Cazelles, 'Der Gott der Patriarchen', *Bibel und Leben* 2 (1961),
pp. 39–49.
[20]IC p. 83.

ontological claim hidden in the word 'Yahweh' is elucidated by later Old Testament writers, and notably the Second Isaiah whose formula 'I am He, I am the first and I am the last' (Isaiah 48,12) is accurately rendered in the LXX as *Ego eimi*: I am. In the New Testament, the Johannine literature will take up this theme and apply it in a unique fashion to Jesus of Nazareth.[21] As Ratzinger sums up his investigation

> The formula which first occurs in the episode of the burning bush, which at the end of the Exile becomes the expression of hope and certainty in face of the declining gods and depicts Yahweh's lasting victory over all these powers, now finds itself here too at the centre of the faith, but through becoming testimony to Jesus of Nazareth ... The name is no longer merely a word but a person: Jesus himself.[22]

Jesus is thus the 'invocability' of God.

The paradox of biblical faith, then, consists in the conjunction and unity of these two elements: Being is accepted as a person, and the person accepted as Being itself. The inaccessible is He with whom relationship is possible. And this choice of an image of God was renewed in the early Church – where the philosophical question of God was transformed by revelation through the work of the Fathers. It must also be renewed today. Ratzinger argues – against those who say that patristic Hellenism represented a de-naturing of the Gospel – that for all the differences between the religious philosophy of the Greek sages and the Jewish prophetic and sapiential movements, both constitute a striving towards the *logos*: a critique of myth. Yet

---

[21] Ratzinger supports his presentation by reference to: E. Schweizer, *Ego Eimi* (Göttingen 1939); E. Stauffer, *Jesus: Gestalt und Geschichte* (Berne 1957), pp. 130–146; H. Zimmermann, 'Das absolute *ego eimi* als die neutestamentliche Offenbarungs-formel', *Biblische Zeitschrift* 4 (1960), pp. 54–69.
[22] IC p. 91.

the rational God who is the 'eternal geometry of the universe'
remains very different from the 'creative love' of Scripture.
Here Pascal's contrast between 'the God of the philosophers',
and the 'God of Abraham, Isaac and Jacob' is fully justified.[23]
Perhaps sophisticated people today find the rational God far
more credible: it seems hopelessly anthropomorphic to ascribe
to the Supreme Being such attitudes towards puny mankind.
But the Christian understanding of reality rebuffs this objection
as beside the point. *Non coerceri maximo, contineri tamen a minimo,
divinum est*: 'not to be coerced by the greatest, but to be
contained by the smallest – *that* is divine'.[24] And so the God
who is pure Thought is also absolute Love: and here, Ratzinger
remarks, 'it also becomes possible to glimpse the starting-point
of the confession of faith in the *triune* God'.[25]

Ratzinger's account of the Trinity begins with a very proper
recognition of the importance of *apophasis*, of the role of
'negative theology' in this context.

> we are now touching a realm in which any falsely-directed
> attempt to gain too precise a knowledge is bound to end in
> disastrous foolishness; a realm in which only the humble
> admission of ignorance can be true knowledge and only
> wondering attendance before the incomprehensible mystery
> can be the right confession of faith in God. Love is always
> *mysterium* – more than one can reckon, or grasp by subsequent
> reckoning. Love itself – the uncreated, eternal God – must
> therefore be in the highest degree a mystery, *the mysterium*
> itself.[26]

[23]Ibid. p. 99; for his interpretation of Pascal's 'memorial', Ratzinger has
recourse to R. Guardini, *Christliches Bewusstsein* (Munich 1950²), and to H.
Vorgrimler, 'Marginalien zur Kirchenfrömmigkeit Pascals', in J. Daniélou-H.
Vorgrimler (ed.), *Sentire Ecclesiam* (Freiburg 1961), pp. 371–406.

[24]A maxim taken from Hölderlin's preface to *Hyperion*, and originating
from a funeral oration on Ignatius of Loyola. See H. Rahner, 'Die Grabschrift
des Loyolas', *Stimmen der Zeit* 139 (February 1947), pp. 321–337.

[25]IC p. 103.
[26]Ibid. p. 114.

Such self-restraint on reason's part is, in this context, the only way in which it can be true to itself and its task. Nevertheless, Ratzinger insists, we cannot escape posing the question what is really meant by confessing faith in God the Trinity.

The origins of Trinitarian faith do not themselves, however, lie in thinking. Rather, that faith developed out of the effort to 'digest historical experience'. In the Old Testament, God was encountered as the Father of Israel, the world's creator and Lord. In the New Testament, there comes 'a completely unexpected event in which God shows himself from a hitherto unknown side'. In Jesus Christ, we encounter a man who, at the same time, knows and professes himself to be the divine Son. We find God in his ambassador, since that ambassador is himself fully God and not some kind of inter-mediate being – and nevertheless, that ambassador addresses God with us as 'Father'. The upshot is, inevitably, a *prima facie* paradox. On the one hand:

> This man calls God his Father and speaks to him as to someone else facing him; if this is not to be a piece of empty theatricality but truth – which alone befits God – then Christ must be someone other than this Father to whom he speaks, and we also speak.

On the other hand:

> He is himself the real proximity of God coming to meet us, God's mediation to us, and that precisely because he himself is God as man, in human form and nature, God-with-us ... His mediation would indeed basically cancel itself out and become a separation instead of a mediation if he were someone other than God, if he were an inter-mediate being.[27]

Here, then, God meets us not as Father but as the Son who is

[27]Ibid. p. 115.

simultaneously our brother. Lastly, this new experience of God is followed by a third, the experience of the Spirit who is not simply identical with either the Father or the Son but is the personal mode in which God gives himself to us.

Naturally, these defining experiences of Jewish and Christian salvation history raise the question of how the forms of such historical encounter with God are related to the divine reality in itself. Does the 'threefoldness' involved simply tell us something about man and the various modes of his relationship to God, or does it shed light on what God is like in himself? It might seem that the first alternative is so self-evidently the more reasonable that the question is hardly worthy of discussion. But, as Ratzinger stresses:

> The point at issue here is whether man in his relations with God is only dealing with the reflections of his own consciousness or whether it is given to him to reach out beyond himself and to encounter God himself ... If the first hypothesis is true, then prayer too is only an occupation of man with himself; there are no more grounds for worship proper than there are for prayers of petition. . . . (But) if the other answer is the correct one, prayer and worship are not only possible; they are enjoined, that is, they are a postulate of the being 'man' who is open to God.[28]

The Trinitarian struggles of the patristic epoch were not, then, mere conceptual hair-splitting. Rather did they concern the defence of the principle that 'God is as he shows himself'. On this assertion, which Ratzinger holds to be identical with the doctrine of the Trinity itself, the Christian relationship with God is founded. The alternative logics of Subordinationism and Monarchianism constituted the two main counter-options to the conciliar orthodoxy of the patristic Church. For Subordinationism, God becomes 'a sort of constitutional

[28]Ibid. p. 116.

monarch' with whom faith deals 'only by way of his ministers'. For Monarchianism, Father, Son and Holy Spirit are regarded as merely 'masks of God' uninformative about how God is in himself. Ratzinger views the Idealisms of Hegel and Schelling, and their materialist inversion in Marx, as the philosophical after-life of Monarchianism: the historical form of God becomes the gradual self-realisation of the divine; *logos* is only real insofar as it is identical with the historical process itself; meaning becomes purely and simply the creation of history. Here, by contrast with orthodox Trinitarianism:

> the personal element, the dialogue, the freedom and the love, is merged into the inevitability of the one process of reason.[29]

Its victory signified the end, at least in principle, of the political abuse of theology, by destroying theology's potentialities as a political myth. Once again, as with Bonaventure on saving history, the shadow of the later debate over liberation theology looms before us, but by now it is a shadow cast by a living body, the 'political theology' of Johann Baptist Metz. Here Ratzinger puts to new use Erik Peterson's essay 'Der Monotheismus als politisches Problem', which was in its own time an assault, in part, on a certain Carl Schmitt's *Politische Theologie* of 1922.[30]

As Ratzinger sees it, the doctrine of the triune God may be thought of in terms of both negative or apophatic and positive or cataphatic theology. Negatively, it is a representation of the insoluble character of the mystery of God, a 'piece of baffled theology'. Again, it may be offered as an example of the abbé de Saint-Cyran's description of faith as a series of contradictions held together by grace,except that, in the light of modern

---

[29]Ibid. p. 120.

[30]E. Peterson, 'Der Monotheismus als politisches Problem', *Theologische Traktate* (Munich 1951), pp. 45–141; C. Schmitt, *Politische Theologie* (Munich 1922).

physical theory, the term 'contradictions' here would much better be replaced by the word 'complementarities'. Just as, in physics, light must be conceived both as corpuscle and as wave, though these two analyses can resist integration into a single structure, so similarly in the theology of God.

> Here too we can always look from one side and so grasp only one particular aspect which seems to contradict some other. Yet only when the one is combined with the other is it a pointer to the whole that we are incapable of stating or grasping.[31]

Ratzinger draws in these remarks, as will Yves Congar somewhat later in the same context, on the notion of complementarity put forward by the Danish physicist Niels Bohr. Bohr himself already suggested a possible theological application of his idea, taken further by C. F. von Weizsäcker – director of the Bavarian *Max-Planck-Institut* – in a survey article cited in Ratzinger's text.[32]

But the same doctrine of the Trinity may also be put positively, its formulae commended as meaningful statements, 'indications about the ineffable' though not its 'incorporation into our mental world'. The positive significance of Trinitarian faith lies, first, in its construal of the unity and plurality of reality:

> The Christian confession of faith in God as the Three-in-One, as him who is simultaneously the *monas* and the *trias*, absolute unity and fulness, signifies the conviction that divinity lies behind our categories of unity and plurality. Although to us, the non-divine, it is one and single, the one and only divine as opposed to all that is not divine, nevertheless in itself it is truly fulness and plurality, so that creaturely unity and plurality are both in the same degree copy and share of the divine.[33]

[31]IC p. 124.
[32]C. E. Weizsäcker, 'Komplementarität', *Die Religion in Geschichte und Gegenwart* III. pp. 1744ff.
[33]IC p. 127.

This has the important consequence that the model of unity to which creatures should strive is not an 'inflexible monotony' but the unity created by love, the 'multi-unity which grows in love'. Secondly, Trinitarian faith confirms the insight that, in confessing the Absolute as personal, we are necessarily saying that It is not an 'absolute singular'. The prepositional features of the Greek *prosōpon* and the Latin *persona*: *pros*, 'towards'; and *per*, 'through' already indicate relatedness, communicability, fruitfulness. 'The unrelated, unrelatable, absolutely one could not be person.'[34] Thirdly, the Trinitarian dogma makes it clear that *relation*, which for Aristotle had been simply among the 'accidents' or contingent circumstances of being, by contrast with 'substance', the sole sustaining form of the real, in fact stands beside substance as an 'equally primordial form of being'.[35] With this discovery, it became possible for man to surmount 'objectifying thought': a new plane of being came into view. But though the dogma of the Trinity means in this way liberation for speculative thinking, it is not for all that non-biblical. On the contrary it is, Ratzinger insists, the mere transposition of the *logia* of Jesus in St John's Gospel. Commenting on the declarations of the Johannine Christ that 'The Son can do nothing of himself', which appears to rob him of all power, and yet 'I and the Father are one', Ratzinger remarks in a particularly fine passage:

> Since the Son is nothing beside the Father, claims no special position of his own, confronts the Father with nothing belonging only to him, retains no room for his own individuality, therefore he is completely equal to the Father. The logic is compelling: if there is nothing in which he is just he, no kind of fenced-off private ground, then he coincides with the Father, is 'one' with him. It is precisely this totality of interplay that the word 'Son' aims at expressing.[36]

[34]Ibid. p. 128.
[35]Cf. Augustine, *De Trinitate* V. 5, 6; IC p. 131.

Nor does he fail to draw out the practical implications of this
teaching for us. It belongs to the nature of Christian existence, as
a being with Christ, to 'receive and live life as relatedness', and
in this way to enter into that unity which is the foundation of all
reality. The doctrine of the Trinity should become the 'nodal
point' of all Christian thinking.

and in Jesus Christ ...

Moving on to the second section of the Creed, the adumbration
of the Church's faith in 'Jesus Christ, his only Son, our Lord',
Ratzinger reminds his readers of the scandal of 'positivity'
which Christology causes for the Christian religion. The
Creed's confession of the Son is an affirmation that the meaning
that sustains all being has become one individual point within
history.

> The meaning of all being is no longer to be found primarily in
> the sweep of mind which rises above the individual, the limited,
> into the universal; it is no longer simply given in the world of
> ideas, which transcends the individual and is reflected in it only
> in a fragmentary fashion; it is to be found in the midst of time, in
> the countenance of one man.[37]

So Dante discovered when, his 'desire and will ... revolved by
the Love that moves the sun and the other stars', he saw in the
midst of the Eternal Light the human face of Christ, 'painted in
our likeness', and could not take his eyes off that sight:

> Mi parve pinta della nostra effige;
> per che 'l mio viso in lei tutto era messo.[38]

But the scandalous element in this is that it involves our basing

[36]IC p. 134.
[37]Ibid. p. 141.
[38]*Divina Commedia*, 'Paradiso', Canto XXXIII, lines 31–32.

our lives on a single straw floating on the surface of the ocean of history. In modern Christology, the historicity of God's self-communication in Jesus Christ has proved perhaps the chief preoccupation of theologians and exegetes alike. From Adolf von Harnack to Rudolf Bultmann, scholars have tended to one of two courses: either to reduce Christology to history, or to abandon history altogether as irrelevant to faith. Harnack's call for a return from the 'preached Christ', the object of conflicting and therefore divisive beliefs, to the 'preaching Jesus', with his simple message of the unifying power of love, under one Father, with all men our brothers, turned out to be as much the projection of a benevolent liberal professor as the reflection of the evidence.

> While Harnack was still proclaiming his optimistic message about Jesus, those who were to bury his work were already knocking at the door. At the very same time, proof was produced that the plain Jesus of whom he spoke was a romantic dream, a *fata morgana* of the historian, a mirage induced by thirst and longing which dissolved as he approached it.[39]

It was, therefore, explicable, though not excusable, that Bultmann took the directly opposite course, maintaining that, for faith, the only thing that matters about Jesus is that he existed. In every other respect, faith cannot be made subject to vacillating historical hypotheses, but must rest, instead, on the verbal event of the preaching of the Gospel by whose agency human existence is first made aware of its own true nature. But this approach too has insuperable disadvantages.

> Is an empty event easier to swallow than one filled with content? Is anything gained when the question who Jesus was, what he was, and what he was like is dismissed as meaningless, and we are

[39]IC pp. 146–147.

forcibly limited to consideration of some merely verbal event? Certainly, the latter takes place, for the Gospel *is* preached. Yet such an approach leaves in doubt the authenticity of that Gospel, and the reality of its content.[40]

How does Ratzinger react to this now more than a century old problem of how the 'Jesus of history' is related to the 'Christ of faith'? Essentially, by way of three moves. First, he suggests that the 'shuttle movement' of the modern mind, here summarily represented in Harnack and Bultmann, between 'Jesus' and 'Christ', is a valuable pointer to the truth. Not only are the Jesus of history and the Christ of faith unthinkable without each other, but also:

> one is bound to be continually pushed from one to the other because in reality Jesus only subsists as the Christ and the Christ only subsists in the shape of Jesus.[41]

Secondly, the Christological debate can usefully instruct us on the limitations of the historical method, without diminishing our engagement with the historical process of the Incarnation. The full truth of history eludes documentary verification, just as the truth of being escapes the quantifying and laboratory-repeatable procedures of experimental science. Documents may survive, or perish, quite by chance; and in any case they do not yield the human depths of the happenings they concern in any automatic or necessarily adequate way. So, thirdly, we may, in chastened mood, be willing to re-consider the image of Jesus Christ presented by the confession of faith itself, which, after all:

> has endured for centuries and by its very nature had no other aim but that of understanding – understanding who and what this Jesus really was.[42]

[40]Ibid. p. 147.
[41]Ibid. p. 148.
[42]Ibid.

REFLECTIONS ON THE CREED

The faith represented by the Creed is not 'a reconstruction or a theory, but a present, living reality'.

Ratzinger's exploration of that image as found in the Creed starts out from a comment on the fusion of personal name, Jesus, and office, Christ, by which the Christian's Lord is denoted. This marrying of name and title is not just another example of history's forgetfulness. On the contrary, it takes us at once to the very heart of the understanding of the man from Nazareth which faith obtained. Faith affirms that, in the case of Jesus:

> it is not possible to distinguish office and person; with him, this differentiation simply becomes inapplicable. The person *is* the office, the office *is* the person. ... Here there is no private area reserved for an 'I' which remains in the background behind the deeds and actions, and thus at some time or other can be 'off duty'. Here there is no 'I' separate from the work: the 'I' *is* the work, and the work the 'I'.[43]

The passage is redolent of Karl Barth's statement in the *Church Dogmatics* that 'Christ's being as man is his work'; the importance of the whole section had been brought home to Ratzinger by von Balthasar.[44]

The birthplace of this faith in Jesus as the Christ was Calvary. On the *titulus*, the execution notice of Jesus, drawn up in all the international languages of the day, Pilate ascribed to Jesus the kingly status of the Christ. By a sublime irony, the pagan Roman procurator's whimsy gave faith its true starting-point.

> Jesus' crucifixion is his coronation; his coronation or kingship is his surrender of himself to men, the identification of his words, his mission and his existence in the yielding up of his life ...

[43]Ibid. p. 149.
[44]K. Barth, *Kirchliche Dogmatik* III.2 (Zürich 1948), pp. 66–69; cf. H. U. von Balthasar, 'Zwei Glaubensweisen', in *Spiritus Creator* (Einsiedeln 1967), pp. 76–91.

> From the Cross, faith understands in increasing measure that this Jesus did not just do and say some*thing*. In him, message and person are identical ... He always anticipates what he says by what he is.[45]

The primitive community found, in its ruminations on the oral memories preserved in the Gospel tradition, that Jesus' message, studied retrospectively, is such that it 'always leads to, and flows into, this "I": the identity of word and person'. John's Gospel is the climax, not the exception. Its treatment of faith in the Christ as the message of the story of Jesus indicates the complete unity of Christ and Jesus, a unity which will remain formative for the whole further history of faith. Moreover, *pace* Harnack, such Christological assertiveness does not suppress concern with the love-command, but enhances it. The inseparability of Jesus' person and work, the identity of a man with his act of sacrifice, these things 'signify the hyphen' which joins faith and love.

Yet this radical 'Christhood' of Jesus only remains a rational belief if it be acknowledged that it postulates his Sonship, and that this Sonship includes his Godhood. 'Without this logical consistency, one sinks into myth.' At the same time, the developed christological orthodoxy of the Church also acknowledges, and no less resolutely, that in his radical service of sacrificial love, Jesus is 'the must human of men', and it thus subscribes to the identity of theology with anthropology. For Ratzinger, the Sonship is expressed, historically speaking, in two titles of Jesus: 'Son of God' and – in no way to be confused with this – 'Son' *tout court*. The first title derives from the Jewish theology of the royal Messiah. When ancient Israel 'de-mythologised' the Egyptian myth of the divine begetting of a new king at his enthronement, and preserved its imagery in its own Davidic court ritual, it kept alive a language which could be used to express Jesus' triumphant fulfilment of the royal hope

[45]IC p. 152.

of the Old Testament.

> It is of him, the complete failure, who no longer has an inch of ground under his feet as he hangs from the Cross, for whose garments lots are drawn, and who seems to be himself abandoned by God, that the oracles speaks: 'You are my son; today – on *this* spot – I have begotten you. Ask of me, and I will make the nations your heritage and the ends of the earth your possession.'[46]

This title must be carefully distinguished from the second 'filial' title, that of 'Son' taken without any further qualification.

> Here we are confronted with something quite different, something infinitely simpler and at the same time infinitely more personal and profound. Here we have a glimpse of Jesus' experience of prayer, of the nearness to God which distinguishes his relations with God from those of all other men, yet, far from aiming at some kind of exclusiveness, was designed to include the others in its own relationship with God. It wishes to incorporate them, as it were, in its own kind of attitude to God, so that with Jesus and in him they can say 'Abba' to God just as he does. No set distance shall separate them any longer; they are to be embraced in that intimacy which in Jesus is reality.[47]

The dogmas of Nicaea and Chalcedon were meant to express nothing other than the 'identity of service and being', of function and ontology, in which the content of the prayer-relationship between the 'dear Father' (*Abba*) and the Son comes to light. By expounding the mystery of Christ in this fashion, Ratzinger hopes to overcome, to the degree possible, the polarity between a Christology of the Incarnation, on the Johannine and patristic model, and a Christology of the Cross, of the sort found in Paul and the sixteenth century Reformers.

[46]Ibid. p. 163.
[47]Ibid. p. 167.

The being of Christ – the predominant concern of a Christology of the Incarnation – is a continuous exodus. It is not a resting in self, but the permanent act of being Son, of being servant. Conversely, this act, for which we need verbs, 'doing'-words, and whose supreme manifestation is the Cross, is not simply doing, but is also being. A Christology of the Incarnation and a Christology of the Cross require each other.

Such a Christology is already soteriology, a doctrine of the salvation wrought by the person of Christ. Nevertheless, Ratzinger considers its necessary to look at soteriology in more explicit terms. He reminds his readers that the classical account of Christ's saving activity in the Western tradition since the Middle Ages has been that of Anselm of Canterbury. Anyone who studies the *Cur Deus homo* 'with a little patience' should be able to appreciate its biblical and human insight. He sums up Anselm's teaching by saying that, in relation to the fundamental problem of the damage to the right order of the world which sin causes:

> God himself removes the injustice; not (as he could) by a simple amnesty, which cannot after all overcome from inside what has happened, but by the infinite Being himself becoming man and then, as a man – who thus belongs to the race of the offenders yet possesses the power, denied to man, of infinite reparation – making the required expiation.[48]

However, the 'rigorous logic' of Anselmian soteriology *can* distort the image of God by giving the impression that God is himself 'under an obligation to the concept of order'. Ratzinger's own soteriology will proceed by exploring the possibilities of a different key idea, namely, the principle of 'being-for'.

The portrait of the earthly Jesus offered by St John's Gospel

[48]Ibid. p. 173.

concludes with the event of the lance-thrust. 'One of the soldiers thrust a lance into his side and immediately blood and water came out.' Ratzinger comments:

> After the lance-thrust that ends his earthly life, his existence is completely open; now he is entirely 'for', now he is truly no longer a single individual but 'Adam', from whose side Eve, a new mankind, is formed.... The open side of the new Adam repeats the creative mystery of the 'open side' of man: it is the beginning of a new definitive community of men with one another ... The fully opened Christ, who completes the transformation of being into reception and transmission, is thus visible as what at the deepest level he always was: as 'Son'.[49]

The 'hour' in which Jesus becomes man's salvation has arrived.

Thinking back, surely, to the debate over *Gaudium et Spes*, Ratzinger underlines how little Christian salvation, so understood, has to do with the 'cheerful romanticism of progress'. The man who is 'open', and thus 'opens up a new beginning' is *sacrificed* man. Man finds himself by looking on the Pierced One, and following him on the path he has cleared into the future. Because faith has already seen the face of the Saviour on the Cross, the faithful know in advance what the Lord of the Parousia will look like: he will be the 'man who can embrace all men because he has lost both himself and them to God'.[50]

The same principle of 'being for' expresses, Ratzinger goes on, the true basic law of Christian existence. Christian faith seeks the individual person; but it wants the individual person to be *for the whole*: for the glorification of God and the service of man in an inseparable combination. The primordial Christian prayer position, portrayed in so moving a way on the walls of the catacombs, is the outstretched arms of the *orantes*. This position reflects the final gesture of the Lord on the Cross: at

[49]Ibid. pp. 180–181.
[50]Ibid. p. 182.

once a worshipper of the Father and an embracer of mankind in 'full and undivided brotherliness'. Such being-for is already hinted at on the plane of cosmic nature:

> Truly, truly I say to you, unless a grain of wheat falls into the earth and dies, it remains alone but if it dies, it bears much fruit.[51]

The clue given by the creation points to the fulfilment found in man, or, more precisely, in *the* man *par excellence*, Jesus Christ. By losing himself, he affords access to true life. To be fruitful, all self-sacrifice requires the mediating acceptance of *the* 'other' who is at once mankind's divine Other and yet completely one with it in its humanness: the God-man.

But no account of salvation would be evangelical in which the principle of being-for was left without its complementary law, the 'principle of excess'. Here too we have a principle rooted in the cosmic creation, where life 'squanders a million seeds in order to save one living one'. Similarly:

> excess is the realm foundation and form of the history of salvation, which in the last analysis is nothing other than the truly breathtaking fact that God, in an incredible outpouring of himself, expends not only a universe but his own self in order to lead man, a speck of dust, to salvation.[52]

Only the lover can understand the 'folly of a love to which prodigality is a law and excess alone sufficient'. Yet in contemplating human love, we see that man is a being for whom excess is, paradoxically, a necessity. Ratzinger concludes, in Kierkegaardian vein, that it is because revelation is superfluous that it is necessary and divine: the love in which the meaning of the world is disclosed.

[51]John 12, 24.
[52]IC p. 197.

This principle of excess, which states the *mode* of the divine being-for in Christ, suggests a third ground-rule of Christian faith, enabling Ratzinger to resolve the 'scandal of positivity' with which his 'reflections on the Creed' began. For Christian faith, man comes to himself 'not through what he does but through what he accepts'.[53] This 'primacy of acceptance' is what gives Christian ethics its basic character: *vis à vis* divine grace, human activity is only of penultimate importance, a discovery which brings in its train an inner liberation. We are freed to act responsibly yet in an 'uncramped' way, putting our lives at the service of redemptive love. Even more importantly for Ratzinger's present dogmatic purposes, the primacy of acceptance shows the intrinsic necessity of Christian positivity – in the special sense he has given that term. Because man does not create his identity, using his own resources, but receives it from outside him as a free gift, our relation with God

> demands the positivity of what confronts us, of what comes to us as ... something to be received.[54]

The antithesis, made so much of by the Enlightenment critic of Christianity G. E. Lessing, between *vérité de fait* (contingent truths of fact) and *vérité de raison* (necessary intellectual truths) is surmounted. The contingent is precisely what is necessary to man.

Before leaving the central section of the Creed, governed by the affirmations about God the Son, Ratzinger deals more briefly with the particular Christological mysteries of the birth, crucifixion, descent, resurrection, ascension and return. On the virgin birth, Ratzinger proposes that this teaching does not belong with the dogma of Jesus' divine Sonship but with the theology of grace. Since the conception of Jesus is new creation,

[53]Ibid. p. 202.
[54]Ibid. p. 203.

not begetting by God, the doctrine of Jesus' divinity would not be affected had he been the product of a normal human marriage. Instead, the virginal conception is

> a proclamation of how salvation comes to us: in the simplicity of acceptance, as the voluntary gift of the love that redeems the world.[55]

And Ratzinger finds its extraordinary that, at a time when people, not least Christians, are re-discovering the significance of their corporeality, there should be an attempt to save the Christian faith by disembodying it, and limiting God to the sole sphere of the spiritual. Like von Balthasar, whose influence will never be far from Ratzinger's work in the years to come, he sees the Virgin's Son as disclosing the Father not only on the Cross but also, and especially, in the descent into Hell. On the Cross, the 'inexhaustible abyss of the divine love' both judges man who denies love in murdering the Just One, and also saves him. But, more than this, on Holy Saturday the Church and the individual:

> reach out beyond the Cross, the moment when the divine love is tangible, into the death, the silence and the eclipse of God.[56]

The door of death stands open, since 'Life and Love have dwelt in death's realm'.[57] The greater strength of love in the face of death is what the resurrection means. In his ascension, Christ, through that power, establishes the reality of heaven, the definitive confluence of God and man. The eternal God has handed over to one who, as man, is our brother the giving of verdict on all human history:

[55]Ibid. pp. 210–211.
[56]Ibid. p. 226.
[57]Ibid. p. 230.

The Judge will not advance to meet us as the Wholly Other, but as one of us, who knows human existence from inside and has suffered.[58]

I believe in the Holy Spirit ...

Ratzinger's reflections on the final, pneumatological, section of the Creed are disproportionately brief. The unity of the last part of the Creed consists in the fact that all its statements – from the 'communion of saints' to the 'resurrection of the body and life everlasting' are descriptions of the way in which the Spirit works in history. He confines his attention to two major questions: the holiness of the Church, and the consummation of both matter and spirit in the Age to Come. For, on the first, to many people today the Church has become the main obstacle in the way of belief. Ratzinger reminds his hearers that, in the Creed, despite a widespread misunderstanding,

> the Church is not called 'holy' ... because its members, collectively and individually are holy, sinless men. This dream, which appears afresh in every century, has no place in the waking world of our text.[59]

The holiness of the Church consists, rather, in that power of sanctification which God exerts in her in the face of human sinfulness. The interplay of God's faithfulness and man's infidelity, the typical pattern of the Church's life, is 'grace in dramatic form'. In this 'unholy holiness' of the Church is revealed God's true holiness which is love: not a reserved aristocratic love but one which 'mixes with the dirt of the world so as to overcome it'.[60] The tone of rancorous bitterness which has become a fashionable habit does not understand this; worse,

[58]Ibid. p. 251.
[59]Ibid. p. 263.
[60]Ibid. p. 265.

it feeds on a hidden pride. Ratzinger advises us not to set too much store by ecclesiastical reforms:

> For the Church is most present not where organising, reforming and governing are going on but in those who simply believe and receive from her the gift of faith that is life to them[61]

– words which show that the spirit of his 'Epilogue' on the last session of the Council was no passing mood. Not that such a relativisation of reform entailed quietism, as his remarks on the resurrection of the body indicate. In an account of the re-union of matter and spirit which must take place if the cosmos, and not just the private self, is to be saved, he concluded his lectures and his book:

> The goal of the Christian is not private bliss but the whole. He believes in Christ, and for that reason he believes in the future of the world, not just in his own future ... He knows that there is a meaning which he is quite incapable of destroying. Is he therefore to sit quietly with his hands in his lap? On the contrary: because he knows that there is such a thing as meaning, he can and must cheerfully and undismayed do the work of history.[62]

Though it may *feel* like the endless stone-rolling of Sisyphus, the daily repeated weaving of Penelope, each of whose work was done only to be undone, that nightmare of the pre-Christian world is pierced by the saving, transforming voice of reality:

> Take courage, I have overcome the world.[63]

In the years to come, Ratzinger would develop further his thoughts on the segment of the Creed that belongs to the Spirit: in further essays on ecclesiology, and a major exploration of eschatology, the theme of the End.

[61] Ibid. p. 266.
[62] Ibid. pp. 277–278.
[63] John 16, 33.

Chapter Seven

MORE ECCLESIOLOGICAL ESSAYS

Stimulated by the experience of the making of *Lumen Gentium*, Ratzinger's contribution to ecclesiology did not stop short with his work on 'people and house of God' in Augustine.

Re-visiting old friends

In this connexion, his thoughts would frequently stray back to the Augustinian corpus. He noted the importance of the idea of 'extensive catholicity', the universal (and thus Catholic) Church of all nations, in the renegade Donatist Tyconius, and how this both resembled and differed from Augustine's ideas on the same subject.[1] Belonging to the Church was, for Tyconius, a purely pneumatological affair – spiritual because of the Holy Spirit, without any Christological dimension. The universal Church of the Donatist lay theologian's vision was a purely invisible reality, composed of those who, through faith, communicate in the Spirit. How different was Augustine's picture, in which there is no access to the *ecclesia vera et invisibilis*, the 'true and invisible Church', save through the *visibilis ecclesia catholica*, its visible, Catholic counterpart. In Augustine's case, Ratzinger felt, it would not be excessive to speak of a real piety directed towards the Church.[2] This piety stands out clearly if one looks at early writings like the *Soliloquia*, with their cry *Deus et anima, nihil aliud*,[3] against the foil of the last treatises, like the *Tractatus*

---

[1] J. Ratzinger, *Das neue Volk Gottes. Entwürfe zur Ekklesiologie* (Düsseldorf 1969), pp. 11–23. Cited below as NVG.

[2] NVG pp. 24–48.

[3] *Soliloquia* I. 2, 7.

THE THEOLOGY OF JOSEPH RATZINGER

in Joannem, with their bold statement that 'Inasmuch as anyone loves Christ's Church, to that degree he possesses the Holy Spirit'.[4] Ratzinger regards the development of Augustine's 'ecclesial piety' as re-arranging in drastic fashion the elements of the Plotinian Catholicism he had discovered at Milan. Whereas for the Neo-Platonists, 'political virtue', *aretē polikē*, could only be a secondary kind of virtue, since man's true good, conformity to God, was not based upon it, for the piety of bishop Augustine this was not so. He could recover in a new way the ancient Hellenic primacy of communitarian virtues, since

> he had found in the Church the new *polis*, which means the tabernacling of God in this world. To enter into her unity does not signify the loss of oneself in the world's multiplicity – whatever any appearance may suggest to the contrary. Entering her unity means being conjoined to the unity of God himself, for such unity is found not in detachment, but in service, in imitation of the Son of God who came down from heaven.[5]

Nor had Ratzinger forgotten his second love, Bonaventure, when meditating on the mystery of the Church.[6] Here the context was the articulation of Catholic faith in the universal primacy of the Roman bishop. Though the papal primacy is rooted in Scripture and the witness of the ancient Church, diverse factors in later Church history contributed to its effective explicitation, and to the coming to be of its concrete form. In the thirteenth century, the Western patriarchs used the newly founded Mendicant Orders to help reform the Latin church. In this context, just as the Franciscans bore the brunt of the attack from secular clerics and from monks, so their doctrine of the primacy – the ecclesiological justification of their

---

[4] *Tractatus in Joannem* XXXII. 8.
[5] NVG p. 46.
[6] See ibid. pp. 49–71.

134

activities – was, of all the Orders of friars', the clearest. On behalf of the older pattern of Church life, William of St-Amour put forward a theory of the hierarchy which invoked the authority of Denys the Areopagite for its anti-papalism. For William, one hierarch can only influence another directly below him, in the three-fold *taxis* of bishop, presbyter, and deacon. Ratzinger compares this constriction of the Petrine ministry to the modern attempt to apply the concept of subsidiarity, originally worked out for social ethics, to the life of the Church. Bonaventure's Ultramontanism sought its own theological expression by reference to a cosmological, rather than a sociological principle. Bonaventure borrowed his idea of *reductio* from the Arab Aristoteleanism of Averroes. This principle asserted that for every kind of thing, there is a first or supreme instance which functions as a criterion for all other beings of the same kind. Employing it in a context which would have surprised Averroes, the Franciscan theologian argued that humanity at large 'reduces' to Christ's premier disciple, the Roman pope. Bonaventure's other suggestions, that the vicar of Christ has the same role in the economy of the New Testament as the Jewish high priest in the Old, but *eminentiori modo*; and that the one Church requires one hierarch who will be to her, typologically, head of the Body and groom of the Spouse, are also regarded by Ratzinger as distinctly dangerous arguments. In fact, Ratzinger shows himself here as very much aware of the possibilities of rank and exotic growth such as can be put forth by an over-enthusiastic papalism. Such a papalism will, he implies, breed its own opposite, and sometimes in the same individual. Thus Bonaventure's ultra-papalist disciple Pietro Giovanni Olivi became, over the issue of the Franciscan Spirituals, a doughty opponent of the Papacy which he stigmatised as Anti-Christ. It all shows, Ratzinger concludes, the need for a 'spirit of moderation and the just mean' which, without considering advantages or disadvantages for the individual or group, will seek, quite simply, what is true to Christ's dispensation.[7]

A eucharistic ecclesiology

Such forays in the tradition, though fruitful in providing both inspiration and warning, cannot replace attempts to think through the systematic issues involved. Ratzinger has devoted considerable attention to the question, Which key idea or ideas will best enable us to understand the Church of Jesus Christ, as revelation presents her to us?

Ratzinger points out that the history of ecclesiology shows an oscillation between a stress on the Church's visible, external side, and an emphasis on her contrasting invisible, interior aspect.[8] Each of these emphases may well have its own rationale in the Church of its time. Thus, Robert Bellarmine's accentuation of the Church as a visible society was a necessary constituent of the Catholic response to the Reformers, and led in time to the profound ecclesial apologetic of the First Vatican Council where the Church as a 'sign of God among the peoples' is seen, in her international universality, as the divine fulfilment of Isaiah's prophecy:

> He will raise an ensign for the nations,
>   and will assemble the outcasts of Israel,
> and gather the dispersed of Judah
>   from the four corners of the earth.[9]

In the years between the two World Wars of this century, the need was, rather, for a deeper sense of the Church's interior

[7]Ibid. p. 71.
[8]Ibid. p. 75–76.
[9]Isaiah 11, 12.

nature, and the intimate share therein which each of the baptised possesses. The satisfaction of this need was the task, in German speaking lands, of the Munich philosopher Romano Guardini, and the imaginative writer Gertrud von le Fort.[10] Yet this bias, desirable as it was in its time, has led to a certain disdain for the Church's external structures, an echo of the Lutheran historian Rudolf Sohm's notorious distinction between a 'Church of law' and a 'Church of love'.[11] In reality, however, there exists:

> only one Church which is indivisibly and at the same time a mystery of faith and a sign of faith: mystery-filled life and the visible manifestation of that life.[12]

Ratzinger proposes to show how this is so by a consideration of the Eucharist, at once the most interior and spiritual, yet also exterior and social, reality that could be conceived. Ratzinger bases himself on the Synoptic accounts of the Twelve as spiritual fathers of a new people of God, a conception realised at the Last Supper where the permanent centre of this new Israel is disclosed as being the Lord's own body, a new Temple, as the evangelist calls it, 'not built by human hands'.[13] He also makes use of the Pauline picture of the Church as the body of Christ and the patristic developments of that theme so exhaustively described by the Belgian Jesuit Emil Mersch.[14] This is, in fact, an exercise in 'eucharistic ecclesiology', a movement of thought whose own origins are to be found in the Russian Orthodox

[10]On Guardini, see J. Ratzinger (ed.), *Wege zur Wahrheit. Die bleibende Bedeutung Von R. Guardini* (Düsselfdorf 1985); on von le Fort, see, for the theological aspect, R. Göllner, *Der Beitrag des Romanwerks Gertrud von le Forts zum ökumenischen Gespräch* (Paderborn 1973).

[11]Ratzinger had already discussed Sohm's thesis in an appendix to *Volk und Haus Gottes*, op. cit. pp. 318–322.

[12]NVG p. 77.

[13]Mark 14, 58.

[14]E. Mersch, *Le Corps mystique du Christ. Etudes de théologie historique* (Louvain 1933; 1936²).

ecclesiology of the early twentieth century.[15] The Church is a communion of communities, *Église des églises*, not in the sense of a federalism but of a body rendered an organic unity by the Eucharistic bond.[16]

Ratzinger's adoption of a eucharistic ecclesiology was owed in particular to the example of de Lubac. He noted the hesitations of a number of inter-war ecclesiologists with regard to the idea of the Church as 'Body of Christ', the fear that it might lead to a false glorification of the Church of the Crucified, camouflaging the spiritual poverty of the earthly Church with a 'false aureole'. On the other hand, the model of the Church which such writers as Johannes Beumer, Erich Przywara and Mannes Dominikus Koster sought to put in its place, that of the People of God, was by itself insufficiently characteristic of the New Testament economy, too little Christologically determined. The unique advantage of a eucharistic ecclesiology was, Ratzinger felt, that it could combine the strengths of both approaches, and in combining them, help them to overcome their weaknesses. The Church is 'the people of God by virtue of the body of Christ'.[17]

> The fact of being People of God is something which the Church has in common with the people of the old Covenant; but the Church's being such in the Body of Christ – this is, so to say, her specifying difference as a new people. This is what gives her particular mode of existence and unity its proper character.

And in a reference of ecumenical significance to the knotty problem of who should count as members of this Church, Ratzinger proposed that all the baptised (in whatever Christian

---

[15]On this, see my forthcoming, *The Table of our Unity. Church, Fathers, Eucharist in N. N. Afanasiev (1893–1966).*

[16]Here one may now consult J. M. R. Tillard, *Eglise des eglises. L'ecclésiologie de communion* (Paris 1987).

[17]NVG p. 97.

denomination) should be seen as 'belonging fundamentally to the *communio*', even though they may be also 'effectively outside the *communio*'s unity'.[18] Here he seeks to transcend the terms of an earlier debate among Catholic dogmaticians and apologists, who had seen non Catholic Christians as members of the Church solely by desire, *voto* – which lumped them together with avowed pagans. Curiously, the canonical tradition·had preserved a surer ecclesiological tact by regarding every baptised person as the Church's man.

A eucharistic ecclesiology naturally gives much attention to the Church's ministerial pattern, since no eucharistic celebration can be without its president, the 'one who gives thanks'. Yet, oddly enough, Ratzinger's own theology of ministerial office does not take its rise from reflection on the Eucharistic assembly, as with the pure eucharistic ecclesiologists of the Orthodox tradition, but from a wider, if more diffused, picture of the Gospel community. He takes as his emblem the dictum of the fifteenth century Dominican John Stoykovič of Ragusa, a Western envoy to the Byzantine East, that the Church is composed of three elements: confession (of the faith), communion (in the sacraments) and obedience (to the apostolic ministry which Christ founded).[19] Over against the Augsburg Confession's moderate Lutheranism, with its definition of the Church as 'the congregation of the holy people, in which the Gospel is taught purely and the sacraments administered rightly', Ratzinger enquires, how, unless obedience to the apostolic ministry is an intrinsic feature of the Church, we are to determine what counts here as 'pure' teaching and 'right' sacraments. The question brings home the crucial character of the question of the ministry.

[18]Ibid. p. 102.
[19]Ibid. pp. 105–106.

The unity of the Church

Ratzinger presents the ministry in terms of the *unity* of the Church. The Church's unity is, in one of its essential aspects, unity with the apostolic office and authority. Such unity was 'explicated' in the sub-apostolic period, in a twofold form: in the local community by the 'vertical' structure of bishop, presbyters and deacons, and in the world-wide community by the 'horizontal' communion of bishops. Just as Word and sacrament found the unity of the Church, so does this apostolic office testify to it. The first two are its cause, the last its necessary condition. However, a Church which is one need not necessarily be a Church that is unitary. The historical development of the Roman see, by marrying the Petrine idea of universal primacy with the patriarchal functioning of the Papacy in the West, has produced an image of 'centralism' which is perfectly dispensable. In other words, there are many matters of the practical administration of the local churches of the Roman patriarchate which could well be ordered without any necessary reference to Rome itself. What is, however, indispensable to the Church's unity is the attentive obedience of all to the definitive interpretation of faith offered at the chair of Peter – naturally, as preceded and prepared by the Pope's listening to the universal Church, in some appropriate form. Moreover, the ambit of such universal–primatial intervention should not always be restricted simply to such 'extraordinary' occasions as *ex cathedra* pronouncements. At times, the Church's unity will require more of its supreme pastor than this.

The present situation indicates with sufficient clarity that it is not only the 'periphery' which has something to say and bring to the 'centre'. There is still a continuing need for the particular churches to accept correction from the centre which bears the 'person' of all.[20]

[20]Ibid. p. 144.

One ought to avoid the impression, Ratzinger continues, that
the only competence of the Pope, or of the apostolic ministry at
large, is to register from time to time the 'statistical mean' of
faith, as though there could be no decision contrary to what the
'average believer' (itself a problematic notion) is thinking. Faith
has objective norms in Scripture and in dogma, though in 'dark
times' these may, alas, evaporate from the awareness of a
statistical majority of the faithful.

> In such cases, the Pope may and must not hesitate to speak
> against statistics, and the power of opinion with its pretence of
> possessing exclusive validity. This should happen the more
> decisively if, as in the hypothetical case I am imagining, the
> witness of tradition is strongly behind him.[21]

Ratzinger was, then, deeply exercised by the theme of the
Church's unity, an international unity with a salvific
significance in its very transcending of the merely national. He
looked back to the world of Christian antiquity to find his
bearings on this topic, with its obvious contemporary relevance
in the temptation of post-conciliar Catholicism to see itself as a
vine carrying discreet clusters of dioceses, bunched together on a
broadly national basis.[22]

What sources did the patristic Church possess for its
reflections on the problem of the One and the Many as that
affects the worldwide society of mankind? First, there was the
heritage of Greco-Roman antiquity. The Stoics had discovered
the unity of man as something underlying all differences in
culture. All men form one body. However, this doctrine

[21]Ibid. See further on the problems raised by attempts to apply democratic
models to the Church's life, J. Ratzinger – H. Maier, *Demokratie in der Kirche.
Möglichkeiten, Grenzen, Gefahren* (Limburg 1970).
[22]J. Ratzinger, *Die Einheit der Nationen: eine Vision der Kirchenväter*
(Salzburg 1971), cited below as EN.

suffered differing interpretations.[23] From it, Antisthenes (pupil of Socrates, and founder of the school of Cynic philosophers) and his disciple Diogenes inferred an apolitical, individual ideal of the world citizen. Since what is really important is humanity, they found the State's order uninteresting. This, Ratzinger points out, was by no means without its effect on Christians:

> This attitude of inner freedom vis-à-vis the State aiming at an ethical, not a political revolution, at changing men, not structural relationships, undoubtedly gave the Christian opposition a departure point of a decisive kind. It helped Christians to develop that inner freedom which enabled the martyrs to counterpose the conviction of faith to State authority, the interior power of truth to the external power of earthly force....[24]

In Alexander the Great, however, the same fundamental Stoic notion led to a quite discrepant conclusion: Alexander's project was the creating of a kingdom that would embrace the entire *oikoumenē*, the 'living area of cultured humanity'. It was the latter programme which had the more obvious impact. The idea of a universal monarchy found its concrete realisation in the government of the Roman *princeps*. In the Hellenistic part of the empire, God as monarch might hold in his hand the strings of the cosmic marionette theatre, but he entrusted the immediate governance of the nations to various custodians. Politically, that meant a strong stress on the distinctive structures of each nation; religiously, a new justification for polytheism. Ratzinger stresses that in the West, by contrast, the notion of unity was much more prominent. The peace which Augustus wished to bring mankind was a cosmic event, the fulfilment of the unity of the pan-human body.

[23] A. A. T. Ehrhardt, *Politische Metaphysik von Solon bis Augustin* (Tübingen 1959), I. pp. 247–309.
[24] EN pp. 14–15.

From these animadversions on pagan ideology, in which Ratzinger is much indebted to the Tübingen classicist A. A. T. Ehrhardt, as well as to the historical-theological investigations of Erik Peterson,[25] he turned to consider the biblical background of the idea of the unity of the nations. The contrast is stark. For the Bible, the unity of the world, and of humankind within the world, depends on confession of the one God, and the rooting of history in the common ancestors whom God has given. Descended as they are from Adam, men and women are all alike in the image of God; sprung from the loins of Noah, they are also embraced by that primordial covenant imaged in the rainbow spanning the whole earth. Such fundamental presuppositions are incompatible with those of classical thought, for which divinity is itself a part of the world, and the world of divine rank. In this latter case, unity is already found in the world, albeit in a condition of latency. What it needs is to realise itself by its own powers – and this can be achieved through the mediatorial activities of the Roman emperor. The Old Testament contains, providentially, its own answer to these pretensions: the story of the Tower of Babel. As there God is portrayed as scattering guilty men into a multiplicity of separate, and separating, languages, it becomes clear that the restoration of unity will not be carried out by man alone.

> The God who stands opposite man, and has a free power of his own which is quite independent of the world, limits man's power and possibilities. Man cannot spin the unity of the world out of his own substance, since separation is imposed upon him by God's sovereign will. The Old Testament looks out constantly for that coming moment when all the nations will go on pilgrimage to the hill of Zion, and Jerusalem become the capital, the mid-point, of a re-united humanity. But it sees this as

[25]E. Peterson, 'Der Monotheismus als politisches Problem', art. cit.

143

no directly political programme but, rather, an eschatological hope whose final realisation lies with God.[26]

And the New Testament takes us even further away from the Greco-Roman idea of a single *cosmopolis* to be attained by human effort. Mankind is hampered by a defective beginning. Humanity as we know it must be transcended, and this happens through the Cross, in the death and descent of the Son of man. In Christ, as the Crucified and Risen One, the second, and definitive, humanity has been initiated. Thus in the Gospel genealogies, Jesus is not only son of Abraham: he is son of Adam. And so the Church of which he is the Head is

the new cosmopolis, which therefore – consistently enough – promises a truly new world.[27]

In the classical world, Christianity could only be a revolutionary force – not in the sense of a movement for the subversion of political power, but in that of

a penetrating calling into question of the spiritual foundations from which the ancient world lived and on whose basis its cosmos, its form of world-order, rested.[28]

If any religious movement should be termed strictly revolutionary in the late antique period, it was not Catholic Christianity but Gnosis.[29] The Gnostic gospel of the wholly other God is 'a radical form of protest against all that hitherto had been accounted holy, good and right'. Gnosis promised to

[26]EN p. 21. Here Ratzinger draws on J. Jeremias, *Jesu Verheissung für die Völker* (Stuttgart 1959²), pp. 48–60 and R. Schnackenburg, *Gottes Herrschaft und Reich* (Freiburg 1959), pp. 1–47.
[27]EN p. 23; cf. Apocalypse 21, 1.
[28]Ibid. p. 25.
[29]Appealing to the classic study of H. Jonas, *Gnosis und spätantiker Geist* (Göttingen 1934; 1954²; 1964³).

lead one out of what was no better than a prison. Though pagans like Celsus and Plotinus might have difficulty in distinguishing between Gnosticism and the Church, their messages and programmes were widely different. For the Church, the present cosmos, though sinful, was still the work of the Father of Jesus Christ. The current world-order, though passing away, retained a certain 'relative right', expressed most clearly in New Testament exhortations to respect the emperor.

> Thus while the Gnostic revolution was anarchic, fundamentally calling into question as it did any and every kind of inner-worldly order, the Christian revolution was limited. For the latter, though denying the hitherto dominant self-understanding of the State and indeed its spiritual basis, assigned to it a new, if essentially altered, place and validity in Christianity's new spiritual world.[30]

Such, then, were the resources, whether positive or negative, on which the Fathers had to draw in formulating their own vision of the 'unity of the nations'. To this Ratzinger now turns. He frankly admits that in writing this section, he has been inspired by Henri de Lubac's *Catholicisme*, translated into German during the Council under the title, 'Katholizismus als Gemeinschaft': Catholicism as community.[31] Ratzinger explained what 'community' meant here. De Lubac's thesis was that:

> The mystery of Christ is, for the Fathers, inherently and entirely a mystery of unity.[32]

Just as sin is an unholy mystery of separation, so Christ's person and work make up a mystery of re-unification. Two ancient

[30]EN p. 29.
[31]H. de Lubac, *Katholizismus als Gemeinschaft* (Einsiedeln 1963).
[32]EN p. 31.

writers are singled out by Ratzinger for fuller treatment:
Origen and Augustine.

Origen's pagan interlocutor Celsus had argued that
Christians are fellows without a fatherland.[33] His is the
common late antique view: religion is an aspect of nationhood;
the ordering of human beings in nations is an ordinance of
divine world-government. De facto, Origen accepts this division
of the world but proposes a spiritual reading of the Babel story
to account for it: humanity remained of one speech so long as it
remained of one meaning. Israel Origen places in a distinct
category of her own: she is not a nation, but is still 'in the East'.
Free of the angel-rulers of the peoples, she remains subject only
to God: 'what all would and should have been able to be: simply
human, and so directly God's'. As Origen's 36th homily on
Luke candidly explains, the power of the angelic archontes of the
nations is basically unjust.[34]

> Whoever delivers himself over to what is national, and, in place
> of thinking and living humanly, thinks and lives in the confines
> of a nation, such a one places himself under the sway of his evil
> angel.[35]

So much is this the case that Origen can speak of the saving
work of Christ as, precisely, liberation from the prison of the
national into the unity of God. For the Origen of the De
Principiis, a 'theological metaphysic of the nation (is) a factor of
disorder'.[36]

The only concession to a more positive evaluation of the
nation that Origen ever makes, so far as Ratzinger is able to
establish, comes in his commentary on John. Commenting on
Jesus' remark to the disciples, 'Others have laboured, and you

[33]Contra Celsum V. 32.
[34]i.e. on Luke 12, 58.
[35]EN p.48.
[36]Ibid. p. 51; cf. De Principiis IV. 12.

have entered into their labour', Origen identifies the 'others' with the angels of the peoples.[37] Here, then, the work of the apostles would be the eschatological completing of the work of the angel-rulers – a hint, at least, of a genuinely preparatory role for the nations in the manifestation of the international wisdom of Christ.[38]

Into the place of the fatherland steps, for Origen, the Church. It is, as Ratzinger sums up, 'the new form of fatherland, grounded through the Word of God'.[39] The Alexandrian doctor fully accepts Celsus' charge that Christian faith has undermined the link between nationality and religion.

It is instructive to compare Ratzinger's account of Origen with the theology of the *Volk* in one of the German Protestant theologians who made his peace with the National Socialist régime, Paul Althaus, professor of systematic theology at Erlangen in Franconia, the Protestant strip of northern Bavaria.[40] Althaus opposed the Barmen Declaration of the Confessing Church, made in 1934 by Karl Barth and others as an expression of their opposition to Nazi intervention in Church affairs. He considered the Barmen statement to be 'Christomonistic', too exclusively Christological, notably in its suppression of any idea that God might be revealed in nature. Over against this, Althaus proposed that there is an *Ur-offenbarung*, a 'primordial revelation', expressed in the 'orders of creation', *Schöpfungsordnungen*. He defined *Ordrungen* as 'the forms of social life ... the indispensable conditions for the historical life of humanity'. In a lecture of 1937, Althaus tied in with this concept the idea of the *Volk*. Starting from the words

[37]Commenting on John 4, 38 in his *In Joannem XIII.* 49.

[38]Cf. *De Principiis* III. 1, where Origen speaks of a three fold wisdom: of God (revealed in Christ); of the world (in science); and of the 'princes of this world' (Egyptian, Chaldaean, Indian philosophy, astrology, metaphysics).

[39]EN p. 57, with reference to *Contra Celsum* VIII. 75.; cf. VIII. 74 and I 1.

[40]R. P. Ericksen, *Theologians under Hitler. Gerhard Kittel, Paul Althaus, and Emanuel Hirsch* (New Haven and London 1985), pp. 79–119.

of Luther's Catechism, 'I believe that God created me', he goes on:

> The belief that God has created me includes also my *Volk*. Whatever I am and have, God has given me out of the well-spring of my *Volk*: the inheritance of blood, the bodiliness, the soul, the spirit. God has determined my life from its outermost to its innermost elements through my *Volk*, through its blood, through its spiritual style, bestowed on me, stamping me, in – above all – language and history. My *Volk* is my outer and inner destiny. This womb of my being is God's means, his *Ordnung*, by which to create and to endow me. The special style of a *Volk* is his creation, and as such it is for us holy.

Althaus explains the absence of reference to the *Volk* in Scripture and the Reformation Confessions of faith by pointing out that, in the periods when those documents were composed, men had not yet discovered the reality of the *Volk*. That discovery:

> did not occur through theologians as such, but through poets, scholars and thinkers, through Herder, the Romantics, the Idealist philosophers.[41]

It is 'the law of God as newly revealed for the modern German era'.

If this background in the Germany of the 1930s helps to explain Ratzinger's attraction to Origen in the latter's refusal to supply a theology of the nation, the same warning signals from the Nazi period light up his reading of Augustine's *City of God*. For Ratzinger, the *De civitate Dei* is essentially an attack on political religion. Augustine sees two vast disadvantages to such religion. First, such religion rates the State's good higher than truth, especially – in the ancient context – by its canonisation of

[41]P. Althaus, *Völker vor und nach Christus* (Leipzig 1937), pp. 3–5. Cited R. P. Ericksen, *Theologians under Hitler* op. cit. pp. 102–103.

148

custom. Secondly, behind the unreal gods of civil religion stands the only too real power of the demons. The lasting value of the *City of God* consists in major part in its assault on the divinisation of the *polis*. As Ratzinger sees it, Augustine's divine city is not some purely ideal community of believing people, yet it has nothing to do with any earthly theocracy or a 'Christianised world'. Rather is it *eine sakramentale-eschatologische Grösse*, 'a sacramental, eschatological reality' which exists in this world as a sign of the coming world.[42] The State is, despite all Christianisation or apparent Christianisation, an earthly State, and the Church an 'aliens' community', which may use earthly realities but is never at home here.

Though the situations which faced Origen and Augustine were diverse, and Augustine – incredible as this would have seemed to Origen – can expect Christians to serve the Roman state as officials, or even as emperor, their eschatological vision is held in common. Both see this world as something provisional, and stand together as revolutionary comrades in their very relativisation of everything inner-worldly, pointing with the Gospel itself to the 'only Absolute, God, and the only Mediator between God and man, Jesus Christ'.[43] Such patristic witnesses, along with the counter-example of the collaborationist theologians of Hitler's Germany throw light on the diffidence with which Ratzinger would treat any suggestion of the renaissance of 'national churches'.

The Church and the world

His ecclesiological interests were not restricted to consideration of the internal structure of the Church. Equally momentous was the question of how she should relate to the reality beyond her.

[42] EN p. 104.
[43] Ibid. p. 106.

This entailed looking at Catholicism's post-conciliar 'openness to the world', and the implications of its 'dialogue' with the non-Christian religions: openness to the non-Christian world.

Ratzinger points out that hitherto reform councils in the Church's history have set their face against *Verweltlichung*: the Church's becoming more like the world. Their impulse might better be described as towards spiritualisation – a more intense radicalism of Christian living, freeing self from all that is not Christ. At the Second Vatican Council, on the other hand – and here Ratzinger has, once again, the making of *Gaudium et Spes* in mind, people argued that since everything is 'open' for Christ, so it should be similarly 'open' for the Church. The question is, Does such a movement of sympathetic acceptance of the world correspond to the Church's essence and that of her task in history? Or does it, on the contrary, directly contradict it?

Accepting the fundamental metaphor of 'openness', which he had himself already used in the soteriology of *Einführung in das Christentum*, Ratzinger begins his reply by affirming that one thing at least is clear:

> The Church lives from the Trinitarian mystery which has opened itself to her in Christ. That there is a Church at all derives from the fact that God has opened himself.[44]

God, at any rate, has 'become world', has taken flesh. In his Son Jesus Christ he has stepped out of the circle of the Trinitarian love so that we should learn everlastingly what that ancient adage means which holds that *Bonum diffusivum sui*, 'The Good spreads itself'. However, the action of Christ as God's 'self-opening' and 'becoming worldly' does not simply leave the world as it is. God does not just become the world's companion. Theology, taking its cue from Scripture, describes the opening

[44]NVG p. 283.

of God in Christ to the world as *mission*, and that means the penetration of the world by God's Word and its consequent transformation by a union of love with God himself.

Given that the Church has no other meaning or purpose except in her being the instrument of Jesus Christ, what her own orientation and programme should be is already sufficiently outlined in what has just been said. She is herself, as Christ's ecclesial body, the 'gesture' of the divine openness. She must ever place herself at the service of that gesture, and actualise it in history. But the one and only aim of the divine gesture of openness is the drawing of all finite reality into that 'holy exchange' which began with the Incarnation. It follows, Ratzinger goes on,

> that there is only one legitimate form of the Church's openness to the world, and so must it certainly always be. That form is two-fold. It is: mission as the prolongation of the movement of the Word's procession, and the simple gesture of disinterested serving love in the actualising of the divine love, a love which streams forth even when it remains without response.[45]

Here we have at last a criterion for judging the appropriateness or otherwise of 'openness to the world' in particular cases. The service of mission and the service of charity form together a 'two-in-one canon'. By reference to this canon, we must make our discernments about what is 'true', that is Christologically fitting, openness on the part of the Church, and what is merely 'worldlified' and so false.

What, in this context, can Ratzinger make of the concept of 'dialogue', so widely employed in the post-conciliar period for a variety of sectorial areas? Ratzinger accepts that the idea of dialogue is already present in the New Testament. It is in there in the discussions of Jesus during the historical ministry. It is in

[45]Ibid. p. 285.

the 'diatribes' of Paul. Yet Christian origins show nothing
remotely resembling the Socratic idea of dialogue which most
moderns have in mind. Jesus' dialogues are presented as
polemics. Indeed, in their Johannine stylisation they are, in
effect, a dialogue on two incommensurable planes. Speaking
without being understood was also a New Testament
experience! From this Ratzinger draws the conclusion that

> the New Testament dialogue is not (as is the Platonic) a matter
> of raising to the consciousness the hidden presence of spirit.
> Rather it is a matter of announcing to man the unthinkable,
> novel, free Act of God, something which cannot be drawn up
> out of the mental depths of man, because it announces God's
> unreckonable, gracious decision. This divine resolve encounters
> resistance, indeed, from man, because it makes him feel
> disturbed, threatens his spiritual autonomy....[46]

Thus, while there is in the Christian message, from the very
outset, an element of dialogue, there is also a limitation to
dialogue. And this makes it intelligible, Ratzinger thinks, that
the dialogue form has never established itself as a *genre* in
Christian literature. The Gospel of redemption cannot be made
an object of dialogical treatment: it is *kerygma*, proclamation.
Yet alongside mission there is a place for dialogue: for the
Christian message can only be heard in its full integrity by way
of response to human questioning. Its offer to non-Christians
presupposes a vital experience of this questioning on the part of
the offerers.

In speaking of 'non-Christians', Ratzinger is careful to
distinguish between the followers of the great non-Christian
religions, on the one hand, and, on the other, what he terms the
'new pagans' in the traditional heartlands of Christendom itself.
Over the last four centuries, Christian Europe has been bringing
to birth a new paganism – not that of atheistic Communism

[46]Ibid. p. 293.

which also derives elements from the Church, but the more widespread rationalistic paganism found within the cultures she has formed. One aspect of such rationalism leads naturally into a discussion of 'non-Christians' in the other sense of adherents to the world religions. Many people, including practising Catholics, no longer regard the Church as the unique divinely established means of salvation. They question her 'absoluteness' and so the gravity of her missionary duty. And indeed one might well ask, If all men and women of good will can be saved *sola moralitate*, why is salvation so simple for them and so complex and difficult for us? Faith comes, in this way, to be experienced as a burden and not a grace.

Ratzinger confesses that many of the attempts, since the time of Robert Bellarmine, to show how God can effectively will the salvation of all, whilst yet preserving the Church's teaching that she alone is the ark of salvation, do sound remarkably artifical. His own attempt at a resolution of the problem turns on the idea that God uses 'the Few', *die Wenigen*, to bring the rest, *die Vielen*, to himself. He sets out from the conviction of the New Testament that all humanity merits condemnation: only through one man, Jesus Christ, has salvation come into the world. Even the highest morality remains otherwise that of sinners. In the Atonement, by a holy exchange, God in Christ takes the evil of man to himself, while freeing the 'place of salvation' for us to occupy. This 'great mystery of representation' is continued in a whole series of representative actions, whose crowning glory is found in the relation of Christ's Church to the non-Christians souls for whose salvation he also thirsts.

> The contrast of Church and not-Church does not mean that there are two parallel realities, *ein Nebeneinander*, or two contrary realities, *ein Gegeneinander*, but that there is a reality of reciprocal relationship, *ein Füreinander*, in which each side has its

own function. To the Few, the Church, is entrusted, in the carrying forward of Christ's mission, the representation of the Many. The salvation of both Few and Many comes about only in their ordering to each other, and in their common subordination to the great substitutionary Act of Jesus Christ which encompasses both.[47]

If the Many who do not belong to the community of faith in any full meaning of that phrase are nevertheless to be saved, this will be because those who are called into the Church are carrying out their tasks as the Few. The lack of Christian faith on the part of the Many should encourage the Christian to a deeper and more intense practice of the faith, since he knows himself to be co-involved in the function of representing Jesus Christ – on which the world's salvation depends.

But if Christ saves the Many, albeit through the representationary mediation of his body, the Few, what is the necessity for the Few to evangelise directly, to add to their own number by subtracting from that of the Many? Here we can only return to that axiom of that anonymous sixth century Syrian writer known as the Pseudo-Denys that 'good spreads itself'. The Church

> only remains faithful to her own meaning, and only fulfils her task, onasmuch as she does not clutch the Gospel she has been given to herself, but carries it abroad to the rest of mankind.[48]

Indeed, Ratzinger goes so far as to say, when we use the word 'Church' what we are naming *is* the *Unterwegssein*, the 'being-on-the-way', of Jesus' message of the Kingdom to all the peoples.[49]

[47]Ibid. pp. 335–336.
[48]Ibid, p. 361.
[49]Ibid. p. 273.

Chapter Eight

THE ESCHATOLOGY THEME

As early as his work on Bonaventure, Ratzinger had decided that the eschatology theme was the central issue of the New Testament. The scheme for a 'Concise Catholic Dogmatics', master-minded by a former Munich colleague, the historian of mediaeval Scholasticism Johann Baptist Auer, gave him the possibility of developing his reflections on eschatology since, in the event, this section of the *Kleine Katholische Dogmatik* as a whole fell to him.

The state of the eschatology question

Ratzinger's *Eschatologie: Tod und ewiges Leben* opens by pointing out that, in recent centuries, eschatology has cut a rather modest figure on the theological stage. Once content to lead a quiet life as the final chapter of the student's manual as 'the doctrine of the Last Things', it has now come to dominate the entire theological landscape. How so? With the aid of modern scholarship:

> people re-established an insight which, in the age of the rationalist Enlightenment, had been virtually dismissed as the brain-child of eccentrics. This insight consisted in the awareness that Jesus' preaching was soaked through with eschatology. The inner impetus of that preaching came from the fact that Jesus, in an authoritative fashion, proclaimed the imminent end of the world, the breaking-in of the Kingdom of God.[1]

[1] J. Ratzinger, *Eschatologie. Tod und ewiges Leben* (Regensburg 1977). Cited below as ETEL, and here at p. 18. All quotations are from my edition of the translation by Michael Waldstein, to be published in 1988 by the Catholic University of America Press.

And Ratzinger declares that the 'novelty and greatness' of Jesus cannot be separated from the momentum which this expectation created. One question he will have to face is whether, in the course of the Church's history, this fact was lost sight of, with gravely damaging consequences for the identity of later Christianity with the primitive Gospel.[2]

For the moment, however, he contents himself with some remarks on the wider human context of this revival of interest in eschatology. He argues that the sudden intensification of our capacity to pick up the eschatological undertones and overtones of the New Testament must have 'something to do with the emerging crisis of our civilisation'. Though premonitions of decline and fall were already registered before the Great War, it was that war which gave this sense its first tragic confirmation. In doing so, it undermined the reigning (Protestant) theological Liberalism of the epoch, with its purely cultural ideal of Christianity. Theology proceeded to move into the new key of Existentialism which, as a philosophy of preparedness and decision, had some claim to count as a fair interpretation of the meaning of Jesus' proclamation about 'the End'.

But more recently, Ratzinger goes on, a second and more powerful tributary, Marxism, has poured its waters into the river of theology. The influx of Marxian thought could not leave the issue of eschatology unaffected, for Marxism:

> draws its passion, and its fascination, from the root of prophetism, which promised a world the signs of whose coming had no rational index.[3]

The Marxist movement, offering its own kind of religious pathos by its very attack on God and the historical religions, also

---

[2] As maintained by M. Werner, *Die Entstehung des christlichen Dogmas* (Bern-Tübingen 1941).

[3] ETEL p. 19.

promises theology a new opportunity to fill out the eschatological message with a tangible and realistic content. Thus, if one wished, one could today write a book named 'Eschatology' which would consist exclusively of dialogue – whether positively or negatively biassed – with the Theology of Futurity, the Theology of Hope, the Theology of Liberation. The classical themes of the doctrine of the Last Things – heaven and hell, purgatory and judgment, death and the immortality of the soul – might be left out altogether, and, in at least one case, *have* been.[4] Ratzinger accepts that the question of the future and its relation to the present, and the search for an appropriate 'praxis of hope' in contemporary society has a perfect right to *Lebensraum* in a study of Christian eschatology. But he also protests that a work of Catholic dogmatics cannot surrender to the transformation of perspective implied by the reduction of eschatology to this and only this.

> Not merely on the extrinsic grounds that a textbook should contain the information classically offered by a work of its *genre*.... These omitted topics belong intrinsically to what is specific in the Christian view of the Age-to-Come and its presence here and now.[5]

No matter how out of keeping with the spirit of the age they may appear, we must give these subjects adequate airing.

But what of the claim that the Church's tradition is marked by a decadent 'de-eschatologisation', a falling into forgetfulness of the original expectations of the first Christians? How can one overlook the discrepancy between the primitive cry *maranatha*, as recorded for us in the first century *Didache*, an expression of a 'joyful hope for the Christ who· will come soon', and the mediaeval *Dies Irae* where we hear only of the fear of judgment,

[4]D. Wiederkehr, *Perspektiven der Eschatologie* (Einsiedeln 1974).
[5]ETEL p. 20.

THE THEOLOGY OF JOSEPH RATZINGER

since it contemplates the End 'under the appearances of horror and of threat to the soul's salvation'?

Ratzinger replies that historical reflection that is 'hooked on to the pegs of a few formulae' must always be problematic – if occasionally illuminating. For instance: the meaning of the *maranatha* cry is by no means self-evident. Some scholars *do* take it as a petition: 'Come, Lord Jesus'. Others regard it as a statement, 'The Lord has come'. Yet others again understand it as a kind of cursing formula for safeguarding the sanctity of the Eucharist, 'As surely as our Lord has come ...'. All that is demonstrably clear is that it belongs with the early Christian celebration of the Eucharist. That Eucharist was simultaneously:

> the joyful proclamation of the Lord's presence and a supplication to the already present Lord that he may come, since, paradoxically, even as the One who is present he remains the One who is to come.[6]

The eschatological hope has never lacked its bond with the 'spiritual experience of prayer' and the 'corporate authority of faith' within the unity of the Church. Though it has known fluctuations, it has never perished or been fundamentally de-natured. To test this claim against the faith-experience of the high mediaeval Church Ratzinger examines not the *Dies Irae*, which he regards as too subjective to constitute a suitable starting-point, but the Litany of the Saints, itself an expression of the shared 'anxiety and hope of the Christian people'. Of that great prayer he writes:

> It absorbed into itself all those concerns with which time harries us, whilst counterposing to them the pledge of hope – through whose agency we may endure them.[7]

[6]Ibid. p. 21.
[7]Ibid. p. 23.

The person praying the Litany, conscious of the perils and dangers of the night of the world:

> finds a shelter in the communion of the saints. He gathers the redeemed of all ages around him and finds safety under their mantle. This signifies that the walls separating heaven and earth, and past, present and future, are now as glass. The Christian lives in the presence of the saints as his own proper ambience, and so lives 'eschatologically'.[8]

In the saints, the Christian promise 'has already proved its worth'. They manifest the Lord's power to save, and that in the present tense. Moreover, as the Litany moves on, a second set of invocations concerns the salvific potency of the great acts of God in history, which those praying summon to their aid. Admittedly, though, only one of these invocations concerns the future, and this is the seemingly negative petition, 'On the Day of Judgment, Lord, deliver us'. *Prima facie*, this appears to favour the thesis of a degenerate de-eschatologising which Ratzinger is here combatting – though he does not deny it a *degree* of truth. However, he deftly turns this verse of the Litany to his own purposes:

> We have to remember that the Lord of judgment is himself addressed as the liberator who has the power to transform the act of judgment into an act of redemption. If one may put it so, the Judge who is to come is confronted with the Saviour who has already come. His coming, his actions, his sufferings and his gifts become so many promises of mercy with which the suppliant steps before him. The believer holds up the mirror of the Saviour to the face of the Judge. Since he cannot place his hope in himself, he finds shelter with the One who was his Saviour and cannot fail to be so everlastingly.[9]

[8] Ibid.
[9] Ibid. pp. 24–25.

Ratzinger's overall evaluation of eschatology then and now is that, whilst the reduction of Christianity to individualism and other-worldliness was a real danger, any attempt to obliterate concern with the person and his dying – the heart of the later 'doctrine of the Last Things' – would be not return to the sources so much as rank barbarianisation. Though he accepts the gains implicit in a recovery of the more ancient corporate, and indeed cosmic, eschatology, he refuses to go along with the relegation of the developed personal eschatology to some dusty corner where it would stand 'bearing the dismissive label, "Salvation for the soul".' The task of eschatology today, as Ratzinger sees it, is:

> to marry perspectives, so that person and community, present and future, are seen in their unity.... While we must not lose sight of the particular preoccupations of the present, we ought not to make it the measuring-yard of everything that we say. Instead, we need to integrate the opposing elements in the light of the Christian centre, to strike a fair balance and come to understand the real promise of faith more deeply.[10]

Eschatology and Scripture

Here Ratzinger deals with some of the most troublesome questions that Christian theology, and apologetics, have to face today. Beginning with the epoch-making study of Jesus' preaching about the Kingdom of God by Johann Weiss, modern exegesis has identified a number of issues that are crucial to the very essence of Christianity.

> To what extent did the historical Jesus include in his preaching the expectation of an imminent end to the world and an imminent epiphany of the Kingdom of God? How central was such an expectation to his proclamation as a whole?

[10]Ibid. pp. 26, 27.

And, more radically still:

> Does his message retain any significant content once the
> expectation of an imminent end is eliminated?[11]

Before launching into these deep waters, Ratzinger offers a
brief excursus on method. He distinguishes between the
questions of the *historian*, which concern what exactly
happened, the character, according to the sources, of Jesus'
proclamation in its time and place, and the questions of the
believer or searcher for faith today, where what is at issue is the
meaning of these data from the past.

> The issue of appropriation, of the transposition of the past into
> the present, should be carefully distinguished from that of
> research into historical data. In no way can it be answered by
> historical methods. It requires quite different methodological
> tools, corresponding to a different modality of the enquiring
> spirit. The very supposition that an ancient text has something
> of value to say to the present and should be interpretatively
> transposed for contemporary digestion already far exceeds the
> departure-point of the historical method.[12]

In cases, especially, where texts contain affirmations that affect
the most fundamental problems of life and death, the concepts
used by textual interpreters necessarily bring into play their own
'pre-understanding'. Indeed, without such sympathetic
understanding 'in which one's own view of reality is risked as in
a wager', the interpreter cannot realistically expect to grasp
anything of his text at all. Thus, for instance, whether or not we
grant any truth to the assertion that 'the Kingdom has come
close' will depend upon what we understand by reality at large.
Furthermore, relying on the historical-critical method in this
domain is particularly problematic when that method is itself

[11] Ibid. p. 30.
[12] Ibid.

understood on the model of the natural sciences, rather than in terms of a paradigm proper to human history. Too often, exegetical results are thought of as

> a sum of fixed conclusions, a body of knowledge with immaculate credentials, acquired in such a fashion that it has left behind its own history as a mere pre-history, and is now at our disposal like a set of mathematical measurements.[13]

But the quantification of the physical world is not a proper analogue for the 'measuring' of the human spirit. The history of exegesis reflects the spiritual history of its age. However, Ratzinger does not intend to be trapped into saying that, at the end of the day, all that we know is ourselves, a solipsism which he has already found cause to reject in the case of Trinitarian theology. He finds the illuminating comparison he is seeking in the history of philosophy where such thinkers as Plato, Aristotle, Thomas, 'remain the originating figures of an enduring approach to the Ground of what is', even though none of them *is* philosophy, or *the* philosopher. Instead:

> it is in the multivalent message of the entire history, and its overall critical evaluation that truth is disclosed, and, with it, the possibility of fresh knowledge.

Analogously, in the case of the Bible:

> only by listening to the whole history of interpretation can the present be purified by criticism and so brought into a position of genuine encounter with the text concerned.[14]

Though historical reason's self-criticism is in its infancy, we can at least say two things: first, a 'definitive acquisition of

[13]Ibid. pp. 32–33.
[14]Ibid. p. 33.

scholarship' does not exist; and second, no past interpretation, if in its own time it turned to the text 'in true openness', is ever wholly *passé*.[15]

These methodological preliminaries concluded, what meaning does Ratzinger attach to Jesus' proclamation of the Kingdom of God? He begins by noting that, as the statistics of occurrence of New Testament words would alone suffice to suggest, the 'Kingdom of God' or 'Kingdom of heaven' is 'the true *Leitmotiv* of Jesus' preaching'. Following the counsel given by the Lutheran exegete Joachim Jeremias, he paraphrases Jesus' announcement that 'The Kingdom of God is at hand' in the words 'God is close'.[16] Fundamentally, Ratzinger locates Jesus within the tradition of *prophetic* expectation. As he writes:

> This is nowhere clearer than in his promise of God's Kingdom to the poor, in the many meanings of that term, and his linking of the gift of the Kingdom, in indissoluble manner, with repentance.[17]

And while no denying that Jesus may have taken up elements from the apocalyptic and what may be termed the 'proto-rabbinic' strands in Jewish eschatological thought, Ratzinger considers that he put forward in prophetic fashion a 'new image of the Kingdom'.

> The Kingdom is announced beneath the signs of joy, festivity and beauty, as in the parables of the Wedding Feast and the Great Banquet, as well as through images of powerlessness, as in the parables of the Mustard Seed, the Leaven, the Haul of Good

---

[15] This appears to reflect Barth's judgment in the preface to his second attempt at a commentary on Romans that 'the critical historians need to be more critical', *The Epistle to the Romans* (London 1950), p. 8. See also on this, R. Smend, 'Nachkritische Schriftauslegung', in *Parrēsia. Festschrift für Karl Barth zum 80. Geburtstag* (Zürich 1966), pp. 215–237.

[16] J. Jeremias, *Neutestamentliche Theologie* I (Gütersloh 1971), I. p. 105.

[17] ETEL p. 37.

and Bad Fish, the Field of Wheat and Tares.... The victory of
God, under the species of insignificance, of the Passion: this is his
new image of the Kingdom.[18]

Ratzinger holds that, although Jesus did not teach an explicit
Christology, the *lignes majeures* of his teaching converge upon
himself as the eschatological sign of God. He interprets the
saying that the Kingdom is 'among you', *entos humin*, as an
ironic reference to the person of the preacher who is, as Origen
would put it, *hē autobasileia*, 'the Kingdom in person'.[19] And
placing alongside this a *logion* about casting out demons 'by the
finger of God' (also found in the Synoptic tradition), Ratzinger
adds that Jesus

> is the Kingdom, not simply by virtue of his physical presence
> but through the Holy Spirit's radiant power flowing forth from
> him. In his Spirit-filled activity, smashing the demonic
> enslavement of man, the Kingdom of God becomes reality, God
> taking the government of this world into his own hands....
> Jesus' actions, words, sufferings break the power of that
> alienation which lies so heavily on human life. In liberating
> people, they establish God's Kingdom.[20]

Jesus, then, *is* the Kingdom because, through him, God's Spirit
acts upon the world. This is for Ratzinger (we may note *en
passant*) the basis of the unity between the preaching *of* Jesus and
the Church's preaching *about* him. The theme of the Kingdom
can be transformed into Christology, since it is from Christ that
the Spirit, the active reign of God, comes.

But what of the expectation of an imminent end of the
world? It can hardly be denied that the New Testament contains

[18] Ibid. p. 39.
[19] P. G. 13, 1197B; the Lucan text appealed to be Ratzinger in this
connexion is at 17, 20f. Compare also F. Mussner, *Praesentia salutis. Gesammelte
Studien zu Fragen und Themen des Neuen Testamentes* (Düsseldorf 1967), p. 95.
[20] ETEL p. 41.

traces of such an idea. Ratzinger does not attempt to deny it, but, rather, to subvert the assumption that a doctrine of the radical imminence of the Parousia belongs with the *oldest* stratum in the Gospel tradition. On his view, the New Testament shows a more complex picture than simple chronological linear development in this regard. Depending on the circumstances of particular communities, 'each period either heightened or relaxed the tension of time'. In some circumstances, the idea of an immediate End to the world may be the result of re-Judaisation: taking place later, not earlier. Ratzinger finds an irreducible plurality in the Synoptic presentations of Jesus' eschatological discourse in Mark 13, and its parallels. On this he comments:

> the New Testament writings leave open the nature of the difference between literary schema and reality in this connexion ... Schema and reality are differently related by different authors, but none of them makes the bald claim to an identity between the two. . . . The schematic character of the statements we are considering is not owing to some accidental absence of ability on the part of the evangelists which could in principle be overcome. . . . Only reality itself, in its own forward movement, can clarify what the schema leaves obscure. Only as the actual course of history unfolds does reality fill the schema with content and shed light on the meaning and inter-relatedness of its various aspects.[21]

Ratzinger hastens to add, however, that, while the 'harvest of historical experience' must be garnered here if the word of Scripture is to gain its full meaning, this should not be taken to imply that the Word of God found in the Bible is in itself vacuous, powerless to resist the hermeneutical advances of any Johnny-come-lately. Faithful appropriation of that Word treads the narrow path between archaism and Modernism:

[21] Ibid. pp. 46–47.

Issuing as it does from the crucified and risen Christ, the Word indicates a given direction which is wide enough to receive all reality into itself, yet clear enough to confront it with a definite measuring-rod of its own.[22]

In sum: Jesus had proclaimed parabolically the Gospel of the Kingdom as a reality at once present and yet to come. The early Church, faithful to this original message, proclaimed Jesus as the Christ who acts in the Spirit, thus constituting himself the 'present form of the Kingdom'. By gazing on the risen Christ, she learned that *a* Parousia had already taken place. The Church knew no pure theology of hope, but rather a 'now' in which the promise was a presence. But this presence was itself hope – it was understood to bear the future within itself.

It in the light of this reading of Jesus' relation to the End, then, that Ratzinger proceeds to evaluate a variety of major contemporary schools or individual writers, from Karl Barth and Rudolf Bultmann to Oscar Cullmann and the English Congregationalist C. H. Dodd (whom he rates extremely highly), finishing with an account of the 'theology of hope', associated with Jürgen Moltmann, and the 'political theology' of Johann Baptist Metz, as well as their offspring in the Third World: 'Liberation theology' and the 'theology of revolution'. In these last mentioned movements, he recognises 'here and there, gleams of real gold'. Yet at the same time, he insists that the Church founded on the Gospel must not only give people hope, but give them truly *evangelical* hope.

The Kingdom of God, not being itself a political concept, cannot serve as a political criterion by which to construct in direct fashion a programme of political action and to criticise the political efforts of other people.[23]

[22]Ibid. p. 48.
[23]Ibid. p. 59.

The transformation of eschatology into political messianism allows the distinctive content of Christian hope to drain away, 'leaving behind nothing but a deceptive surrogate'. On the other hand, this is not to say that the Kingdom is irrelevant to politics: it is supremely relevant, but as an ethical, not an eschatological reality. And in a sentence heavy with consequence for his own future dealings with theologians elsewhere, Ratzinger goes so far as to say that

> The setting asunder of eschatology and politics is one of the fundamental tasks of Christian theology.[24]

Death and immortality

Consonant with his introductory remarks on the 'state of the eschatology question', Ratzinger divides up his material on the further implications of scriptural teaching into its individual and corporate dimensions – which are to be distinguished, though not separated.

He points out that Western society has at present two contradictory attitudes towards death. On the one hand, it wants to hide it away. Grave Sickness and death are becoming 'purely technological problems to be handled by the appropriate institution'. The typical pattern of modern living is such that the family home, rather than being 'that sheltering space which brings human beings together in birth and living, in sickness and dying', is too often more like a 'sleeping bag'. On the other hand, the very same society also puts death on show, via the media, as a 'thrilling spectacle, tailor-made for alleviating the general boredom of life'. Though seeming contraries, these two attitudes have the same ulterior motive: to deprive death of its character as 'a place where the metaphysical

[24]Ibid. p. 60.

breaks through'. Thus, whereas people used to pray for deliverance from sudden and unprovided death, a contemporary Litany of the Unbelievers would ask for just the opposite: a way of dying that left them no time for reflection or suffering. Alas: when things reach such a pass that accepting death in a human way becomes too dangerous, being human itself has become too dangerous as well. Perhaps the perplexity to which positivism and materialism thus bring us will at least encourage us to seek out what may be the 'wisdom of the tradition' on the matter.

But this is more easily said than done, thanks to a certain muddying of the waters in contemporary theology. For some writers, belief in immortality is alien to what they deem 'biblical thought', belonging rather to a dualistic tradition indebted to Plato. Not the body alone, but the entire human being perishes: the resurrection of Christ attains its full meaning only against this stark background. For others, such a dismantlement of the tradition is not radical enough. Arguing that the ideas of both immortality *and* resurrection are entirely peripheral in the Jewish Scriptures, they find the same conviction of the 'totality' of death in the (hypothetically reconstructed) 'Q' community – the body of early Christians to whom the transmission of many of the sayings of Jesus in the Synoptic tradition are ascribed by a number of modern exegetes. Ratzinger finds the progression from the first to the second of these positions unsurprising:

> A resurrection juxtaposed with total death in an immediate and unconnected manner *does* become a fantastic sort of miracle, unsupported by any coherent anthropological vision.[25]

But here faith – if the term can be used – resigns itself to a final absence of meaning.

[25]Ibid. p. 70. Ratzinger has especially in mind here the writings of Jacques Pohier. See, most recently, the latter's *God – in Fragments* (London 1985).

In revisionist mood, Ratzinger offers his own reading of the supposed criminous architect of Western belief in immortality: Plato. So far from forming part of a philosophy of flight from the world, Plato's thinking about immortality is, Ratzinger holds, essential to his view of the human city, the *polis*.

> Man, to survive biologically, must be more than *bios*. He must be able to die into a more authentic life than this. The certainty that self-abandonment for the sake of truth is self-abandonment to reality and not a step into the night of nothingness as a necessary condition for justice. But justice is the condition on which the life of the *polis* endures.[26]

Faithful to his early work on Augustine, Ratzinger insists that Platonism had, and has, much to offer Christianity, by way of assisting the latter's 'philosophical unfolding'. Yet he also holds that the Church has much to do in order to 'correct and purify' Plato's intention.

At the origins of the Judaeo-Christian tradition in ancient Israel, the fulness of life was held to consist in seeing one's children, and one's children's children, so as to participate through them in the future of Israel. Following a widespread concept of death among primitive peoples, the dead individual was regarded as

> cut off from the land of the living, from dear life, banished into a non-communication zone where life is destroyed precisely because relationship is impossible.[27]

In Sheol Yahweh is not, nor is he praised there. In relation to him also, communication breaks down. The state of death is, at one and the same time, being and non-being, existence, yet not life. But because this 'non-being' is something other than utter

[26]ETEL pp. 73–74.
[27]Ibid. p. 75.

THE THEOLOGY OF JOSEPH RATZINGER

THE THEOLOGY OF JOSEPH RATZINGER

nothingness, death is not in any straightforward way a happening in the order of nature. According to Ratzinger, it was because ancient Israel realised this, notably in her life of prayer, that she developed a 'phenomenology of sickness and death' in which these things were interpreted as spiritual phenomena. In this way, he argues:

> Israel discovered their deepest spiritual ground and content, wrestled with Yahweh as to their import, and so brought human suffering before God and with God to a new pitch of intensity.[28]

The upshot of these reflections was that life, real, life, means communion, whereas death, the heart of death, is the absence of relationship. And here it became increasingly evident to Israel's spokesmen that, if death be a barrier which limits the God of Israel to his own finite sphere, then the all-encompassing claims of Yahwistic faith are overthrown. He who is Life itself cannot tolerate such a limitation. And so in the end, the alternatives were:

> either to abandon faith in Yahweh altogether or to admit the unlimited scope of his power, and so – in principle – the definitive character of the communion with man he had inaugurated.[29]

The first possibility was canvassed, implicitly, in that intellectual and spiritual crisis of the Wisdom schools which has left us Job and Qoheleth as its monuments. In this situation, the faith of Israel was sustained by the 'new level of insight' to which prophets and pious men had broken through. Ratzinger instances as examples of what he is talking about the Servant Songs of the second Isaiah, where sickness, death and

[28]Ibid.
[29]Ibid. p. 76.

abandonment are understood as vicarious suffering, suffering on behalf of others, but also – and especially – Psalm 73, one of Augustine's favourites:

> My flesh and my heart may fail,
>   but God is the strength of my heart and my portion for ever.[30]

The psalmist, without the benefit of any theory of immortality, equipped only with a stupifyingly sober confidence, puts forward a certitude of experience. 'Communication with God *is* reality.' Ratzinger describes this as one of those texts where the Old Testament 'stretches forward to touch the New, and most fully possesses its own deepest implications'. Its teaching would soon be further spread by a new Jewish experience: martyrdom.

The New Testament does not need to put forward any new ideas about death and the after-life.

> Its newness consists in the new *fact* which fathers acceptingly to itself all that went before and gives it its wholeness. This new fact is the martyrdom of Jesus, the faithful witness, and his resurrection. The martydom and raising to new life of the just one *par excellence* clothes in flesh and blood the vision of the author of Psalm 73 and the hope-filled confidence of the Maccabees (the Jewish martyrs). In the risen Christ, the cry of troubled faith has at least found its answering response.[31]

God in Christ, entering the realm of death, transforms the 'space of non-communication' into the 'place of his own presence'. Because where men and women die with Christ and into him death is vanquished, the Church must necessarily oppose herself to the modern wish for instantaneous death. It is in the transforming acceptance of death, present not just at the clinical

[30]Psalm 73, v. 28.
[31]ETEL p. 83.

moment of biological dying but time and again in the 'inauthenticity, closedness and emptiness' of everyday living, that we mature for true life, the life everlasting. We permit ourselves to be inserted into the passion of Christ since it is there that the resurrection breaks forth.

> Communion with God, which is the native place of life indestructible, finds its concrete form in sharing in the body of Christ.[32]

Just as death's realm extends into the midst of daily living, so does that of the deathless life of Christ's resurrection.

> The border-line between Sheol and life runs through our very midst, and those who are in Christ are situated on the side of life, and that everlastingly.[33]

Whenever someone enters into Christ's life, through baptismal faith and the banquet of the Eucharist, he enters straight away into the 'space of unconditional life'. This, for Ratzinger, explains why such New Testament writers as the author of the Fourth Gospel do not raise the question of an 'inter-mediate state' between death and resurrection. Nevertheless, that question must be confronted, for

> If the 'Last Day' is not to be identified with the moment of individual death, but is accepted as what it really is, the shared ending of all history, then the question naturally arises as to what happens 'in-between'.[34]

Belief in the existence of an 'inter-mediate state' was firmly entrenched in inter-testamental Judaism, as a variety of

[32]Ibid. p. 101.
[33]Ibid. p. 103.
[34]Ibid. p. 104.

documents, from the book of Enoch and Fourth Ezra to diverse early rabbinic texts can testify. In the New Testament and the Fathers, all the images that Jews created for the inter-mediate state recur: Abraham's bosom, Paradise, the Tree of Life, water, light, and so on. But what became clear with the transposition of such images to a new context in the life of the Church was that

> these images do not describe places, but transcribe Christ himself, who is true light and life, the very *arbor vitae*.[35]

Beginning from this perception, Christians proceeded to use the instruments provided by Greek thinkers so as to grasp more clearly what it means to say that, after death, we shall be 'clasped by the person whose love embraces us all'.

Where the patristic age advanced haltingly, the Middle Ages showed greater doctrinal self-confidence. Ratzinger devotes considerable attention to the dogmatic Bull *Benedictus Deus* which Pope Benedict XII promulgated in 1336, to settle the dispute about eschatology which had troubled the pontificate of his predecessor, John XXII. As Ratzinger presents Benedict's teaching;

> after Christ, there is no longer a closed heaven. Christ is in heaven: that is, God has opened himself to man, and man, when he passes through the gate of death as one justified, as someone who belongs to Christ and has been received by him, enters into the openness of God.[36]

Although this insistence on the 'openness of heaven' after Christ's ascension could not leave untouched such early Christian notions as that of the 'sleep' of the departed, the papal

---

[35] Ibid. p. 107. Ratzinger is indebted here to P. Hoffman, *Die Toten in Christus* (Münster 1966).
[36] ETEL p. 118.

intervention maintained, in accordance with the tradition, that there is still something provisional about the state of the separated soul. Reunification with the body, and final judgment, are yet to come.

But is not this the definitive triumph of body-soul dualism in the Church of the Incarnate, the abomination of desolation standing in the place where it should not be? Ratzinger thinks not. According to his analysis, Christian theology had to maintain two truths. First, not even death can destroy life with Christ. Secondly, before the final 'resurrection of the flesh' that life is incomplete. To fashion an anthropology which would sustain both of these insights, the mediaeval divines, and above all St Thomas, welded together the philosophies of man found in Plato and Aristotle 'precisely at the points where their doctrines were mutually opposed'.

> There was a need to take over Aristotle's teaching on the inseparable unity of body and soul, yet without interpreting the soul as an 'entelechy'. For, in the latter case, the soul of man would be just as much bonded to matter as is organic life at large: dependent on matter for being what it is. Instead, the special, spiritual nature of the soul had to be highlighted, without letting the soul drop into some murky ocean of an *anima mundi*.[37]

Thomas' wonderful contribution to Christian anthropology lay in his showing how the spirit could be *both* personal *and* the form of matter. And so Ratzinger finds this account of the soul 'a product of the Christian faith, and of the exigencies of faith for human thought'.

[37]Ibid. p. 125. Here Ratzinger makes much use of A. Pegis' writings on Thomas' anthropology, notably *At the Origins of the Thomistic Notion of Man* (New York 1963), and 'Some reflections on *Summa contra Gentiles* II. 56' in *An Etienne Gilson Tribute* (Milwaukee 1959), pp. 169–188. Nb. by 'entelechy' is meant the formative principle of material reality in general.

Resurrection and parousia

Here Ratzinger confronts the question whether, 'beyond the being-with-Christ which awaits the believer after death one should posit something more'. *Does* faith require the affirmation that there will be a truly 'Last Day', an end to history as such? And does it expect a transformation of matter, and thus 'something very like corporeality' in the risen state? Some exegetes deny that the New Testament makes didactic claims about this cosmic dimension of the future. But as Ratzinger points out, a great deal turns here on how one defines 'didactic' and 'cosmic'.

As we have seen, Ratzinger has argued that, for the New Testament, the inter-mediate state is subtly but unmistakeably distinguished from the resurrection. The resurrection constitutes a further stage as yet unrealised, and thus the proper object of fresh expectation. He now adds that the same corpus of documents boasts a number of quite explicit statements about bodiliness in the risen state. These are not, he maintains:

> simply linguistic devices lingering on from traditional eschatological discourse, but are consciously formulated in a novel way on the basis of the Christian reality.[38]

In First Corinthians, Paul faces an opponent has tried to reduce resurrection faith to the absurd by asking, 'How are the dead raised? With what kind of body do they come?'.[39] In his attempt at an answer, Paul by transposing the Easter experience of Christ's risen bodiliness into an understanding of the resurrection of all the dead.

To his mind, body exists not only in the Adamic mode of the

[38]ETEL p. 140.
[39]I Corinthians 15, 35.

ensouled body but also in the christological mode prefigured in the resurrection of Jesus, a corporealty stemming from the Holy Spirit.[40]

Paul embraces a 'pneumatic realism', which should be contrasted both with physicalist realism and with spiritualism. Although the New Testament offers no further theoretical enlightenment as to the relation between Christ's body and the risen bodies of believers, Ratzinger holds its claim that all God's creation, in some form, will enter upon its definitive salvation at the close of time to be 'so palpable that any reflective systematisation of the biblical data must do it justice'.

In the Apostles' Creed, the ancient Creed of the West, we hear not of the resurrection of the *body*, but of the *flesh*. Taken over, perfectly serenely, from Judaism this phrase denotes the salvation of the human creature in its entirety. But as yet no clear distinction had been drawn between man's creaturehood and his embodied condition. In the early Church, this Jewish usage came up against the Pauline insistence that 'flesh and blood cannot inherit the Kingdom of God' – where the term 'flesh' has the quite different sense which it acquired in Paul's personal vocabulary. Ratzinger calls the resultant affray a 'wrestling match between Pauline and Johannine terminology', in which something of enormous importance was at stake – the concrete content of Christian realism itself. Gnostic teachers, in an effort to reconcile the biblical texts with ideas favoured by the dominant rationality of the age came up with conclusions remarkably akin to some modern positions, arguing, for example, that 'the resurrection is *now*'. Thus, for the second century Egyptian Gnostic Valentinus:

Since the truth lies beyond history, i.e. since the definitive reality

[40]ETEL pp. 140–141. Ratzinger's account is indebted to F. Mussner, *Die Auferstehung Jesu* (Munich 1969).

which awaits us on the far side of death is timeless, the resurrection must be understood as ever-present there. To the extent that we understand both ourselves and reality aright, we transcend the flux of historical becoming and participate in that true present, in the already realised resurrection.[41]

Here the formula 'the resurrection of the flesh' is preserved, yet the Christian hope is spiritualised out of all recognition. Over against all such deformations, Ratzinger acclaims as 'glorious' a sentence in the treatise *De resurrectione* (probably to be ascribed to the early Christian Apologist Justin Martyr):

If the gospel of salvation is proclaimed to humanity, then salvation is also proclaimed to the flesh.[42]

The Church's rejection of Valentinian Gnosis derived from her conviction of God's faithfulness to the *whole* of his creation. She remembered that healing activity had punctuated the public ministry of the Saviour, attesting God's fidelity not least towards the body, towards 'this earth which God has made'. At the winding-up of this debate, it had become clear that the resurrection of the flesh can mean the resurrection of the creature only if it also means the resurrection of the body. An *a priori* speculative construction had been excluded in the interests of maintaining the 'inner logic' of the New Testament itself.

But what *is* a 'risen body'? In the patristic period, under the influence of Origen's intellectualism, that question degenerated into a mathematical conundrum about the ideal form of the body (usually identified as that of a sphere). In reaction, Churchmen felt obliged to 'protect a human resurrection over against a mathematical one'. But the conceptual tools with

[41]ETEL p. 144. Compare G. Kretschmar, 'Auferstehung des Fleisches. Zur Frühgeschichte einer theologischen Lehrformel', in *Leben angesichts des Todes. Festschrift Thielicke* (Tübingen 1968), pp. 101–137.
[42]Cited ibid. p. 134.

which to do so were really lacking until the entry of Aristotle into Christian thinking during the course of the thirteenth century.

> With the help of Aristotle . . . a non-sensualist realism could be formulated, and in this way a philosophical counterpart to the pneumatic realism of the Bible could be found.[43]

The decisive step was taken (as we have seen) by St Thomas, in whose interpretation of the formula *anima forma corporis*, 'the soul, the form of the body', both soul and body are realities only 'thanks to each other and as oriented towards each other'. Though not identical, they are one, and, as one, constitute the single human being. Ratzinger shows that this insight carried with it two vital consequences.

First, the soul can never entirely abandon its relationship with matter.

> If it belongs to the very essence of the soul to be the form of the body, then its ordination to matter is inescapable. The only way to destroy this ordering would be to dissolve the soul itself.[44]

Here we see emerging an 'anthropological logic' which shows the resurrection to be 'a postulate of human existence'. Secondly, just as the soul is defined in terms of matter, so the living body is defined by reference to the soul.

> The material elements from out of which human physiology is constructed receive their character of being 'body' only in virtue of being organised and formed by the expressive power of soul.[45]

The soul builds itself a living body as its 'corporeal expression'.

[43]ETEL p. 147.
[44]Ibid. p. 148.
[45]Ibid.

Although Ratzinger declares that the 'simple re-pristinisation of a thorough-going Thomism' is not for him. He finds in this idea a 'sign-post for us to follow'. He will return in a moment to the question of the inter-relation of matter and spirit in the Age to Come.

But the Church's faith is not simply in resurrection: the resurrection concerned is, more specifically 'on the Last Day'. Of course, when I die, history is concluded, in preliminary fashion, for me. But I do not lose my relation to history. The 'network of human relationality' belongs to human nature itself.

> Every human being exists in himself and outside himself; everyone exists simultaneously in other people. What happens in one individual has an effect upon the whole of humanity, and what happens in humanity happens in the individual.[46]

Though everyone is judged and reaches his destiny after death, his final place in the whole can be determined only when the total organism of the body of Christ is complete, 'when the *passio* and *actio* of history have come to their end'. And so the gathering together of the whole cannot leave anyone unaffected.

> Only at that juncture can the definitive general judgment take place, judging each man in terms of the whole and giving him that just place which he can receive only in conjunction with all the rest.[47]

And this suggests a profitable line of thought for the difficult problem of the marriage of matter and spirit in the resurrection world. Ratzinger points out that the temporality of the universe, which 'knows being only as becoming', has a certain

[46]Ibid. p. 157.
[47]Ibid.

direction. He describes this, in Teilhardian langauge, as disclosed in the gradual construction of 'biosphere' and 'noosphere' from out of the physical building-blocks which it then proceeds to transcend. Being a progress to ever more complex unities, it calls for a 'total complexity: a unity which will embrace all previously existing unities'. This exigence for unity found in matter is fulfilled by non-matter, by spirit. In the world of the resurrection, this search reaches the point of integration of all in all where 'each thing becomes itself precisely by being completely in the other'.

> In such integration, matter belongs to spirit in a wholly new and different way, and spirit is utterly one with matter. The pancosmic existence which death opens up would lead, then, to universal exchange and openness, and so the overcoming of all alienation. Only where creation realises its unity can it be true that 'God is all in all'.[48]

Faith cannot imagine this new world; but it can and must affirm that, since Christ is the origin of all created being, he who is 'without' can fulfil what in the cosmos is most deeply 'within'.

So far Ratzinger has said nothing directly about the Parousia, Christ's return. But this too is a nettle he must grasp. He points out that tradition seems to speak about the Parousia with two seemingly contradictory voices. On the one hand, it maintains that Christ's coming cannot in any way be calculated from the evidence of history.

> Christ is not the product of evolution or a dialectical stage in the processive self-expression of reason, but the Other, who throws open the portals of time and death from the outside.[49]

The only answer to the request for 'signs' of his return is, 'Be

[48]Ibid. p. 158.
[49]Ibid. pp. 160–161.

watchful!'[50] But on the other hand, another substantial segment of the tradition maintains quite distinctly that there *are* such signs. Ratzinger follows the late cardinal Jean Daniélou in his attempt to resolve this discrepancy.[51] According to Daniélou, Christ is the fulfilment, *telos*, of all reality and so cannot be measured against the continuous time of this world and of history. Yet he is also the chronological end, *peras*, of historical time.

> Christ's coming is thus at one and the same time a pure act of God without precedent in history and which no periodisation of history can attain, *and also* the liberation of man, a liberation not achieved by man, yet not achieved without him either. And in this latter respect, while the Parousia does not permit of being calculated, it does allow the possibility of signs.[52]

Ratzinger reminds his readers of the curious remark of the Swabian seer-philosopher Martin Heidegger that in the situation into which humankind has blundered our only hope is to 'prepare the way for the readiness to receive the appearing of the god'.[53] Ratzinger finds in this dictum of a post-Christian pagan a genuine insight into the Parousia. Readiness to expect is itself transforming for the world. And readiness, in its turn, differs depending on whether

> it waits before a void, or goes forth to meet the One whom it encounters in his signs, such that precisely amid the ruin of its own possibilities, it becomes certain of his closeness.[54]

[50]Mark 13. 37.

[51]J. Daniélou, 'Christologie et eschatologie' in A. Grillmeier-H. Bacht (eds.), *Das Konzil von Chalkedon* III (Würzburg 1954), pp. 269–286.

[52]ETE: p. 161.

[53]Some notion of what this dark saying might mean can be gleaned from F. Kerr O.P. 'Metaphysics after Heidegger: for his eighty-fifth birthday', *New Blackfriars* 55. 651 (August 1974), pp. 344–356.

[54]ETEL p. 165.

But the theme of the Parousia is not a speculation about the unknown. Rather is it an intepretation of the Liturgy and of the Christian life in their intimate inter-connexion. As Ratzinger puts it, if only we realised that every Eucharist is Parousia, the Lord's coming, and yet the Eucharist is even more truly 'the tensed yearning that he would reveal his hidden glory', then we should gladly accept our

> obligation to live the Liturgy as a feast of hope-filled presence directed towards Christ, the cosmocrator. . . . In the Liturgy the Church should, as it were, in following him, prepare for him a dwelling in the world. The theme of watchfulness thus penetrates to the point where it takes on the character of a mission: to let the Liturgy be real, until that time when the Lord himself gives to it that final reality which meanwhile can be sought only in image.[55]

Hell, Purgatory, Heaven

Ratzinger's account of the doctrine of Hell begins a good deal more combattively than it ends. He opens by telling us that here no quibbling is of avail. The idea of everlasting punishment has a firm place in the teaching of Jesus, as well as in the New Testament writings. However, Ratzinger is also at pains to point out how many of the Eastern fathers – and, on one occasion, the Western voice of Jerome – followed Origen in his conviction that, given the logic of God's relationship with history, there must be a universal reconciliation at the End. For the Bavarian theologian, Origen's universalism comprised two elements, one deriving from a philosophical system but the other a genuine reflection of Scripture. The Middle Platonism of the *Peri Archōn*, the first sketch of a truly systematic *summa* of Christian thought, over-accentuated the notion that evil is in

[55]Ibid. p. 168.

fact nothingness, God alone being real. More important, however, was his biblically-derived hope that, in and through the 'divine suffering ... which brought God down into death':

> the reality of evil is taken prisoner and overcome, so that it loses its quality of definitiveness.[56]

Though the Church found herself constrained to admit that the universalist *doctrine* derived from the system. She has allowed the echo of the universalist *hope* to resonate through the centuries.

Two points must be retained from this battle of long ago. First, we should hold on to the 'fact of God's unconditional respect for the freedom of his creature'. The Christ who descended into Hell does not, for all that, treat man as an immature being deprived in the last analysis of any responsibility for his own destiny:

> Human life is fully serious. It is not to be de-natured by what Hegel called the 'cunning of the Idea' into an aspect of divine planning.[57]

But secondly, in the event of the death of the God-man, which Ratzinger calls, again with reference to Hegel, 'not a "speculative Good Friday" but a Good Friday that was most real', we glimpse a divine response to human evil that is able to draw freedom to itself. And drawing on von Balthasar's explorations of the 'Hell' experienced by such mystical saints as John of the Cross and Thérèse of Lisieux, Ratzinger writes:

> For the saints, 'Hell' is not so much a threat to be hurled at other people, as a challenge to oneself. It is a challenge to suffer in the dark night of faith, to experience communion with Christ in

[56]Ibid. p. 177.
[57]Ibid. p. 178.

solidarity with his descent into the Night. One draws near to the
Lord's radiance by sharing his darkness. One serves the salvation
of the world by leaving one's own salvation behind for the sake
of others ... Hope can take this on, only if one shares in the
suffering of Hell's night by the side of the One who came to
transform our night by his suffering.[58]

But despite this attempt at a revival of the so-called
'*misericordia*-doctrine' (one recalls that the old Roman breviary
contained a collect for the alleviating of the sufferings of the
damned), Ratzinger devotes the bulk of his attention to a more
securely founded dogmatic topic, that of Purgatory. By this
doctrine, the Church hung on to one aspect of the primitive
concept of the inter-mediate state, namely the insistence that:

> even if one's fundamental life-decision is finally decided and
> fixed in death, one's definitive destiny need not necessarily be
> reached straight away. It may be that the basic decision of a
> human being is covered over by layers of secondary decisions,
> and needs to be dug free.[59]

Ratzinger traces the historical emergence of this teaching,
whose explication had to wait on the 'gradual unfolding of
Christian anthropology and its relation to Christology'. From a
history-of-religions standpoint, it crystallised out of the
materials offered by three sources: Late Antique sensibility,
Judaism and Christianity.[60] The common element is the idea of
a suffering on the part of the dead that may be lightened through

[58]Ibid. See H. U. von Balthasar, *Schwestern im Geist. Therese von Lisieux und
Elisabeth von Dijon* (Einsiedeln 1970); ibid., 'Christlicher Universalismus', in
Verbum Caro. Skizzen zur Theologie I (Einsiedeln 1960), pp. 260–275; ibid.,
'Über Stellvertretung', in *Pneuma und Institution. Skizzen zur Theologie* II
(Einsiedeln 1974), pp. 401–409.
[59]ETEL p. 179.
[60]Ratzinger draws in this on J. A. Fischer, *Studien zum Todesgedanken in der
alten Kirche* I (Munich 1954); Kl. Schmöle, *Läuterung nach dem Tode und
pneumatische Auferstehung bei Klemens von Alexandrien* (Münster 1974); A.

prayer. In the West, where Tertullian, Cyprian and the unknown author of the *Passio Perpetuae* (possibly Tertullian, or one of his circle) mark essential mile-stones, the nascent doctrine was formed not in a philosophical ambience but in that of popular Christian belief. The penitential way of purification, people held, exists not only for weak and sinful Christians in this world, but also in the world to come. At Alexandria, by contrast, the idea of Purgatory (not the word) was worked out in debate with the Hellenistic philosophical schools, notably Platonism and Stoicism: it forms part of the divine educational process or *paideia*. Ratzinger notes that, according to these witnesses, death does not destroy, or even disrupt, the anchoring of a person in the Church:

> The decisive step is taken in baptism: while the fundamental option of the baptismal candidate becomes definitively established in death, its full development and purification may have to await a moment beyond death, when we make our way through the judging fire of Christ's intimate presence in the companionable embrace of the family of the Church.[61]

But because this idea of the purifying fire had become linked in the Eastern Christian mind with the Origenistic notion of *apokatastasis*, general restoration, it was combatted by Chrysostom whose doctrine became and remains official in the Orthodox churches. Although the living can bring 'respite and refreshment' to the dead through the Eucharist, prayer and almsgiving, the 'unhappiness' which such actions are meant to alleviate no longer includes a purifying or atoning suffering.

Nevertheless, turning back now from the story of Christian tradition to the classic 'proof-text' of the doctrine of Purgatory

---

Steiber, *Refrigerium interim. Die Vorstellungen des Zwischenzustandes und die frühchristliche Grabeskunst* (Bonn 1957).
[61]ETEL p. 185.

in First Corinthians, Ratzinger feels able to affirm that, when Purgatory is grasped christologically, with the Lord himself as the judging fire which transforms us and conforms us to his own glorified body, it cannot be excluded from Paul's meaning. Entering the realm of the risen Christ is an immersion in eschatological fire. Purgatory is

> the inwardly necessary process of transformation in which a person becomes capable of Christ, capable of God and thus capable of unity with the whole communion of saints. Simply to look at people with any degree of realism at all is to grasp the necessity of such a process. It does not replace grace by works, but allows the former to achieve its full victory precisely as grace.[62]

But if Purgatory is to be 'christologically determined', so must Heaven be also. Heaven's existence, for Ratzinger, depends upon the fact that Christ as God is also man, and has made 'space for human existence in the existence of God himself'. By being with Christ we find the locus of our existence as human beings in God. Ratzinger insists on the 'shaping' of the reality of Heaven by the paschal mystery of Christ's death and resurrection.

> The paschal sacrifice abides in him as an enduring presence. For this reason, Heaven, as our becoming one with Christ, takes on the nature of adoration. All cult pre-figures it, and in it comes to completion. Christ is the temple of the final age; he is heaven, the new Jerusalem; he is the cultic space for God.[63]

Christ: but the total Christ, Head and members. If heaven depends on being with Christ, then it must entail a co-being with all those who are members of his body.

[62]Ibid. p. 188.
[63]Ibid. p. 191.

Heaven is a stranger to isolation. It is the open society of the communion of saints, and in this way the fulfilment of all human communion. This is not by way of competition with the perfect disclosure of God's Face, but, on the contrary, is its very consequence.[64]

This is why, Ratzinger explains, there can be such a thing as the Christian cult of the saints. Heaven will only be complete when every last member of the Lord's body has been gathered in. Whereas the Lord's exaltation in the mysteries of Easter and the Ascension give rise to the new unity of God with man, and so to heaven, the perfecting of his body in the *plērōma* of the 'whole Christ' is what brings heaven to its cosmic completion. In that moment, Ratzinger concludes, in one of the frequent lyrical passages which characterise this work:

> the whole creation will become song. It will be a single act in which, forgetful of self, the individual will break through the limits of being into the whole, and the whole take up its dwelling in the individual. It will be joy in which all questioning is resolved and satisfied.[65]

[64]Ibid.

[65]Ibid. p. 193. For further enlightenment on Ratzinger's eschatology and the discussion it aroused in the German-speaking countries, see G. Nachtwei, *Dialogische Unsterblichkeit. Eine Untersuchung zu Joseph Ratzingers Eschatologie und Theologie (Leipzig 1986).*

Chapter Nine

THE PREACHER

The activity of preaching, from the pulpits of cathedrals and churches, or via the mass media enabled Ratzinger to reach a wider audience and to rehearse favoured themes in more popular ways. He also reflected on what the task of preaching involves. Nowadays, he mused, the path from dogma to preaching seems so tortuous that many preachers simply leave dogma by the wayside. But in that case, the proclamation of the Gospel loses its objective content, becoming instead merely speech in one's own name. This is essentially the path travelled by liberal theology in the Protestant tradition, as described by Eric Peterson.[1]

> The inner tension of the sermon derives from the objective arc of tension connecting dogma, Scripture, the Church, the world of today. None of these pillars may be removed, except at the cost of the crumbling of the whole thing.[2]

Ratzinger finds the clue to successful resolution of the preacher's dilemma to lie in recognising that both the 'place' and the ultimate acting 'subject' of preaching is not the individual's experience and identity but those of the *Church*. The Church is not the Word, but she is the locus of the Word's habitation. Nor is this a 'static' conception, for he indwells her only as her ever new ground of possibility. Behind preaching stands the 'universal I' of the Creed. The preacher must yield himself to the impulse of this 'all': *omnes*. Nor is this simply a matter of those alive today: the 'I' of the Church is diachronic as well as

[1] E. Peterson, *Was ist Theologie?* (Bonn 1926).
[2] J. Ratzinger, *Dogma und Verkündigung* (Regensburg 1973), cited below as DV, and here at p. 7.

synchronic. Such ecclesial universalism will, Ratzinger predicts, inject 'a measure of reality' (in both senses of that phrase!) into the preaching of the Gospel in the 'confusion of today'.[3] What form, then, does his own preaching take?

Here I shall simply draw attention to three basic aspects of Ratzinger's preaching: its Trinitarian character; its concern with the present and (especially) the future of Catholicism; and its willingness to accept inspiration from the Liturgy, notably from the temporal and sanctoral cycles – the celebration of the Church's year, and the memory of its saints.

The Word of the Triune God

The Holy Trinity is never far removed from this preacher's sensibility. The meditations, *Betrachtungen*, that Ratzinger offers are deeply felt thinking: he aims, as he says, to 'bond together theology and spirituality'.[3] The question of the proofs of God's existence, which, in any case scarcely lend themselves to homilectics, belong to a later stage of prayerful reflection on the Godhead than meditation on how the sense of God arises in the first place. Ratzinger traces the origins of our awareness of God to a sensation of feeling oneself known. In the religious history of the species, God appears in a variety of cultures as the Watcher, the Being full of eyes.[4] Man

> knows that absolute security does not exist, that his life is always exposed to the gaze of Someone, that his living is a being-seen.[5]

[3]DV p. 24.

[4]J. Ratzinger, *Der Gott Jesu Christi. Betrachtungen über den Dreieinigen Gott* (Munich 1976), preface. I have had access only to the Italian translation: *Il Dio di Gesù Cristo* (Brescia 1978), cited below as DGC.

[5]Cf. R. Pettazzoni, *L'onniscenza di Dio* (Turin 1955); E. Biser, 'Atheismus und Theologie', in J. Ratzinger (ed.), *Die Frage nach Gott* (Freiburg 1972), pp. 89–115.

But this sensation, of which in the Hebrew Bible Psalm 138 is a wonderful expression, can precipitate two contrary reactions. Either one can react negatively, angry at the existence of this Witness who threatens man's unlimited capacity to will and act. Or one can respond positively, opening himself to love through his enveloping presence, finding in it the 'confidence which allows him to live'.[6]

In the biblical revelation, this watchful presence reveals his Name, *YHWH*, an act which signifies his desire to be addressed, to enter into communion. Ratzinger contrasts with this understanding of the divine *Name* the *number* of the Beast, the negation of God, in the Johannine Apocalypse.[7] What that number means, Germans have seen in the concentration camps, which were peculiarly horrendous in that they cancelled face and history, reducing men to the norm of machines. But the ultimate fulfilment of the revelation of the Name must await the New Testament, where it is given as Jesus.

> His Name is not new. He himself is the face of God, the Name of God, the possibility of invoking God as a Thou, as person, as heart. The proper Name of Jesus unveils the mystery of the Name pronounced in the Burning Bush. It now appears that God had not pronounced definitively his own Name, that his discourse had been temporarily interrupted. The Name of Jesus, in fact, contains the word *YHWH* in its Hebrew form, and adds to it a further concept: 'God redeems', 'I am who I am' signifies 'I am he who redeems you'. His being is redemption.[8]

How does Ratzinger speak of God the *Father*? Though the divine image in man offers us a certain grasp of our own sonship, the divine Fatherhood is revealed in its true colours only in

[6]DGC, p. 15.
[7]Apocalypse 13, 18
[8]DGC p. 21.

Christ. For Jesus' whole existence was as that of one 'propelled into the abyss of truth and goodness which is God'.

> A Jesus who was not continually immersed in the Father, who did not communicate continually and profoundly with him, would be a being quite different from the Jesus of the Bible, the real Jesus of history.[9]

But if relationship with the Father is constitutive of the being of the Son, the converse is also true. Before the world was made, God was already the Love between the Father and the Son. It is because there never was a time when God was not Father that he can be the norm of all fatherhood.

This thought leads Ratzinger by a fairly natural progression into consideration of God's Creatorhood, which the Creed too links in a single phrase with the being of the Father. Though the role of the rational proofs of God's existence as Creator may have been exaggerated in some Catholic apologetics, their abandonment, he warns, will dissolve the relation between faith and human rationality: truth will transmute into folklore. He shows an interest in what natural scientists may have to say about the character of the cosmos in this connexion. After all, many listeners to a modern preacher will have a much fuller scientific education than they will literary or artistic. The physicist Werner Heisenberg, best known for his 'uncertainty principle' in molecular analysis, had been led by his concern with the structure of the cosmos to face the question of its foundation. He used, for God, the term 'central order'.[10] More practically, the belief in God as creator which contemporary

[9]Ibid. p. 28.

[10]Ratzinger refers here to W. Heisenberg, *Der Teil und das Ganze* (Munich 1969); see also his own 'Ich glaube an Gott den Vater, den Allmächtigen, den Schöpfer des Himmels und der Erde', in W. Sandfuchs (ed.), *Ich Glaube. Vierzehn Betrachtungen zum Apostolischen Glaubenserkenntnis* (Würzburg 1975), pp. 13–24.

physical theory may place some part in reinvigorating, raises the question of how we are to relate to reality at large.

Here Ratzinger finds evidence that a 'new Marcionitism' is stalking the land. As with the second century Asiatic heresiarch who denied the identity of the Father of Jesus with the world's Creator spoken of in the Old Testament, so today we can observe a certain convergence between ascetic distaste for the sphere of the bodily, and a cynical libertinism in its regard. But this has grave consequences for man in his place in the cosmos.

> the body's exclusion from the sphere of morals, of spiritual responsibility, is simultaneously an exclusion from man's own human sphere, from the dignity of the spirit. Thus it becomes a pure object, a thing, and in such fashion human life is made banal.[11]

However, any satisfactory response to Marcionitism, whether new or old, must take with full seriousness the problem of theodicy – if God be all-powerful Goodness, whence comes evil? – which was surely Marcion's own point of departure. No question of doctrine or theology exercises ordinary men and women in the pew more than this. For Ratzinger, the reply given by the Creator-Father to the reproaches of Job about his ill governance of the world, is found in the Son's Cross and Resurrection. The response to Job, and to all subsequent theodicists, is 'not an explanation but an action'. Ratzinger recalls the great images of the crucifix and the *pietà*: these tell us that 'in our suffering, God suffers, and our wounds make us like him'. Remembering too the example of such saints as Francis and the Franciscan-influenced Elizabeth of Thuringia, he claims that

> the Crucified has not taken suffering from the world, but with his Cross he has transformed men. He has turned their hearts to

[11]DGC p. 35.

the suffering brothers and sisters in need, and so has re-invigorated and purified both the one and the other. He it is who has inspired that 'respect for the inferior' which pagan nations lack, and which is progressively extinguished when faith in the Crucified grows less.[12]

Turning, then, to God the *Son*, Ratzinger states frankly that 'the Incarnation of God is the central article of the Christian creed'. Attempting to revive the notion that the Word Incarnate, as preached on and contemplated, is essentially found in his mysteries, that is, the events of his life, Ratzinger devotes much attention to such particular events, from the sacred Infancy right up to Good Friday and Easter. For, as he puts it, only the 'totality of the temporal course of an individual's life constitutes a human being'. The religious devotion of the Middle Ages and the early modern period understood this very well: hence its meditation on the different phases of the Saviour's earthly journey.

Ratzinger presents the childhood of Jesus as lived in close contact with his most personal mystery, the Sonship. The 'real content' of the home of Nazareth, so often sentimentalised, was – as Charles de Foucauld discovered in his own hidden life in Palestine – poverty.

The New Covenant did not begin in the temple nor on the holy mountain; it began in the little dwelling of the Virgin, the house of the worker, in one of the forgotten places of 'pagan Galilee' from which no good could be expected.[13]

The public ministry which had this household as its matrix was marked by a two-fold solitude. One turns on the rejection of Jesus and his mission.

[12]Ibid. p. 42.
[13]Ibid. p. 71; cf. M. Carrouzes, *Charles de Foucauld, explorateur mystique* (Paris 1958), p. 93.

Whoever acts in public does not only win friends: he also exposes himself to contradiction, incomprehension and abuse.[14]

The other variety is that well described by William of Saint-Thierry in his *Golden Epistle*: whoever is with God is 'never less alone than when he is alone'.[15] Ratzinger finds that the unity of the public ministry with the climactic events of the death and resurrection is disclosed by an episode which has received less attention in the West than in the East, at least in modern times: the Transfiguration. On Mount Thabor, it became clear that the 'inner basis' of the Resurrection was already present in the Jesus of the historic ministry. This inner basis is:

> the immersion of the heart of his existence in his dialogue with the Father. That dialogue was both the glory of the Son and the content of his Sonship. His passion and death would signify that his entire earthly existence was re-moulded and consumed in a total dialogue of love.[16]

In Christ's death, what was ruptured was more than in any other death that had ever been or could be: what was 'ripped away' was the dialogue that is the 'axis of the whole world'. The meaning of the resurrection, then, is that the humanity assumed by the Word is

> re-inserted into the triune exchange of eternal love in such a manner that it can never fall away again.[17]

By contrast with the Son, the *Holy Spirit* remains God the Unknown. Alas, these movements in the Church that are born from appeal to him – Montanism, Joachimism – are part of the

[14]DGC p. 71.
[15]William of Saint-Thierry, *Epistola aurea* I. 4, 10.
[16]DGC p. 74.
[17]Ibid. p. 76.

reason why the Church has spoken with 'ever greater discretion' about the Spirit. For Ratzinger, the condition of a sound pneumatology is the affirmation that the locus of the Spirit is the Son. Mindful that, in St John's Gospel, the Spirit is presented as the 'breath of the Son', Ratzinger declares:

> The more we are with Jesus, the more truly are we with the Spirit in his increasing presence with us.[18]

The proper name of the Third Person is, paradoxically, what is common to God: *spiritus*. Precisely. This person is the commonwealth of Father and Son, their unity, which he personifies in the strongest sense: he personally *is* it.

> The Father and the Son are not unified to the point of dissolving one in the other. They remain counterposed, since love is founded on such counter-position of a kind that cannot be eliminated. If each remains himself, and does not suppress himself in the other, his being does not for all that remain enclosed in itself. Rather does it express itself in a fecund way, where one gives himself to the other while remaining what he is. Both are one single thing because their love is fecund and transformative. They are themselves, *and* they are one single reality in the Third, in which they give themselves, in the Gift.[19]

Such a 'given' of the faith appears as mere speculation, rather than the blatantly obvious, if the Church herself ceases to be inhabited as a Trinitarian communion, and begins to be conceived as an association of persons who happen to find themselves thrown together.[20] Preaching the Triune God is

[18]Ibid. p. 101.
[19]DGJC p. 29. See further, J. Ratzinger, 'Der Heilige Geist als *communio*. Zur Verhältnis von Pneumatologie und Spiritualität bei Augustinus', in C. Heitmann and H. Mühlen (ed.), *Erfahrung und Theologie des Heiligen Geistes* (Hamburg-Munich 1974), pp. 223–238.
[20]Ibid. p. 30; see also J. Ratzinger, 'Taufe, Glaube und Zugehörigkeit zur Kirche', *Internationale Katholische Zeitschrift* 25 (1976), pp. 218–234.

ineluctably connected, then, with preaching about the state of the Church.

Being the Church in the world

The theme of the present and future state of the Catholic Church, or animadversions thereon, recurs time and again in Ratzinger's sermons and conferences.[21] Naturally enough, the Church is considered, in this homilectic context, not simply in itself, as a matter of pure ecclesiology, but in relation to the world, within whose mental space the preacher's hearers spend most of their working hours. In both the Church and the world the sense of time is, nowadays, a constant accompaniment of life. Perhaps never before, Ratzinger remarks, has the element of temporality, or development, struck people so forcibly as it has today. Our age is future-oriented. Yet the city of man, to many the symbol of all they desire, inspires in others only feelings of melancholy and *ennui*. Technology creates new possibilities for the human – and for the anti-human as well. It would, says Ratzinger, be too easy to bring down the 'wooden mallet of the theologian' at this point, and cry: Let us be saved *from* technology, not *by* technology. After all:

> The Christian God came not as a *deus ex machina* to set everything eternally in order, but as the Son of Man in order to share interiorly in the passion of mankind. And this too is precisely the task of the Christian: to share in the passion of mankind from within, to extend the sphere of human living so that it will find room for the presence of God.[22]

The City which is above will, when it descends, spell the end of all our planning and its collapse. Yet that City only comes because, and when:

[21] See especially *Glaube und Zukunft* (Munich 1970), cited below as GZ.
[22] GZ p. 86.

man has run, and suffered, the entire course of his human
existence, to the limits of his capacities.[23]

What, then, of the Church which must live her life in such a
technological age? Though Ratzinger disclaims any talent as a
soothsayer, he does risk offering a conference on the topic,
'What will the Church look like in the year 2000?'. In fact, he
approaches ecclesiastical futurology in the spirit – paradoxically
– of an historian.

> Looking back into the past does not yield a prediction of the
> future, but it does limit our illusion of complete uniqueness, and
> shows us that, while exactly the same thing has not happened
> before, something very similar has. The dissimilarity between
> then and now is the reason for the uncertainty of our statements
> and for the newness of our tasks; the similarity is the basis for
> orientation and correction.[24]

According to Ratzinger, two periods resemble ours at any rate
in significant part: that of Modernism, and the age spanning the
Enlightenment and the Great Revolution of the West, referred
to in German cultural history as that of the Rococo.

Ratzinger makes the connexion with the world of
Modernism briefly enough. The crisis of Modernism:

> never really came to a head, but was interrupted by the measures
> taken by Pius X and by the change in the intellectual situation
> after the First World War. The crisis of the present is but the
> long-deferred resumption of what began in those days.[25]

---

[23]Ibid. p. 88. It might have been useful here to note that, in this human
'course', technology is simply a complement to civilisation – as pointed out by
the Guinean novelist Camara Laye in his *Le Mâitre de la parole* (Paris 1978); ET
The Guardian of the Word (London 1980), p. 18.

[24]GZ pp. 91–92.

[25]Ibid. p. 92.

He lingers much longer over the comparison with the *Rokokozeit*. That age resembled ours, he alleges, in its systematic preference for rationality over against tradition, and also in its curious *mélange* of exaggerations with genuinely fruitful beginnings. That age too had its eminently desirable liturgical movement, and its honourable effort to vindicate the just place within Catholic consciousness of the local church in all its particularity. Yet both became extreme, finishing in such highly ambiguous phenomena as the 1786 (Tuscan) Synod of Pistoia,[26] or the career of the Saxon ecclesiastic Ignaz Heinrich von Wessenberg (1774–1860).[27] Between the two of them, they would have reduced the Catholic liturgy to a Calvinist austerity, abolished all extra-liturgical devotions and expressions of piety, decreed the monastic and mendicant orders out of existence, and erected their respective churches into a law unto themselves, all animated by what Balthasar has called *der anti-römische Affekt*.

Following the impulses of the same cultural epoch, individuals could veer off in dizzily different directions. On the one hand, there was a Jean-Baptiste Gobel, the archbishop of Paris who was the first, in 1790, to sign the Civil Constitution of the Clergy, and in the following year to consecrate nine similarly 'juring' clergy to the episcopate without the mandate of the Holy See.[28] Having abandoned his office under the anti-Christian pressure of the *Assemblée nationale*, he took part in the inauguration of the 'Goddess of Reason' at Notre Dame de Paris in November 1793 prior to being executed for atheism the

[26]See on this M. Vaussard, *Jansénisme et gallicanisme aux origines du Risorgimento* (Paris 1959).

[27]W. Müller, 'Wessenberg, Ignaz Heinrich Freiherr von', LexTHK 10 cols. 1064–1066.

[28]See N. Pisani, *Répertoire biographique de l'épiscopat constitutionnel 1791–1802* (Paris 1907); or, more widely, A. Latreille, *L'Eglise catholique et la Révolution française* (Paris 1946–1950).

following spring. Or again, the same period provides the instructive example of Matthäus Fingerlos, rector of the pastoral institute called the *Herzögliches Georgianum* in Landshut from 1804 to 1814. Declaring ethics to be the essence of religion, he looked forward to the day when the highest office of the Catholic clergy would be the instruction of others in agricultural improvement.[29] Against such figures, Ratzinger sets Johann Michael Sailer, whom we have already encountered,[30] and Clemens Maria Hofbauer, the Moravian baker's apprentice who, ordained as a Redemptorist in 1785, built up an extraordinary influential apostolate which earned for him the name of 'Apostle of Vienna'.[31] And pondering the work of Sailer and Hofbauer, Ratzinger concludes:

> The thing that outlived the ruins of the declining eighteenth century and was reborn as the future was very different from what Gobel and Fingerlos and expected. It was a Church reduced in size and diminished in social prestige, yet become fruitful from a new interior power, a power that released new formative forces for the individual and for society, a power manifested both in great lay movements, and in the founding of numerous Religious Congregations.[32]

Whereas a Church that 'celebrates the cult of action in political prayers' will prove to be superfluous and self-destructing, the Church of the future will 'once again, as always, be re-shaped by the saints' who see further than others since their lives embrace a wider reality.

[29]E. Weigl, 'Fingerlos, Matthäus', LexTLK 4 cols. 138–139.
[30]See above, p. 13.
[31]J. Hofer, *St Clement Maria Hofbauer* (New York 1926).
[32]GZ pp. 100–101.

Saints and seasons

Ratzinger did not, indeed, neglect the inspirational resources of the sanctoral cycle, the celebration of the Church's saints. He compared the saints to the *Hochaltarbilder*, the images of the reredos in the Baroque churches of 'our Bavarian homeland', artworks which, architecturally speaking, 'close' the church building, yet iconographically function as a door, taking the believer through to the greater and more intensely real world of God. In the saints of the Church's year, he wrote

> the single invisible Light of God is broken up in the prism of our human history, so that we may encounter the everlasting glory and radiance of God in our own human world, in our brothers and sisters.[33]

The saints are our elder siblings in the family of God. They take us by the hand, and would lead us. They make us say, If one Christian could do these things, then why not I? For, as Ratzinger remarks in a homily on Augustine, Christian holiness does not consist in being supermen, or in receiving some power that others have not. It consists, rather, in the obedience which responds when God calls, knowing that only in service and self-abandonment shall be truly find ourselves. So it was that Augustine abandoned the 'ivory tower of high intellectuality', to be a man among men, a servant among the servants of God. He who could have been such an aristocrat of the spirit relinquished his exalted educational ideals, and spoke to his brethren in the cathedral of Hippo 'in an ever more simple, ever more homely way'. The Augustine who had stood with his mother at a window in Ostia, as they spoke together of the

[33]DV p. 421.

eternal Today of God, which shall be when, for us, earth and sea sink away, and past and future are no more[34]

thus became himself what every saint should be, a window into eternity.

This is supremely so in the greatest of the saints, the Mother of God. The greeting of Elizabeth to Mary, with its promise that 'all generations will call you blessed' is well-founded because

> she is the great believer, who humbly opened herself, like a glass that receives God's dark mystery, and let her own life's plan fall from her hands without a murmur ...[35]

Mary takes Elizabeth's praise and directs it from herself to God to whom all praise belongs. In her *Magnificat* she gives us the model for all Marian devotion; she herself is a hymn to God, the mirror of the gracious mercy he has shown to man. Ratzinger insists in his meditations on the Church's Marian belief, *Die Tochter Zion*, that the canticle of the Blessed Virgin Mary is a carpet, woven from the threads of Old Testament speech. In it the whole history of Israel becomes a single act of praise of the gracious and steadfast One. The *Sophia* of the sapiential books of the Old Testament refers not only to the divine Word who establishes wisdom, but also to the womanly answer which 'receives wisdom and brings it to fruition'. Thus, in the moment of the Annunciation:

> the figure of the woman, until then seen only typologically in Israel, although provisionally personified by the great women of Israel also emerges with a name: Mary.[36]

---

[34] Ibid. p. 428.

[35] Ibid. p. 412.

[36] J. Ratzinger, *Die Tochter Zion* (Einsiedeln 1977); ET *Daughter Zion* (San Francisco 1983), and here at pp. 27–28. Ratzinger notes that where typological exegesis has been rejected, the unity of the Testaments is lost, and with it Mariology, ibid. pp. 32–33.

In the Child born of the Virgin's womb, the earth has borne its greatest fruit – because there God has acted, truly acted, and not simply provided us with an interpretation of the course of nature. The birth from the Virgin Mary is not a 'tiny, private chapel' owned by the evangelists Luke and Matthew:

> The alternatives are simple. Does God act or not? Can he act at all? If not, is he really 'God'?[37]

On right Marian belief turns the assurance, and the hope of Christians.

That assurance and hope are summed up in the two great Marian feasts which correspond to them: the Immaculate Conception, and the Bodily Assumption. On the first, Ratzinger tells his hearers:

> the doctrine of the *Immaculata* reflects ultimately faith's certitude that there really is a holy Church – as a person and in a person. In this sense it expresses the Church's certitude of salvation ... God's covenant in Israel did not fail but produced a shoot out of which emerged the blossom, the Saviour.[38]

And on the second:

> This dogma was intended to be an act of veneration, the highest form of Marian praise.... The veneration refers to one who is alive, who is at home, who has actually arrived at her goal on the other side of death.

In her, death is swallowed up by the victory of her Son. Through bearing him who is the death of death, her divine Motherhood already points to her Assumption: 'from this birth comes only life, not death'. By her entry into glory, the

[37]Ibid. p. 61.
[38]Ibid, p. 70–71.

Church's *promised* certitude of salvation becomes its *bodily* certitude also. In celebrating this feast, the Lucan commission to 'call her blessed' is put into supreme effect.

But the sanctoral cycle, even when its festivals honour the God-bearer herself, plays its part within the greater drama of the temporal cycle, which celebrates the unfolding of our salvation through the Father's sending of the Son and of the Holy Spirit. That cycle has two moments of climax: Christmas–Epiphany, preceded by Advent, and Easter–Pentecost, preceded by Lent. Ratzinger's homilies and meditations on these seasons are, I find, comparable in the English homilectic tradition to those of the Anglican Austin Farrer, who died as Warden of Keble College, Oxford: hard thinking, in which are embedded bright, crystalline images. This makes them stimulus for contemplation as well as for reflection.

The symbolism of light binds together his Christmas and Easter preaching. In a homily on Advent, he compares the lights that dot the landscape in the deep darkness of a South German winter's night to the light of Christ's Parousia, the real meaning of 'Advent'. These lights are both comfort and warning. They comfort, for

> the Light of the world has already arisen in the dark night of Bethlehem. The unholy night of man's sin has been changed into the holy night by God's pardon.[39]

At the same time, they also warn, since

> this Light wills to spread its illumination, and can only spread it, by shining forth in others – in Christians who carry on the work of Christ through the ages.[40]

[39]Ibid. pp. 73–74.
[40]DV pp. 373–374.

Ratzinger presents the liturgy of Advent as a triptych in which John the Baptist and Mary point to the central figure of Christ. The Church knows, he explains, that man lives more by concrete images than by abstract truths. Via those images we learn what celebrating Advent is: the manifestation of the hidden presence of God in our lives. When Christmas comes, Ratzinger hails it in an ironic use of the pagan language for the winter solstice: 'the birthday of the Unconquered Light'. Christ's birth means

> winter's turn of the sun for world history, bringing with it the certainty that, in all the risings and fallings of that history, here at least the Light will not die for it has the final victory already in possession.[41]

In the holy night of Bethlehem, the God who elected the tiny, forgotten people of Israel to be his own, has finally made the sign of littleness the decisive sign of his presence in this world. To dwell in this night is 'to find truth and love under the same sign', the highest, most god-like values as they are – and the 'quietest, the most forgotten'.[42]

This same symbolism of light in darkness recurs in Ratzinger's homilies and meditations on the Easter triduum. In a sermon for Holy Thursday, preached in the *Liebfrauendom* in Munich, he presents the Lord as going out into the threefold night of Gethsemane, the Cross and the grave. His stepping outside the boundary of the protective walls of the city is a gesture of victory.

> He summons us to dare to accompany him on his path; for where faith and love are, he is there, and the power of peace is there which overcomes nothingness and death.[43]

[41] Ibid. p. 396.
[42] Ibid. p. 398.
[43] J. Ratzinger, *Schauen auf den Durchbohrten* (Einsiedeln 1984), ET *Behold the Pierced One* (San Francisco 1986), p. 109.

His Church, then, is 'not a bunker or a sealed fortress but an open city', since her rampart is faith in, and love of, him. At the end of the liturgy of the Lord's Supper, we must make of our following him, in the procession with the Blessed Sacrament,

> a commitment on our part to be continually entering into Jesus' forsakenness . . . to stand by him wherever men do not want to know him.[44]

Again, in a meditation delivered before Pope John Paul II and the members of the Roman Curia, Ratzinger adds that the imitation of Christ entails not only such passive enduring, but also active engagement. For the Liturgy of Holy Thursday also includes the *mandatum*, the Foot-washing with its command of love. And here:

> to receive this washing means to continue with Christ to wash the soiled feet of the world.[45]

On Good Friday, Jesus dies praying, and, according to Ratzinger all the evangelists are agreed in this, that the Lord's dying was itself an act of prayer.

> Death which by its nature is the end, the destruction of every relationship, is by him transformed into an act of communication of himself; and this is the salvation of humankind, in that it signifies that love conquers death[46]

And so at last to Easter which is both divine response to the Cross, and its divine interpretation. In the light of the Paschal candle; in the baptismal waters; and in the alleluias of the Church's chant the 'Christ drama' comes to its completion:

[44]Ibid.
[45]J. Ratzinger, *Il cammino pasquale* (Milan 1985); ET *Journey towards Easter* (Slough, 1987), p. 99.
[46]Ibid. p. 105.

the encounter of God and the world, the triumphant breaking in
of God to the world which would give him no room, yet now at
the end can debar him from none whatsoever.[47]

[47]DV p. 341.

Chapter Ten

THE LITURGIST

'Nothing is sacred – nothing in church at least', remarks one Anglican critic of liturgical reform.[1] Naturally, to oppose all liturgical reform on principle would be as idiotic as to suppose that all achieved reform is, *eo ipso*, a good thing. Criticisms of the particular liturgical reform that the last twenty years have seen in the Catholic Church of the Latin rite, as in the Anglican communion, are not necessarily made from the standpoint of root-and-branch opposition to everything which the Liturgical Movement in the Western Christendom of this century has attempted to achieve. On the contrary, they may be motivated by profound attachment to that Movement's aims. The point may be missed by those who, easily satisfied, or so it would seem, with the diet offered in their churches, dismiss malcontents as bangers of antique drums who would be better

---

[1]P. Mullen, 'A mess of pottage for the poor old C of E', *The Observer*, 19. 4. 1987, p. 8. Mr Mullen's article may be taken as representing what is now a substantial body of articulate Anglican criticism of much contemporary liturgical reform. See, for example, the comment of Professor David Martin, that 'a very deep sense of despair can grip the Christian intellectual who is seeking to re-present the resources of traditional Christianity and is, at the same time, deprived of the resources of the traditional liturgy', in C. A. A. Kilmister, *When will Ye Be Wise? The State of the Church of England* (London 1983), p. 156; or again, R. K. Fenn's expression of doubt as to whether those 'alienated from the local community, distasteful of traditionalists and of the uneducated laity, accustomed to bureaucratic routine and to the fellowship of commissioners can produce a liturgy worthy of acclaim', in M. D. Bryant (ed.), *The Future of Anglican Theology* (New York – Toronto 1984), p. 104, as typical examples. For an analogous British Catholic reaction, one might consult K. Flanagan, 'Resacralising the Liturgy', *New Blackfriars* 68. 802 (February 1987), pp. 64–75, an article partly indebted to Ratzinger's liturgiological writing.

employed in seeing to the needs of their neighbours. As Ratzinger puts it:

> Faced with the political and social crisis, of the present time, and the moral challenge they offer to Christians, the problems of liturgy and prayer could easily seem to be of secondary importance.

But this would be a tragic misconception. As he explains:

> The question of the moral standard and spiritual resources that we need if we are to acquit ourselves in this situation cannot be separated from the question of worship. Only if man, every man, stands before the face of God and is answerable to him, can man be secure in his dignity as a human being. Concern for the proper form of worship, therefore, is not peripheral but central to our concern for man himself.[2]

A theology of the Liturgy

Establishing a healthy liturgical *practice* can only be done on the basis of a sound liturgical *theology*. Ratzinger's starting point is that liturgy is an instance of praying, itself the most transparent moment in the dialogue between God and man which gives the Christian Gospel its entire pattern. What is unique to Christianity is that it

> ascribes to the God of the philosophers the fundamental traits of the gods of the old religions, namely, relationship with men, albeit now in an absolute form insofar as it calls God the Creator.[3]

This 'paradoxical conjunction' – that the Absolute is itself

[2]J. Ratzinger, *The Feast of Faith* op. cit. p. 7. Cited below as FF.
[3]FF p. 17.

relationship – constitutes both the novelty of the Christian message, and also its fundamental difficulty and vulnerablity. In this light, arguments against prayer prove to be arguments against Christianity itself. Anti-metaphysicians reject prayer – because, for Christian faith, prayer is address to the God who is that Creator and Ground of all things who has himself spoken to us. Rationalists of a deist variety reject prayer – because, for Christian faith, prayer implies that the world is not governed by the 'chance and necessity' into which the biologist Jacques Monod analysed it.[4] It includes among its constitutive elements freedom and love, and indeed, if the personality which is postulated by such freedom and love is not characteristic of the Ground of all reality, then it is not a possibility at all, and man's claim to transcend mechanical causalilty is delusion. Most acutely of all, there is an Aristotelean objection to prayer according to which:

> eternity by its very nature cannot enter into relationship with time, and similarly time cannot affect eternity.... If anything new were to be initiated in eternity, eternity would have become time. And if eternity were to get involved with the changing stream of time, it would forfeit its nature as eternity.[5]

This is, Ratzinger confesses, a serious problem for Christian thought, and one that suggests the need to work out a concept of 'the creativity which eternity exercises with regard to time'.[6] He holds, moreover, that a non-Trinitarian monotheism will be unable to meet this objection. Its God will become a *Deus otiosus*, separated from man by an unbridgeable chasm. He will fade into a mere 'transcendence'; the idea of prayer being 'heard' then evaporates, and faith becomes that hopelessly elusive thing

[4] J. Monod, *Chance and Necessity* (London 1971).
[5] EF. pp. 20–21.
[6] Ibid. p. 21.

'self-transcendence'. Wherever, despite the relegation of the dogmatic content of Christian faith to the status of a piece of outmoded Western metaphysics or mythology, there remains a deep religious or spiritual impulse in people, we increasingly find an option for the 'way of Asia', of Great Vehicle Buddhism, or Advaita Hinduism. Though the Church can learn from the classic Asiatic religions, Ratzinger predicts that one day, where spiritual life is concerned, our civilisation will have to decide between their search for the serene identity of the illusorily distinct 'I' with the Ground of all being and the biblical prayer which is essentially 'a relation between persons and hence ultimately the affirmation of the person'.[7]

While such a theology of prayer is valuable, Ratzinger has said nothing so far about that supreme instance of prayer which is the Church's Liturgy. The way into the subject is via his hint that only a *Trinitarian* monotheism will be able to relate in satisfactory fashion the realms of eternity and time. For Christianity, God himself is 'speech' or 'word'.

> His nature is to speak, to hear, to reply, as we see particularly in Johannine theology, where Son and Spirit are described in terms of pure 'hearing'; they speak in response to what they have first heard. Only because there is already speech, *Logos*, in God can there be speech, *logos*, to God. . . . The divine Logos is the ontological foundation for prayer.[8]

Ratzinger offers as a translation of the opening sentence of the Prologue of the Fourth Gospel:

> In the beginning was the Word, and the Word was in communication with God.[9]

[7]Ibid. p. 24.
[8]Ibid. p. 25.
[9]Ibid.

The term 'communication' here adverts to the relationship of the Logos to God. Since there is a relationship within God himself, there can also be a participation in this relationship. Through the Incarnation of the Logos, such participation is offered to us. Through the economies of the Son and the Spirit:

> man is able to participate in the dialogue within God himself, because God has first shared in human speech and has thus brought the two into communication with one another.[10]

The 'place' of this insertion of man into God's own speech is the *Church*.

Only in the common fellowship of the Church can we make our own the prayer of Christ, for the Church is so identified with him that she can be called his 'body'. The content of Christian prayer is, fundamentally, the Son's adoring and intimate prayer, recorded for us by the Gospel tradition in its original Aramaic form: *Abba*. This prayer, which is the Son's act of being, and is thus rooted in the ultimate depths of reality, is, as Ratzinger presents it, an affirmatory 'act of consent' to the goodness of the world's Ground.

> Prayer is an act of being; it is affirmation, albeit not affirmation of myself as I am and of the world as it is, but affirmation of the Ground of being, and hence a purifying of myself and of the world from this Ground upward.[11]

All such purification, which Ratzinger associates with the classical *via negationis* of mystical theology, is only possible on the rock-like foundation of affirmatory consent: As Paul writes to the Corinthian Christians, the Son of God was 'not Yes and

[10]Ibid. p. 26.
[11]Ibid. p. 27: this section is indebted to J. Pieper, *Zustimmung zur Welt. Eine Theologie des Festes* (Munich 1963).

No. ... In him it is always Yes'.[12] But this Son who guides us along the path of purification through the gateway of the 'Yes' is himself only encountered as a living person in that foretaste of his presence which is the Church. It is here, in reference to this divine and human co-being of the Church's mystery, that Ratzinger situates the possible future contribution of the non-Christian religions of Asia to the Gospel. There is, alas, a constricting and excessive personalism, which sees individual identity as an encapsulated 'I', over against the similarly encapsulated 'Thou' of God, Here, partnership between God and man is conceived so straitly in I-Thou terms as to deprive God of his infinity and exclude others from the unity of being. In the Liturgy we learn, by identification with the Church, how to find our true identity in the Christ who as the 'firstborn of all creation' holds all things together.[13] And so the aim of prayer may be defined as 'that man should become an *anima ecclesiastica* – the personal embodiment of the Church'. Through the Liturgy:

> the language of our Mother becomes ours; we learn to speak it along with her, so that gradually, her words on our lips become our words. We are given an anticipatory share in the Church's perennial dialogue of love with him who desired to be one flesh with her, and this gift is transformed into the gift of speech. And it is in the gift of speech, and not until then, that I am really restored to my true self; only thus am I given back to God, handed over by him to all my fellow men; only thus am I free.[14]

I learn to pray by learning in the Liturgy to respond with the Church, *sentire cum Ecclesia*.

[12] II Corinthians 1, 19ff.
[13] Colossians 1, 15ff.
[14] FF p. 30.

Liturgy and music

However, despite his stress on the *words* of the Liturgy, words 'lived and prayed by countless people', Ratzinger does not neglect its other dimensions: music, silence and gesture. A recurrent aspect of Ratzinger's liturgical interests – perhaps connected with the fact that his brother Georg is the cathedral chiormaster of Regensburg – is the Church's *music*.

> Liturgy and music have been closely related to one another from their earliest beginnings. Wherever man praises God, the word alone does not suffice. Conversation with God transcends the boundaries of human speech, and in all places, it has by its very nature called to its aid music, singing and the voices of creation in the harmony of instruments. More belongs to the praise of God than man alone, and liturgy means joining in that which all things bespeak.[15]

However, as Ratzinger goes on the point out, the relation of liturgy and music has not infrequently been strained, especially at 'turning-points of history and culture'. The immediately post-conciliar period saw a certain amount of minor skirmishing between pastoral liturgists and Church musicians, with the latter trying to bring out the inherent dignity of good music as a pastoral and liturgical norm in its own right.

At the time, this discussion seemed to be about the mere nuts and bolts of how to apply in practice things that everyone agree to in theory. But since then, a feeling has emerged which is hostile to the very existence of a rite as such. Rather than the Church supporting the liturgy of an individual group by its historic tradition, the group takes over. 'Rite' becomes a negative term, signifying attempts to constrain 'real' liturgy, which arises on the spot, springing from the creativity of the

[15] J. Ratzinger, 'Liturgy and Sacred Music', *Communio* 13. 4 (1986), p. 377.

assembled persons. By contrast, traditional liturgy and Church music appear as mystifications which, it is insinuated, have as their covert intent the preservation of a particular form of power in the Church. Using as exemplar the entry 'Canto e musica' in the authoritative *Nuovo dizionario di liturgia*, Ratzinger puts the position he wishes to question as follows:

> A certain administration of power, we are told, feels threatened by processes of cultural transformation and reacts by masking its striving for self-preservation as love for the tradition. Gregorian chant and Palestrina are tutelary gods of a mythicised, ancient repertoire, elements of a Catholic counter-culture that is based on re-mythicised and super-sacralised archetypes, just as in the historical liturgy of the Church it has been more a question of a cultic bureaucracy than of the singing activity of the people.[16]

The last thing Christian worship should do, on this account, is to prop up the historic Church with its lamentable history of decline from the New Testament fulness and simplicity. Rather, the liturgy should take its cue from Mary's *Magnificat* and help pull down the mighty, whether temporal or spiritual, from their thrones. Much more to the linking of such writers are the revolutionary chants of the *Missa Nicaraguensis*, aiming as these do to create solidarity between the members of a new people of God. Unfortunately, Ratzinger comments, 'God' here really means 'the people itself and the historical energies realised in it.'[17]

The makers of such liturgies have rightly perceived that freedom is the essence of Christianity, Yet Christianity is not freedom as they have conceived it. Where members of a group make themselves the true acting subject of the liturgy, both the common subject (the Church) and the transcendent Subject (God) disappear from view. People forget that the liturgy is *opus*

[16]Ibid. p. 379.
[17]Ibid. p. 381.

Dei, the work of God. First and foremost it is he who is active in it, and we, the worshippers, become redeemed people only because that is so. By celebrating itself, the group celebrates nothing, generating that tedium which many have reported in connection with the *Novus Ordo Missae*.

What, then, can be done? For inspiration, Ratzinger turns to the writings of Romano Guardini, himself a founding father of the Liturgical Movement.[18] Guardini insisted that a Catholic vision of liturgy depends on the dogmatic faith that, despite the Church's sometimes appalling human frailty, the presence in her of the Incarnate Lord continues. Without the discovery that in the Church Jesus Christ shares our time, there can be no true liturgy. For the liturgy is not the mere recalling of the paschal triumph but its *real presence*, and so a sharing in the divine conversation of Father, Son and Holy Spirit.

The Church, as the 'communion of saints' of all times and places, is the proper subject of the liturgy, and this fact withdraws the liturgy from the arbitrariness of any group or individual – be they cleric, be they specialist. Any creativity which aspires to be an expression of human autonomy lies at the opposite pole from liturgical creativity, which issues from readiness to receive and partake. Following Guardini, Ratzinger identifies the three 'ontological dimensions' in which the liturgy lives as the cosmic, the historical and, finally, the mysterious. It is by the systematic denigration of these three elements that we arrive at do–it–yourself liturgy whose characteristics are

> caprice, as a necessary form of refusal of every pre-given form or norm; unrepeatability, since the performation of a repetition

[18]R. Guardini, *Liturgische Bildung: I. Versuche* (Rotenfels 1923); revised edition: *Liturgie und liturgische Bildung* (Würzburg 1966). Ratzinger discusses Guardini more fully in his 'Von der Liturgie zur Christologie', in J. Ratzinger (ed.) *Wege zur Wahrheit. Die bleibende Bedeutung von R. Guardini* op. cit.

would already imply dependence; and artificiality, since it is necessarily a question of a merely human creation.[19]

Since man can be himself only through 'reception' and 'participation', the flight from dependence on tradition makes us play false with the human condition, thus condemning us to cultural decline.

Consonant with this account, Ratzinger offers a sketch for a theology of Church music. It begins from the Johannine prologue, with its proclamation that the Word has become flesh. In the Incarnation, a God who is Meaning communicates himself by becoming man. In Johannine perspective, this sparks off a process which reaches its climax in the Cross and Resurrection. From the Cross, the Lord Jesus draws everything to himself, bearing man, and, with man, the entire sensuous order, into the eternity of God. The existence of music as an aspect of human reality shows that the 'Word' – the continuing, dynamic presence of the Incarnate Son – cannot be mere speech. The sacramental signs, themselves more than just language, belong within a liturgical life which, including as it does art and music, echoes the relation of the Incarnate Lord to the whole created order.

The Word, therefore, 'becomes music'. In doing so, God draws to himself our pre-rational and super-rational powers as musical beings, thus uncovering for us the 'song which lies at the foundaiton of all things'.[20] The flesh becomes spirit; brass and wood become sound; what is unconscious, unsettled, turns into orderly and significant resonance. Church music must correspond to these demands of the Incarnation.

It follows, Ratzinger goes on, that such music cannot be Dionysiac, using the forms of rock and pop to weave an illusion

[19]'Liturgy and sacred music', art. cit. p. 38.
[20]Ibid. p. 386.

of escape from the ego and the limitations of the everyday. Nor can it employ those modes of musical expression which belong essentially to political or erotic arousal, or the simple desire to entertain. Nor, finally, can it be rationalistic, though, we are informed, many modern hymns designed to commission belong in this category. For Ratzinger, the greatness of the music of the Latin church, from plainsong through Renaissance and Baroque to Bruckner and beyond, constitutes, by its superb unification of the spiritual and the proface, a kind of aesthetic verification of the Christian doctrine of man and human redemption. Only those who are living wholeheartedly within this vision can create a music appropriate to it.

What, then, of the future of sacred music? Ratzinger hopes that, in combining appeal to the traditional inheritance with the best of popular music a new renaissance of *Musica sacra* might be possible. Certainly, music of the highest standard and constructed according to such a formula exists. In Britain, one might think of Vaughan Williams' *Mass in G Minor*, or Kenneth Leighton's *An Easter Sequence*. Looking beyond Europe, Ratzinger muses that from the churches of Africa, Asia and Latin America new cultural forms may be budding. In the West, we should not be frightened of the word 'sub-culture', he counsels, if this is the only way to encourage such music. It may be that the purification of culture, and the re-integration of a scattered mosaic, will only be possible on 'islands of spiritual composure'.[21]

With regard to the frequently banal and unworthy music which has too frequently, since the Council, perpetuated the worst of the pre-conciliar practice at the expense of the plainsong and polyphony which was its best, Ratzinger is putting questions of importance. Has the Church the right to renounce her mission to baptise culture, especially that 'high'

[21] Ibid. p. 390.

culture which is the bearer of human insights and values attained at most cost? Has she ceased to seek the cultural expression of that glorious transfiguration of the human which is *la vita nuova*, the new life in Christ? In other words: has not the triumph of liturgical populism been achieved at too high a price?[22]

Western music tradition has indeed displayed that 'cosmic and universal character' which Ratzinger considers appropriate for the celebration of the Liturgy.[23] As a recent historian of the relation between music, philosophy and cosmology has shown: the Hellenic (Pythagorean) account of music as a revelation of divine order and a moulder of human conduct was not dismantled when, with Synesius, Martianus Cappella and Boethius, the Classical merges into the Christian world.[24] The threefold *musica* of Boethius, for example, which is at once *musica instrumentalis* (music made through man–constructed instruments, using dead matter in the interests of spiritual life), *musica humana* (music uttered by human voices) and *musica mundana* (the music of the spheres)

> is a penetration of the very heart of providence's ordering of things. It is not a matter of cheerful entertainment or superficial consolation for sad moods, but a central clue to the interpretation of the hidden harmony of God and nature in which the only discordant element is evil in the heart of man.[25]

This tradition continued through the Renaissance, flourished in both the Enlightenment and the age of Romanticism, and survives in modern music in such figures as Webern and

[22]See C. Fabro, 'Spiritualità ecclesiale nella Musica Sacra', *Rivista di Ascetica e Mistica* 9. 6 (1964), pp. 3–14.

[23]FF p. 64.

[24]See J. Godwin (ed.), *Music, Mysticism and Magic. A Sourcebook* (London 1987), reviewed by W. Mellers as 'Audible Truths', *Times Literary Supplement* No. 4000 (31. 7. 1987), p. 813.

[25]H. Chadwick, *Boethius. The Consolations of Music, Logic, Theology, and Philosophy* (Oxford 1981), p. 101.

Messaien, thus showing that a high doctrine of music as repository of truth is by no means implausible today. As John Henry Newman put it:

> Music is the expression of ideas greater and more profound than any in the visible world, ideas which centre, indeed, in Him whom Catholicism manifests, who is the seat of all beauty, order and perfection whatever.[26]

Silence and gesture

So much for music; what of its essential counterpart, silence? This Ratzinger connects with our need for re-education in inwardness, the *Innerlichkeit* of the German mystics. If there is to be true 'active participation' then, paradoxically, there must be silence.

> In this silence, together, we journey inward, becoming aware of word and sign, leaving behind the roles which conceal our real selves. In silence man 'bides' and 'abides'; he becomes aware of 'abiding reality'.[27]

In the Roman rite, such silence is appropriate before and after communion, as well as at the preparation of the Gifts. Ratzinger also recommends a partial reversion to the silent recitation of the Canon – as an antidote to the excessively didactio wordiness of much contemporary celebration. The continual recitation of the canon aloud results in the demand for 'variety'. But this demand is insatiable, however much new eucharistic prayers – whose content frequently leaves much to be desired – may proliferate. And so, Ratzinger concludes:

[26] J. H. Newman, *The Idea of a University* (London 1936[6]), p. 80. Cf. E. Bellasis, *Cardinal Newman as a Musician* (London 1892), pp. 5–7.
[27] FF p. 72.

This is why, here especially, we are in such urgent need of an education towards inwardness. We need to be taught to enter into the heart of things . . . The only way we can be saved from succumbing to the inflation of words is if we have the courage to face silence and in it learn to listen afresh to the Word. Otherwise we shall be overwhelmed by 'mere words' at the very point where we should be encountering *the Word*, the Logos, the Word of love, crucified and risen, who brings us life and joy.[28]

But the Liturgy is framed with the assistance not only of music and silence but also with that of the *gesture*. Standing, sitting, bowing, beating one's breast, making the sign of the cross, all these have an 'irreplaceable anthropological significance' as the way that spirit is expressed in flesh. Ratzinger appeals to an essay of Joseph Pieper's in this connexion; in it, that attractive Thomist writer argues that such gestures bring together the 'inside' and the 'outside' of the person in a reciprocal relationship which is equally important for both.[29] *Das Fest des Glaubens* selects three gestures for sustained comment: kneeling; the eastward position in Eucharistic celebration; and walking in procession.

Ratzinger expresses concern over the threatened disappearance of the practice of kneeling. He points out that Jesus himself knelt to pray, as did, according to the book of Acts, the apostles Peter and Paul and the proto-martyr Stephen. He offers a theological reflection on the custom of kneeling based on Paul's Letter to the Phillipians.

The hymn to Christ in Phillipians 2, 6–11 speaks of the cosmic liturgy as a bending of the knee at the name of Jesus, seeing in it a

[28]Ibid. p. 73.
[29]J. Pieper, 'Das Gedächtnis des Leibes. Von der erinnernden Kraft des Geschichtlich-Konkreten', in W. Seidel (ed.), *Kirche aus lebendigen Steinen* (Mainz 1975), pp. 68–83.

fulfilment of the Isaian prophecy ... of the sovereignty of the God of Israel. In bending the knee at the name of Jesus, the Church is acting in all truth; she is entering into the cosmic gesture, paying homage to the Victor and therefore going over to the Victor's side. For in bending the knee we signify that we are imitating and adopting the attitude of him who, though he was 'in the form of God', yet 'humbled himself unto death'.[30]

Secondly, he advocates an eventual return to the practice of eastward celebration of the Eucharist. Celebration in the westward position, 'facing the people', does express one aspect of the Mass, the dialogue between priest and people. But its danger is that it makes the congregation into a 'closed circle', no longer aware of the

> explosive Trinitarian dynamism which gives the Eucharist its greatness.[31]

The *inner* direction of the Eucharist is certainly Trinitarian: from Christ to the Father in the Holy Spirit. The question is, How can this best be expressed in liturgical form? Drawing on the work of Erik Peterson, of the the historian of the Liturgy Josef Jungmann, and, more recently, of Father Everett Diederich, Ratzinger argues for the superiority of the eastward position.[32] The fact that this disposition of the celebrant can now be described as 'the priest turning his back on the people' shows how dramatically its meaning had been lost in the pre-conciliar period, and explains in great part the astonishing rapidity with

[30] FF pp. 74–5.
[31] Ibid. p. 142.
[32] E. Peterson, 'Das Kreuz und die Gebetsrichtung nach Osten', in ibid., *Frühkirche, Judentum und Gnosis* (Freiburg 1959), pp. 15–35; J. A. Jungmann, review of O. Nussbaum, *Der Standort des Liturgen am christlichen Altar vor dem Jahre 1000* (Bonn 1965) in *Zeitschrift für Kirche und Theologie* 88 (1966), pp. 445–450; E. A. Diederich, 'The unfolding presence of Christ in the celebration of Mass', *Communio* 5.4 (1978), pp. 326–343.

which the westward orientation succeeded it, without mandate as it is in the new liturgical books. The true significance of the gesture was that by it:

> priest and people faced the same way in a common act of Trinitarian worship.... (They) were united in facing eastward; that is, a cosmic symbolism was drawn into the community celebration – a factor of considerable importance. For the true location and the true context of the eucharistic celebration is the whole cosmos. 'Facing east' makes this cosmic dimension of the Eucharist present through liturgical gesture. Because of the rising sun, the east – *oriens* – was naturally both a symbol of the Resurrection (and to that extent, it was not merely a christological statement, but also a reminder of the Father's power and the influence of the Holy Spirit), and a presentation of the hope of the Parousia.

The Mass of the Roman rite was celebrated, not facing the altar, much less the tabernacle, but facing the *cross*, as embodying in itself the entire theology of the *oriens*. That cross pre-supposes the theology of the icon which is, as Ratzinger says, 'a theology of incarnation and transfiguration'. In the wake of the Council there has been a loss of a sense for holy images, yet they are a constitutive sign of the economy of the Son, who, in the Holy Spirit, is now depictable to the eyes of faith.[34] Ratzinger concludes that, though it would be pastorally inadvisable to restore the eastward position in the very near future (too many people have suffered too much from changes in their way of worship), we might at least see to it that the altar crucifix is so

[33]FF p. 140.

[34]Ibid. pp. 143–144, with reference to C. von Schönborn O. P., *L'Icône du Christ. Fondements théologiques* (Fribourg 1976). I may perhaps be allowed to mention here my own *The Art of God Incarnate. Theology and Image in Christian Tradition* (London 1980), whose argument is that the making and veneration of holy images and the Christian view of the form of divine revelation are mutually entailing.

placed that both priest and people can see it, even in a westward-facing celebration.

> At the eucharistic prayer they should not look at one another; together they ought to behold him, the Pierced Saviour.[35]

A third gesture discussed at some length by Ratzinger is walking in procession – notably in the context of Corpus Christi. The expression of our relationship to God calls for

> this celebratory walking along together in the community of the faithful, together with the God in whom we believe.[36]

In the Christian Liturgy we can identify two elements which gave rise to the Corpus Christi procession, itself a product of German soil. First, there are the two 'processions' embedded in the events of Holy Week: Jesus' entry into Jerusalem on Palm Sunday, a procession of triumph, and his ascent of the Mount of Olives on the evening of Holy Thursday, a journey, this second, 'into the darkness of night, of betrayal and of death'. In the mediaeval West, the Liturgy began to re-enact these two processions of the Lord. On Palm Sunday, in certain parts of France, the Blessed Sacrament was carried in the procession of palms: the victorious Christ re-entering his house to take possession of it. The Holy Thursday procession, which survives in the reformed Roman missal of Paul VI, is likewise a 'walking with the Lord as he goes to deliver himself up for us'. In Holy Week, these partial features of the mystery of the Atonement cannot be long dwelt on; we need Corpus Christi to bind them together into a great feast. In the triumphal procession of that day, we invite the crucified and risen Lord to 'take possession of our streets and squares'. In the countryside, one becomes more

[35]FF p. 144, with references to Zechariah 12, 10, and Apocalypse 1, 7.
[36]FF p. 132.

aware of the second element in the synthesis of this procession: ceremonies of rogation, seeking God's blessing on field and beast. In this relation with the productivity of the earth:

> the eucharistic Bread imparts its blessing to the daily bread, and each loaf of the latter silently points to him who wishes to be the bread of us all.[37]

In this way the Liturgy moves beyond the church walls, embracing heaven and earth, present and future. In the Corpus Christi procession, the link of faith with the earth is represented by the act of walking, 'of treading the ground, our ground'. Except that on this day we do not manhandle the earth, with the hands that 'so often exploit and violate it'; rather do we carry the Creator himself over the ground, he who willed to give himself in the wheat-grain and the vine-fruit. Ratzinger encourages people not to look anxiously over their shoulders and see if everything is in keeping with the latest theological theory, but to walk on joyfully in the procession of the redeemed. For after all:

> True liturgy signs with the Angels, and is hushed with the awaiting deep places of the world. And so true liturgy redeems the earth.[38]

[37]Ibid. p. 134.
[38]'Liturgy and sacred music', art. cit. p. 391.

224

Chapter Eleven

BACK TO FOUNDATIONS

The somewhat disorganised, not to say anarchic state in which Catholic theology found itself in the post-conciliar period encouraged Ratzinger to address the question of the foundations of theological activity. Although he did not produce a unified, systematic work along those lines, he offered what he termed *Bausteine*, 'building blocks', for such a work in the future.[1]

The foundations of dogmatic theology

In Ratzinger's view, there is one essential problem which underlies all the difficulties of dogmatic theology today. That problem is the nature of historical process, in relation to the transcendence of God and his truth. In a wide variety of cultures, the contemporary mind-set considers all being as *Gewordensein*, 'having-become-ness'. By contrast, in the past, at least until the nineteenth century:

> the Christian reality had been conceived as the Absolute, the self-manifestation of immutable divine truth. But now it has to let itself be interpreted in terms of the categories of history, and of historicity – and that in such a way that, the more it involves itself in the problem of historicity, the more it seems that the absolute character of Christian truth is resolved into the process of historical becoming.[2]

[1]Compare the sub-title of his essay collection on fundamental-dogmatic theology: *Theologische Prinzipienlehre. Bausteine zur Fundamentaltheologie* (Munich 1982); cited TP.

[2]J. Ratzinger, *Storia e dogma* (Milan 1971) collects (in Italian) some of his more crucial articles on the relation of dogma to its history. It will be cited below as SD, and is here found at p. 14.

Such a *reductio theologiae in historiam* is one cause, at least, of the 'crisis of the Christian fact'. Thought no longer leads back the process of historical transformation to the permanent truth of God, but turns even what is apparently stable into the process of historical transformation.

There are, nevertheless, so Ratzinger points out, two major declarations of the doctrinal magisterium of the Catholic Church which could indicate – if very generally – right orientation in these realms. To begin with, there is the teaching of the First Vatican Council which, in opposition to theological evolutionism, affirmed that Christian doctrines are not teachings which little by little attain to their perfection through human efforts, rather as might a philosophical system. Instead, they form a divine deposit, entrusted to Christ's bride, the Church, to be faithfully guarded and infallibly explained. One must preserve for the dogmas of the Church, therefore, 'in perpetuity' that sense which on some one definite occasion, *semel*, Holy Mother Church has expounded, not departing from it on the pretext of appeal to some higher criterion.[3] This frontal attack on what Ratzinger terms an 'ideological' concept of dogma, 'heterogeneous and modernising', did not exclude, however, the possibility that faith has nevertheless a genuine history all its own.[4] For after all, the Council cited in just this connexion the *Commonitorium* of Vincent of Lérins which speaks of a growth and deepening of understanding of dogma on the part of the whole Church, or of individuals within it, the meaning of the dogma remaining itself invariant.[5] Were there not a self-identical element persisting unchanged in every transformation it would not be possible, indeed, to speak of a

---

[3]H. Denzinger – A. Schönmetzer, *Enchiridion Symbolorum, Definitionum et Declarationum de rebus fidei et morum* (Freiburg 1967[34]), 3020. This reference work will be cited below as D.-S.

[4]SD p. 15.

[5]*Commonitorium* 2; PL 50, 640.

true history: a mere juxtaposition of unrelated data cannot be called such. And yet, by directing theological attention to the Gaulish semi-Pelagian monk who was so hostile to the later Augustine, the Council did Catholic theology a disservice. For Vincent's definition of Tradition as that which has been believed 'always, everywhere and by everybody' was not simply a 'specious rejection' of Augustine's inference from the Pauline corpus, but also an attempt to constrict doctrinal development, sealing it within a snail's shell of rigidity.

The second magisterial intervention Ratzinger has in mind is the decree of Pius X's Holy Office *Lamentabili*, issued during the Modernist crisis.[6] The individual articles of this document should not, Ratzinger suggests, be 'over-valued'. The value of the text lies simply in its condemnation of a 'radically evolutionist and historicist direction' for the interpretation of doctrine – in a word, and for want of a better word, 'Modernism'. The more particular assertions which fell under *Lamentabili*'s executioner's axe may have, taken in themselves, an acceptable sense: but they ought not to be taken in themselves but taken, rather, as symptoms of a *Weltanschauung*. And Ratzinger compares his own exegesis here to Ronald Knox's estimate of the condemnation of Quietism in *Enthusiasm*.[7] Unfortunately, though, in the theology of the turn of this century, when the 'great danger' of relativising the assertions of faith pressed upon the Church, an anti-historical reaction led her to assume a defensive position in a precipitate and inflexible fashion.[8]

Naturally, as Ratzinger emphasises, this could not have come about without precedent of some kind. At the very beginning of the modern era, the (Lutheran) Centuriators of Magdeburg

[6] D.-S. 3421–2.
[7] R. A. Knox, *Enthusiasm. A Chapter in the History of Religion* (Oxford, 1950), pp. 311–314.
[8] SD p. 16.

had compiled a mass of historical documentation with a view to proving, over against the claims of the Catholic Church in the Counter-Reformation period, that the post-apostolic history of Christianity was nothing but a story of endless decline and deviation from primitive Gospel purity.[9] Catholic spokesmen were obliged to show that, on the contrary, the present Church was identical with the Church of the apostolic age. The most erudite product of this effort was the *Annales* of the Oratorian cardinal and Librarian of the holy Roman church, Cesare Baronio.[10] There was, then, a built-in tendency to see dogma in static fashion, which not even the most historically sensitive students of doctrine, such as Joseph Tixeront, could fully overcome.[11] Whereas, post-Tridentine Catholicism thus appeared incapable of writing a genuine history of dogma, Protestantism, in sharp contrast, was incapable of *not* writing a history of Christian doctrine, though of a sort where the concept of development would inevitably take on a negative meaning. From Harnack's *Lehrbuch der Dogmengeschichte*,[12] with its thesis of the unnatural Hellenisation of the Gospel, to Martin Werner's *Die Entstehung des christlichen Dogmas*[13] with its key-idea of the de-eschatologising of the original faith, this is exactly what we find, with the added refinement that, in the contemporary period, the notion of a decadent Catholicising of the primitive kerygma has been pushed back, by the use of Ernst Käsemann's notion of *Frühkatholizismus*, into the time of the New Testament writings themselves.[14]

[9]P. Meinhold, 'Flacius', LexThK 4 pp. 161ff.

[10]See A. Cesare Baronio. *Scritti vari* (Sora 1963), with full bibliography.

[11]On Tixeront, see C. E. Podechard, *Joseph Tixeront* (Lyons 1925).

[12]A. von Harnack, *Lehrbuch der Dogmengeschichte* I (Tübingen 1931[5]), pp. 340ff.

[13]M. Werner, *Die Entstehung des christlichen Dogmas* (Bern-Tübingen 1953[2]).

[14]E. Käsemann, *Exegetische Versuche und Besinnungen* I (Göttingen 1960), pp. 214–223; II. pp. 239–253. On the whole controversy about the 'decadence'

Though Newman's *Essay on the Development of Christian Doctrine* was a turning-point in Catholic appreciation of the positive side of the idea of historical change, it did not result in a really satisfying account of the meaning and task of the history of dogma, even if such an account might be said to be slowly taking form.[15]

Ratzinger's own contribution to the problem entails identifying three areas in which the non-historical theology of identity hitherto reigning might be overcome. In *Christology*, we learn that the earthly Jesus and the glorious, risen Christ who will come again are one identical person. From this we should see that Christian faith is turned both to the past and to the future, and so founds the possibility of 'a Christian history as the history of the Christian fact'.[16] Although the original event of the historical ministry of Jesus provides this 'Christian fact' with its definitive and permanent norms, the fact itself cannot be limited to the original event. As the Greek fathers loved to say, the movement of the Incarnation, whereby humanity is assimilated to the Godhead, is begun in Jesus Christ but does not reach its final term in him. Or, in more modern language, the encounter between man and God in Christ goes on until all its possibilities have been developed.

Again, in the theology of *revelation*, the biblical revelation is

---

of the Church vis-à-vis the Gospel, see A. Grillmeier, 'Hellenisierung und Judaisierung des Christentums als Deuteprinzipien der Geschichte des kirchlichen Dogmas', in *Scholastik* 33 (1958), pp. 321–355; 528–558.

[15]Ratzinger points out that it is, in one sense easier to write a series of monographs on the development of various Christian doctrines, as in the *Handbuch der Dogmengeschichte* edited by M. Schmaus and A. Grillmeier than to give an account of what is going on in such development. Among surveys of theories on development, he lists H Hammans, *Die neueren katholischen Erklärungen der Dogmenentwicklung* (Essen 1965), and W. Schutz, *Dogmenentwicklung als Geschichtlichkeit der Wahrheitserkenntnis* (Rome 1969), not least for their extensive bibliographies.

[16]SD p. 22.

best thought of as an event which both happened once and for all in the past, and yet happens again, repeatedly, constantly, for faith. For the believer, the God-man relationship has reached its ultimate perfection already, in Christ. It cannot be transcended, yet it can be re-received time and again. In accepting the rule of faith, and the canon of Scripture, the Church submits herself for ever to a fixed interpretative norm. Yet the affirmations of the Creed and the Bible are not themselves the revelation, but its explication in the words of men.

Finally, in the theology of *tradition* where by 'tradition' should be meant:

> the explication, in the history of the Church's faith, of the event of Christ witnessed to in Scripture.[17]

In the primitive community, 'tradition' was that manner in which the New Testament commented Christologically on the Old, conferring on the inherited Scriptures of the ancient people of God their true meaning. This process continues today. The historian must accept as a constant of the phenomenon of Christianity which he is studying that, for the believer, such interpretation takes place under the guidance of the Spirit of the risen Christ. Historians investigate the human factors at work in this explicative process, but they must also take note of this conviction, and of the identity which endures through all transformations.

As Ratzinger presents it, the history of dogma is neither a sad saga of decadence, nor is it a tremendous tale of ever accelerating progress – as certain Catholic authors, like the learned A. M. Landgraf in his *Dogmengeschichte der Frühscholastik*, would present it. For Landgraf, the pilgrimage of doctrinal history ascends steadily towards the temple mount of the Neo-

---

[17]Ibid. p. 26.

Scholastic sanctuary, firmly constructed as that is of 'solid concepts, joined together by a natural sequence of argumentation'.[18] In fact, that history, insofar as it is a human story, is marked, and marred, by all those features which are typical of man's historical development. Nevertheless:

> the believer, as a man of faith, must bear in mind that this all too human history is a demonstration of the potent originality of God, who not least in abasement and decadence can and does bring about the movement of conservation and assimilation despite everyting that is changing and new.[19]

But if the relation between history and dogma *is* of the kind which these considerations suggest, then not only is a history of dogma in the Catholic context possible. More strongly, 'dogmatics is not conceivable except as the history of dogma'.[20] And indeed, this is how the Second Vatican Council proposed that doctrine should be studied: first in its biblical foundation, and subsequently in the building upon that foundation which doctrinal history reveals to us.[21]

But this nuanced acceptance of the historicity of dogma requires some underpinning by way of discussion of what a dogma is anyway. Ratzinger observes that the history of the changing forms of dogmatic declaration in the Church is one of the most important tasks for historical theology to carry out.[22] Dogmatic affirmation, in his view, has its origins in the interrogation of baptismal candidates. Their threefold response to questioning about the mystery of Father, Son and Spirit formed the basis of the primitive creeds. These developed by

[18]A. M. Landgraf, *Dogmengeschichte der Frühscholastik* (Regensburg 1952–1956), I. i. p. 13.
[19]SD p. 28.
[20]Ibid. p. 29.
[21]*Optatam totius* 16.
[22]SD p. 42.

way of the more complex credal statements of the ancient Councils into the creation of anathemata. In the mediaeval period, dogmatic assertions take the form of decrees and doctrinal chapters with relevant canons appended, of the sort which can be seen in their mature state in the *Acta* of Trent. Finally, in the modern period, we reach the *genre* of dogma as single proposition, examples of which are the 1854 definition of Mary's Immaculate Conception, and its 1950 counterpart on her Assumption. To grasp what dogma is we must return, Ratzinger advises, to the beginnings of this development: the baptismal dialogue.

> 'Dogma', that is, the self-engaging affirmation of faith, has its primary home in the event of baptism, and so in the liturgical sealing of a process of conversion wherein a man turns from belonging to himself alone and accepts in its place the bond of existence in the way of Jesus Christ.[23]

The pattern of the baptismal dialogue, where it is the representative of the Church who identifies the content of the shared faith, and the individual candidate who appropriates this with his 'I *do* believe', highlights what Ratzinger terms the 'anthropological structure of faith' at large. Faith, as the Letter to the Romans puts it, 'comes from hearing', that is:

> not from reflecting (as in philosophy). Faith's essence consists in the re-thinking (*Nach-denken*) of what has been heard.... In faith, the word takes precedence over thought, whereas in philosophy thought precedes the word in a typical product of the meditation which seeks its own translation into words that are themselves secondary in relation to the thinking concerned, and so may be replaced by alternative terms as time goes on.[24]

[23]Ibid.
[24]Ibid. p. 43.

Faith is not self-invented but comes to man from without in all its 'positivity': the term Ratzinger had lighted on in his 'Reflections on the Creed'. For this reason, the word in which the message of faith is spoken, striking me and summoning me to response is ever 'pre-ordained and precedent to my thinking'.

Thus the language of dogma is, in its origins, a 'symbol' in the ancient sense of that word which passed into Christian currency to denote the early Creeds.[25] Dogma creates a unity of spirits through a unity in the word, all for the sake of the common service of God, communion in the sacred reality itself. Dogma is, then, an essential instrument for the life of faith. It is only an instrument, a means, yet it is an irreplaceable means. It is

> not a closing-off, but an opening which places us on the right road. Only by way of the infinite rupture of the Symbol can faith advance as the permanent self-transcendence of man towards his God.[26]

And Ratzinger offers an example of this communitarian, liturgical and linguistic character of dogma by some comments on the doctrine of the Trinity. In the world of antiquity there was no direct possibility of expressing the 'relationality' of the triadic form of revelation together with the unity of the being of God, though these were two absolutely vital constituents of the biblical message. In the last analysis, the early Councils are stages in the elaboration of a *regula loquendi* in which these scriptural contents could be expressed. By contrast, the early heresies are the resistance of human language and thought to those same contents. Our situation is defined in part by the fact that this movement of dogmatic construction has already taken place, with ourselves as the gainers. Yet at the same time we are not exonerated from all further effort. Language has broadened its

[25]See above, Chapter Six.
[26]SD p. 44.

THE THEOLOGY OF JOSEPH RATZINGER

compass in the continuous explicative endeavours of the human spirit. Because of this, the presuppositions for the understanding of dogma are different now. And so we are obliged to penetrate anew, in language and concept, what the patristic dogmas truly signify.[27] The separating out of the two planes of *ousia* and *hypostasis*, and the counter-posing of *persona* to *essentia* enabled what had hitherto been inaccessible to thought in the divine revelation to become both attainable and capable of expression.[28] The particular manner in which this feat was executed was in itself fortuitous. Had the main missionary drive of the Church been to the Indian sub-continent, rather than to the Greco-Roman world, the articulation of the tri-personal nature of God would have happened quite differently. Yet it is only because the process of articulation has been conserved in the patristic dogmas that our own permanent task of comprehending anew is possible. But Ratzinger stresses, in those cases where a transformation of the language of doctrine may prove necessary, that:

> this does not happen by a merely personal judgment, even though it cannot take place without the co-participation of individuals in this struggle and suffering.... Such a change can only be enacted through the community (of the Church), though it does not dispense with the individual, with his courage and his patience.[29]

[27]Ibid. p. 46. For Ratzinger's view of the *consensus patrum* as the crucial element in the Church's reception of biblical revelation and therefore authoritative for all later faith, see his 'Die Bedeutung der Väter im Aufbau des Glaubens', in TP pp. 139–159.

[28]Cf. J. Ratzinger, 'Zum Personverständnis in der Dogmatik', in J. Speck (ed.), *Das Personverständnis in der Pedagogik und ihren Nachbarwissenschaften* (Münster 1966), pp. 157–171.

[29]SD p. 48. For the inter-relation of faithful, bishops and theological specialists in this task, see, if briefly, 'Kirche und wissenschaftliche Theologie', TP pp. 339–348, and especially p. 348.

The foundations of moral theology

But if dogmatic theology is in need of steadying by a return to the foundations, so also, to Ratzinger's mind, is moral theology. Nor is it simply a matter of the methods by which moral theology is to reflect on its own materials: values, whether simply humane or additionally Christian. For the perception of those values is itself in flux. Writing in 1975, Ratzinger declared:

> This crisis of faith that is increasingly making itself felt among Christian people is also revealing itself with increasing clarity as a crisis which concerns the awareness of fundamental values in human living. It is nourished by the moral crisis of mankind, and at the same time it intensifies this crisis.[30]

Current moral theological discussion prompted by this wave of questioning is itself vastly heterogeneous. At one pole, some moralists exalt 'orthopraxy' over 'orthodoxy'. On this view, if Christianity wishes to contribute to a better world, it must come up with a better praxis: 'not seeking truth as a theory, but producing it as a reality'. At the opposite pole, others claim that there is no specifically Christian morality, the Church being obliged to draw its norms of conduct from the anthropological insights of its time. On this view:

> Faith does not develop a morality of its own, but adopts the practical reason of contemporary men and women.[31]

Historical investigation appears on first viewing to back up this claim since there seems to be no single moral proposition found

---

[30]See J. Ratzinger, H. Schürmann, H. U. von Balthasar, *Prinzipien christlicher Moral* (Einsiedeln 1975); ET *Principles of Christian Morality* (San Francisco 1975), cited below as PCM, and here at p. 47.

[31]PCM p. 49.

exclusively in the Old Testament that can be regarded solely as the fruit of faith in Yahweh; while, in the New Testament, the lists of vices and virtues in the apostolic letters reflect Stoic ethics. Consequently, what is significant about the moral reflection carried on in Scripture is not its content but its structure: it points to reason as the only source of moral norms. These two types of ethical theory have little in common, Ratzinger comments, except their rejection of any right of Church authority to lay down specific moral norms on the basis of a divinely given commission.

What response does he make to these searching questions? He points out that the fact that the Bible's moral pronouncements can be traced to other cultures or to philosophical thought does not entail that biblical morality is a function of reason alone. For:

> What is important is not that such utterance can be found elsewhere, but the particular position they have or do not have in the spiritual edifice of Christianity.[32]

What is 'original' in Christianity is not that which has come to be in clinical purity, without contact with 'other milieux'.

> Christianity's originality consists rather in the new total form into which human searching and striving have been forged under the guidance of faith in the God of Abraham, the God of Jesus Christ.[33]

Nor, historically speaking, did Israel simply take over, lock, stock and barrel, the morality of the surrounding cultures. As these texts written by or about the prophets show, there was a struggle, often dramatic in its intensity, between those elements

[32]Ibid. pp. 53–54.
[33]Ibid. p. 53.

236

of the juridical and moral tradition of the nations around Israel which she could properly assimilate, and those which she was bound to reject. The 'reason' of the nations, and the revelation of God, do not necessarily confront each other as pure paradox: there may well be an 'analogy' between them. In both Old Testament and New, the recipients of the revealed tradition are found making critical discernments, on the basis of faith, about the deliverances of (fallible) practical reason in their pagan neighbours. Take, for example, the case of Paul.

> Anyone who reads the Pauline letters carefully will see that the apostolic exhortation is not some moralising appendix with a variable content, but a very practical setting forth of what faith means; thus, it is inseparable from faith's core. The apostle is in fact only following the pattern of Christ, who, in this central theme of his preaching, linked admission to the Kingdom of God and exclusion from it with fundamental moral decisions, which are consequences intimately related to the way God is conceived.[34]

In mentioning the apostolic exhortation, Ratzinger has moved beyond the discussion about the relation of faith and morals, and entered on to that of the teaching authority of the Church in the ethical domain. Drawing on the work of Heinrich Schlier, a former Lutheran exegete who became a Catholic through reflection on the ecclesiology of Ephesians, Ratzinger points out that Pauline moral exhortation comes

> clothed with the Lord's authority, even when it does not appear in the form of a command or an official doctrinal decision.[35]

The 'substantive basis' of Christian ethics lies in the

[34]Ibid. p. 65.
[35]Ibid. p. 67; cf. H. Schlier, *Besinnung auf das Neue Testament* (Freiburg 1964), pp. 340–357.

development of such apostolic exhortation as a normative tradition, but *vis à vis* particular situations whose contours change with the movement of history itself. The Church's teaching authority, which, so far from coming to an end with the age of the apostles, is a permanent dominical gift, includes the task of 'making concrete the demands of grace and of working them out in detail with regard to the contemporary situation'.[36]

The proponents of the orthopraxy model are right in this: Christian faith involves a praxis, which is nourished by faith's own essence: the grace which appeared in Jesus Christ and is appropriated in that primordial sacrament of Christ that is the Church. But in this, contrary to a concept of orthopraxy which would fain leave orthodoxy behind, faith's praxis

> depends on faith's truth, in which man's truth is made visible and lifted up to a new level by God's truth.[37]

At the same time, those who see ethics as basically an exercise in rational reflection also have a point: since the Redeemer God is also the Creator, grace and faith will be concerned with the protection of the created order, and thus enter spontaneously into happy relations with reason which is created spirit's reflection on itself. As Ratzinger puts it:

> Since grace refers to both the creation and the Creator, apostolic exhortation (as a continuation of Old Testament admonitions), is involved with human reasons.... There must be a correspondence with basic insights of human reason, even if these insights have been purified, deepened and broadened through contact with the way of faith.[38]

[36]CTAFM pp. 69–70.
[37]Ibid. p. 70.
[38]Ibid. pp. 70–71.

238

On the other hand, reason is not absolute in the moral sphere; or rather, that reason which is absolute, since it manifests the reason of God, must be distinguished from apparent reason, the defective rational endeavours of each age. For this reason needs faith, just as faith needs reason. Indeed:

> faith . . . finds its language in communication with the reason of the nations through a process of reception and dialectic.[39]

In this, as in every significant process of discernment in the Church, three agencies are at work. First, there is the Christian and human experience of the Church at large; second, there is the work of scholars; and third, there is the 'watchful attention, listening and deciding undertaken by the teaching authority'.[40] The last, which is the one most keenly under question in the Church today cannot be sacrificed without losing hold on the apostolic tradition itself.

It is not difficult to correlate these three agencies with the three elements that a contemporary British historian of the 'making of moral theology' has found in the attaining of ecclesial judgment about ethical questions.[41] Two of these are comparatively uncontroversial. The first or experiential element functions in seemingly intuitive fashion as a 'global instinct' of faith for what is right and proper. The second, or learned, element, consists in the exploration, by moral philosophers and theologians, of the possibilities of rational argumentation in this area. It is the third or magisterial element whose task in relation to the other two is currently in dispute. For Ratzinger, the role of the magisterium is, in continuity with the ethical element in the original apostolic preaching, the

[39]Ibid. p. 71.
[40]Ibid. p. 73.
[41]J. Mahoney, *The Making of Moral Theology. A Study of the Roman Catholic tradition* (London 1987), pp. 280–289 especially.

assessment of the consonance, or coherence, of moral norms proposed in the Church community with the vision of creation and redemption provided by revelation as a whole. Pope and bishops, when offering authoritative guidance on such questions, actualise in the realm of ethics the distinctive charism of episcopal and papal office. That charism is not meant to substitute for the exercise of the experiential and learned elements in the Church but to 'place' the results of the latter within a wider whole: the apostolic Church in its response to the apostolic revelation. This does not preclude the development of doctrine in morals; but it does not presume its necessity either. The spirits must be discerned. In this way, Ratzinger's attempt to re-call moral theologians to the fondations of their discipline (as he sees it) echoes his appeal to their dogmatic *confrères*. In each case, what is at stake is the cognitive, and not simply canonical, relation of the individual to the community in its diachronic as well as synchronic dimensions, spread out in time as well as space, and entrusted to the care of pastors who cannot truly be in the 'apostolic succession' unless they are simultaneously *doctores*, teachers of the faith.

Chapter Twelve

THE PREFECT

Ratzinger's summons from Munich to Rome in November 1981 in order to take up the position of Prefect of the Congregation for the Doctrine of the Faith gave him the opportunity to reiterate for a wider audience and with the enhanced ecclesiastical authority of the Roman dicastery over which he presided, many of the emphases and insights which have emerged in these pages so far. As observers were quick to note, and indeed could hardly help noticing, he departed from customary curial practice by seeking wide publicity for the principles which he proposed to put into practice as head of the main doctrinal organ of the universal primacy. This he did in public lectures and in interviews, and it is this material, when combined with the documents promulgated by his Congregation, which enable one to gauge the bearings of his policy as a whole.[1]

The attempt to combine the roles of Prefect and theologian arouse considerable criticism. To more traditionally-minded members of the Roman Curia it was innovatory and imprudent. No previous Prefect, since the foundation of the Congregation by the reforming Farnese pope Paul III in 1542, had behaved in this manner. The arousing of debate about the state of the Church in general, and of its theological schools in particular, by way of interviews, articles and books was regarded as encouraging error by airing it. Criticism of tendencies in the episcopate, though possibly shared in private, was thought to be, if it went public, a tasteless offence against the

---

[1] It was characteristic of Ratzinger's style as prefect that he arranged the publishing of all such recent documents in book form.

respect that was the bishops' rightful due. To 'liberal' or 'progressive' forces in the Church beyond Rome, what appeared to be a hardening of doctrinal discipline, comparable with the anti-Modernist reaction, was anathema. It was not always realised that a number of the cases which the Congregation found itself adjudicating under pope John Paul II and cardinal Ratzinger had been initiated under their predecessors Paul VI and the Croat cardinal-prefect Franciszek Šeper. What was new was not somuch papal anxiety about the state of Catholic doctrine and theology but the papal determination to do something about it. To those hostile in principle to such doctrinal interventions, the co-existence within Ratzinger of the two roles of Prefect and personal theologian provided a stick with which to beat him. What was this but the palming-off, as the common faith of the Church, of an essentially private theology? For such critics, there was no significant different between Ratzinger's activities in the 1980s, and the papal enforcement of Thomism in the pontificates of Pius X and Benedict XV in the 1910s and 20s. At least the theology of Thomas had venerability and generally acknowledged intellectual excellence to commend it.

To these criticisms, which, as danger-signs, marking the whereabouts of possible temptations, are not without value, three points may perhaps be made. First, the reform of the Congregation for the Doctrine of the Faith by Paul VI expressly requires it to adopt the positive function of encouraging good theology in the Church, alongside its historic negative function of discouraging bad.[2] But if the exercise of this function is not to dissolve into mere platitudes, it must be carried out concretely, specifying the kind of values, themes and trends which should be fostered. Secondly, unless the Holy See, in its capacity as guardian of the unity and continuity of the faith of the Church is

---

[2] Through the motu proprio *Integrae servandae* of 1965.

to abnegate its responsibilities entirely,[3] it must occasionally carry out doctrinal intervention where circumstances appear to the best judgment available to require this. Such intervention must be made in theological language, for one cannot criticise Chinese literature in the terminology of electrical engineering. In the absence of a *theologia communis*, a doctrinal authority is obliged to improvise such language, seeking the most adequate discourse it can from within the resources of theological tradition as known to it. Thirdly, in point of fact, the object of these criticisms, as the concluding section of this chapter will show, is fully committed to the desirability of a *plurality* of theologies in the Church such that, taken together, they can exhibit the rich intelligibility of revelation and doctrine more fully than can any one taken singly. The orchestra of Christian truth has many instruments, to use Ratzinger's own preferred metaphor, but they contribute to the harmonious performance of the same piece of music.

In what follows, I shall concentrate on four areas to which Ratzinger has given attention in the years of his prefecture: ecclesiology; the relation between the Church and political ethics; ecumenism; and what may be called the simultaneous unity and plurality of Christian wisdom. Consonant with the aim of this study, as stated in the preface, I shall restrict my attention to Ratzinger's personal theology. Excluded from this account, therefore, are the documents of his Congregation and the decisions bearing on a variety of individual theologians – such as Edward Schillebeeckx, Leonardo Boff, Charles Curran – decisions which would, in any case, necessitate a careful and thorough examination of the theologies which were their objects if superficial and harmful generalisations are to be avoided.

---

[3] This seems to be the desire of G. Alberigo, in his 'Institutional defence of orthodoxy', *Concilium* 192 (1987), pp. 92–93.

Ecclesiology

In his most recent writing on the Church, Ratzinger shows himself to be, above all, a man of *Lumen Gentium*, the Second Vatican Council's Dogmatic Constitution on the Church to which, as we have seen, he devoted so much attention in the 1960s.[4] In one sense, he points out, that great document did no more than sum up the gains of the period from 1920 to 1960 in ecclesiology. These were not just a matter of ecclesiological theory, but of the re-awakening of a vital sense of what the Church is. And yet, in doing this, *Lumen Gentium* formally constituted those gains as a precious patrimony for the entire Church.

Ratzinger stresses the importance of the opening phrase of the text: *'Lumen Gentium cum sit Christus'*. It is Christ, not the Church, that is the 'Light' of all peoples. The Church is only healthy to the extent that her attention is concentrated on *him*. The image of the Church as Christ's mystical body tells us that the Church is more than an organisation. It is the organism of the Holy Spirit, something vital, which works intimately within us and makes the mystery of the Incarnation present in our lives. As that mystical body, the Church is our contemporaneity with Christ, and his with us. Ratzinger insists in the first place on the role of *interiority* in all this. The Church grows 'from within', from intimate communion with Christ, through faith, hope and love, as these are at work in the spiritual, and especially the sacramental, life.

Yet to say that it is truly the *Church* which grows 'from within' is at once to imply a complementary truth which must be affirmed in as close to the same breath as we can manage. Christ has given himself a *communitarian*, and so public and

---

[4]See the section 'Zu Wesen und Struktur der Kirche', in J. Ratzinger, *Kirche, Ökumene und Politik* (Einsiedeln 1987), cited below as KÖP.

historical 'body'. The Church is a 'We', composed of both the living and the dead. This is an 'open' We, one that throws open sealed frontiers – both socio-political frontiers, and those which separate earth from heaven. The We-form of the Church is the foundation of the co-responsibility of all its members for its life and mission. At the same time, it is also a call on me personally, to collaborate with the rest in my own name, in the discharge of my duties in freedom. Corresponding to these two aspects of responsibility, corporate and personal, the Church recognises the possibility of a two-fold criticism. There is a right to criticise others, including the hierarchy; and there is also my duty – which comes first – to criticise myself.

The concept of the Church's *growing* also puts Ratzinger in mind of Newman's idea of development an idea which he terms one of the truly fundamental concepts of Catholicism. Ratzinger commends the Second Vatican Council for incorporating, for the first time in a magisterial document, the idea of development as used in a positive sense. This should help to save us from 'archaising sterility', which has nothing to say to contemporary people, but also from its opposite – the vain effort to overleap the centuries in a desperate attempt to find a lost original. For

> there is a real identity with the origin only where there is at the same time that living continuity which develops the origin, and, in so developing it, guards it.[5]

Reflection on the Church as the body of Christ leads Ratzinger to touch, once again, on the notion of eucharistic ecclesiology which he has far from abandoned. He reminds us that it was cardinal de Lubac who first grasped that, in the Fathers and early mediaevals, the notion of the Church as

[5] KÖP p. 16.

THE THEOLOGY OF JOSEPH RATZINGER

Christ's body is inseparably connected with the fact that the Church not only celebrates, but is founded upon, the Eucharistic mystery, which is the sacramental body of the Lord. Ratzinger identifies eucharistic ecclesiology with an ecclesiology of communion, finding in the latter the heart of *Lumen Gentium*. According to Eucharistic ecclesiology, the Church was born at the Last Supper, with the Mass the essential law of her being. In the Mass, which is the present actualisation of the 'new Covenant' made by God in Christ's death and resurrection, men are joined to each other by being conjoined with Christ. So it is that they become Church. By the Mass, the Church adores God and thus serves mankind, transforming in the world in relation to God.

However, as Ratzinger reminds us in cautionary tone, the Council felt itself obliged, nevertheless, to correct a certain imbalance in the idea of eucharistic ecclesiology as that had originated in the Orthodox theology of the Russian diaspora. For in some of its exponents, and here Ratzinger has Nikolai Nikolayevič Afanasiev especially in mind, the external union of local churches with each other in a world-wide Church can add nothing to the ecclesial reality of the local church. After all, if the local church with its Eucharistic assembly is already the presence of Christ, how can it be further amplified or exalted? Union with other local churches can only add a desirable dimension inasmuch as it better *manifests* the fulness of Christ to the outside world. For Ratzinger, on the other hand, such union is not simply an optional extra but is constitutive of the being of the local church. He echoes the Orthodox criticism of Afanasiev's congregationalism made by Professor (now bishop) John Zizioulas when he writes:

I can have the one Lord only in the unity that he himself is – in unity with the others who are also his body and who, in the Eucharist, must always become it anew.[6]

[6]Ibid. p. 19.

246

The local church must enter into a 'structure of reception' or of 'encounter' with other local churches, on pain of ecclesial extinction. Ratzinger offers a rich exposition of this structure to fill out the dry and somewhat inadequate words of *Lumen Gentium* for which the whole Church is present in the local episcopal community (only) when the latter is 'legitimately constituted'.[7]

Consideration of the Church as a communion of necessarily inter-related churches leads Ratzinger on, naturally enough, to the subject of episcopal collegiality. As the co-consecration of bishops – the principal ancient expression of collegiality – demonstrates, such collegiality is ordered to the service of the Church as a liturgical totality. A bishop's job is to preserve his community within the greater unity of the whole Church. The manner in which he carries it out cannot be evaluated in isolation from his duties as a member of the entire *ordo* which he entered by his consecration.

> A bishop is not a bishop by himself, but only in Catholic communion with those who were bishops before him, are bishops with him, and will be bishops after him.[8]

To this we must link the second element in the idea of collegiality, namely, that of apostolic succession. Just as the apostles were what they were only within the unified whole of the community of the Twelve, so one becomes a successor of the apostles by entering into the communion of those in whom their ministry endures. In practice, the most immediate expression of this is the ecumenical Council, but there can be other secondary

---

[7]*Lumen Gentium* 26:: Haec Christi Ecclesia vere adest in omnibus legitimis fidelium congregationibus localis, quae pastoribus suis adhaerentibus, et ipsae in Novo Testamento ecclesiae vocantur. Hae sunt enim loco suo Populus novus a Deo vocatus, in Spiritu Sancto et in plenitudine multa (cf. I Thessalonians 1, 5).

[8]KÖP p. 21.

mediations, synods of bishops, episcopal Conferences and the like.... The workings of all of these must be measured in terms of the fundamental principle involved: which Ratzinger defines as

> crossing the threshold of the local horizon, so as to arrive at the common content of Catholic unity.[9]

This brings him to the name for that unity which he had studied, thirty years earlier, in Augustine: the Church as 'People of God'. The reasons for its reintroduction in the German Catholic ecclesiology of the 1930s Ratzinger regards as rather superficial. These were, in brief, the claim that the main alternative, 'Mystical Body', was an image, not a concept; and the feeling that the idea of the People of God would lend itself better to 'sociological and juridical mediation', in other words, to a contextual specification of the rights and duties of all the Church's members. He considers that at the Council itself there were better reasons than this for employing it. First, there were ecumenical reasons: the notion allowed more easily of a relationship to the Church of those outside her visible unity. The image of the Mystical Body, on the other hand, offered only one status, that of 'member', and between being a member and being a non-member there is nothing. Secondly, there were reforming reasons: in order to stress that the Church is *semper purificanda*, she must be shown as standing before Christ, rather than as being identified with him. And this the People of God idea could do much better than its chief rival. Thirdly and finally, there were reasons connected with the renaissance of eschatology, for

> In this way, it was possible to express the Church's historical position as a pilgrim. She will be completely herself only when

[9]Ibid. p. 22.

she has travelled to the end of the road of time and passed into the hands of God.[10]

However, Ratzinger's own research into the People of God theme in Augustine had alerted him to the comparative rarity of its appearances in the New Testament: on just two occasions is it used for the Church, rather than for Israel. Only by undergoing a Christological transformation could it come to signify the Church. Thus, just as for the Old Testament the People of God is not the empirical Hebrew nation, but that nation inasmuch as it is turned towards Israel's Lord, so for Catholicism:

> if we are to speak of the 'People of God', then Christology must remain, for all that, the centre of the Church's teaching.[11]

For the Council, the Church is not only the People of God; she is also the sacrament of Christ. And this means that her integral differentiation – into laity and ordained ministry – is as significant, because as sacramentally based, as her being itself. In an historical excursus, Ratzinger reveals the grounds for his opposition to a unilateral, or exclusive, use of the People of God idea in Catholic ecclesiology. As early as Eusebius, Constantine the Great's ecclesiastical counsellor, that idea was turned to political use: in their case, against pagans and Jews.[12] In the Eastern church, where the *motif* remained vigorously alive, it had one mis-application which was, in Ratzinger's eyes, uncannily prophetic of contemporary Catholic abuse rather than use. This was the schism of the *raskolniki*, the 'Old Believers', who in the context of sixteenth century Russia established their own priestless, though in other respects hyper-

[10]Ibid. p. 24.
[11]Ibid. p. 26.
[12]Here Ratzinger refers to V. Twomey, *Apostolikos Thronos. The Primacy of Rome as reflected in the Church History of Eusebius and the historico-apologetic writings of Athanasius the Great* (Münster 1982), pp. 13–229.

Orthodox, community.[13] Similarly, in the post-conciliar period, the formula 'People of God' is in danger of becoming the vehicle for an anti-hierarchical ecclesiology, a revolutionary category in which to appropriate the concept of a 'new' Church.

Ratzinger does not, however, leave the area of ecclesiology today without devoting two essays to the dual structure of responsibility in the Church. He has already defined this as simultaneously co-responsibility and personal responsibility 'by name'. To these two aspects correspond, he now suggests, the Church's 'synodal' and 'primatial' dimensions.

He considers 'synodicity' with special reference to the Synods of Bishops which, following the express wish of the Second Vatican Council, meet at regular intervals in Rome.[14] For Ratzinger, these Synods are pastorally important but juridically of necessarily limited authority. He opens by looking at what is said about such a Synod in the new Code of Canon Law of the Latin church. He finds that the canons – actually canon 342 – specify three aims for the Synod. First, bishops chosen from different parts of the world come together so as to promote closer relations between the episcopate and the Pope. Secondly, the Synod offers the Pope its counsel: counsel not only for the preservation of the integrity of *faith* and *morals* and their 'expansion', but also for the consolidation and strengthening of ecclesiastical *discipline*. (Ratzinger points out that in this last statement there is both a conservative and a dynamic element: guarding, yet also enlarging.) Thirdly, according to the canons, the Synod should consider questions relating to the Christian mission in the wider world. It has, therefore, a threefold rationale: collegial, primatial and evangelical or, as Ratzinger puts it, somewhat colourlessly, 'external'. The *collegial* aspect

[13]Cf. E. von Ivànka, *Rhomäerreich und Gottesvolk* (Freiburg-Munich 1968) for the Eastern fate of the term.
[14]KÖP pp. 49–63.

serves the unity and catholicity of the Church by facilitating the reciprocal relations of Pope and episcopal college; the *primatial* aspect consists in help for the Pope in the duties of his universal primacy; the 'external' aspect is meant to clarify issues arising from the situation of the Church in the contemporary world.

What then of the status of the Synod which has these aims? Here the canons speak of the Synod as definitely subordinate to papal authority. It does not take decisions, or issue decrees, though the Pope may, at his discretion and in particular cases, bestow such power upon it. So the juridical status of the Synod is more straitly confined than the breadth of its pastoral goals would lead one to expect. Why? The explanation is to be found in the doctrine of *Lumen Gentium*. There we find that the episcopal college is the bearer of plenary power in the Church only when it meets in ecumenical Council or when found in the common concert of all the bishops together, spread throughout the world.[15] The college cannot delegate its competence to a selection of its members. Either there is moral unanimity or there is no collegial action at all. Moreover, as Ratzinger underlines, the ecclesiological point of there being a college of bishops in the Church is not to provide for its central government, but quite the opposite. Through the college, the one Church is to grow as a single organism in those living cells which are the local churches. To make an episcopal Synod the effective central governmental agency in the Church would be to introduce a centralism far more burdensome than that of the papal Curia. Centralism in the Church should indeed be overcome: but this will happen through the judicious correlation of two poles: the living plurality of local churches, and the primatial office, which expresses the whole Church's unity-in-plurality.

Having thus established the ecclesiological basis of the Synod,

[15]*Lumen Gentium* 22.

both by saying what it is, and by saying what it is not, Ratzinger moves on to various projected schemes for its reform. One idea is that the Pope should delegate decision-making power to the Synod on a regular and systematic basis. But this would be a second, re-duplicated Curia. It would also deprive local churches of their residential bishops for considerable periods, thus resurrecting that figure buried by the Council of Trent, the late mediaeval absentee bishop. And if the residential bishops simply popped in for a short spell, they would scarcely have adequate time for studying any issue in depth. Another idea is to make the Roman 'Synod Secretariat', which includes pastoral bishops elected by the synodal assembly, into a permanent synod on the Byzantine pattern, the *synodos endemousa* still found in the patriarchate of Constantinople today. But historians of the Byzantine church generally agree that the experience of such a synod has not been entirely happy because, once again, of the problem of the absence of the bishop from his diocese which it brings in its train. To hear some people talk, Ratzinger remarks, one might think that the Second Vatican Council had deliberately reversed the provisions of Trent for episcopal residence, as though bishops were essentially itinerants, wandering round the world, meeting fellow bishops and working out with them answers to the problems of the universal Church. For Ratzinger, such a development would implicitly overthrow the true nature of the Church which is to be a communion of local churches. Because the local or particular churches are the fundamental forms of the Church's life and constitution, the one Church entrusted to the bishops to guide is entrusted to them precisely as guides of their particular churches. If the individual bishop's good guidance of his church, as he leads it towards the Lord and thus into the 'reciprocal unity of all', is weakened or dissolved, then the very foundation of collegiality disappears. No assembly will be of avail. There is already an organ of the convergence of episcopal churches as they move together in the direction of Catholic unity. It is called the bishop of Rome.

How, then, does Ratzinger currently view the papal office?[16] He observes that the decline of monarchy as an ideal in political life has rendered the Papacy an unattractive subject to many people. Just as the First Vatican Council, with its teaching on the primacy, cannot wholly be severed from its setting in the European society of its day, where the dominant political forms were still royal or imperial, so the Second Vatican Council, with its teaching on collegiality, cannot entirely be separated from reaction against those forms. Yet both papacy and college are needful, for, whereas collegiality represents the We-element in the Christian religion, so the primacy reflects its complementary I-element.[17] As the Old Testament makes clear, the We of the community does not obliterate the I of personal responsibility. Just as God has a Name, so man stands in the history of revelation with a name of his own. It is as a 'name-bearing being' that he is a responsible being in the working out of the story of salvation. In the New Testament, this aspect of things is further highlighted. The new People of God arises not by birth but through call and response. Baptism, which is the sacramental entry into the life of that People, can only be received by individual persons, called out by name, and the same is true of the repairing of the baptismal life, the sacrament of Penance, which, in grave cases, must also be a person-to-person affair. In the Liturgy, we find the names of the saints, and of those individuals who personify the churches with whom we communicate. There is in the Church no such thing as anonymous, communitarian guidance. Ratzinger thinks here of the phenomenon of episcopal lists, which appeared as early as

[16]KÖP pp. 35-48.
[17]On the 'We-structure' of collegiality, Ratzinger refers back to his own, 'Die pastoralen Implikationen der Lehre von der Kollegialität der Kirche', Concilium I (1965), pp. 16-29.

Hegesippus in the early second century. He finds the ultimate confirmation of this principle in martyrdom, whose personal testimony is the primordial form of the imitation of Christ.[18]

Ratzinger feels justified, therefore, in speaking of a 'martyrological principle' at work in the Church. It is in this principle that the Petrine office is rooted. The great primatial text, Matthew 16, 17, has always generated the question. But is the Church's rock-like foundation Peter's person or Peter's faith? Discussed by Augustine, it returned with a vengeance in the sixteenth century Reformation. Ratzinger's answer is that it must be inseparably *both*.

> A confession of faith exists only as an act of personal responsibility. For this reason, confession is bound to the person. And vice versa, the foundation is not a person thought of, so to say, on some neutral metaphysical plane. It is the person precisely as the bearer of confession.[18a]

The unity of the Christian We is held together by personal bearers of responsibility for that unity. And their task is itself represented in a personalised way by Peter. In receiving his name, Peter, rock-man, Simon is raised up to become the beginning of an institution in history, but an institution which can only exist as a person with a nameable, personal responsibility of his own. The new name, being the name of the rock, contains that continuity, 'continue-ability', which the Church's journey towards the final Parousia requires.

The Church and political ethics[19]

Ecclesiology, however, must not give the impression that the

[18]Cf. E. Peterson, 'Zeuge der Wahrheit', *Theologische Traktaten* op. cit. pp. 165–224.

[18a]KÖP p. 40.

[19]I am grateful to the Editor of *New Blackfriars* for his permission to re-use here material originally published in that journal.

Church is the only reality. As in his sermons, Ratzinger was deeply exercised by the Church–world relationship. From recent essays on that relationship I take six themes in what seems to be a coherent conceptual order. First, Ratzinger offers picture of the relation between theology, the magisterium of Pope and bishops, and political activity. Secondly, he considers how such activity stands in relation to eschatology: this is crucial for his estimate of liberation theology, and also helps to 'place' politics within the human and divine scheme as a whole. Thirdly, he stresses the vital role of the concept of conscience in the Christian practice of politics. This brings us to, fourthly, the question of what service Christian witness has to offer in the pluralist democracies of the West, under whose *régime* he happens to live. In connexion with this we shall note, fifthly, the special weight he attaches to the historic destiny of Europe. Finally, as that destiny is, for Ratzinger, bound up with the idea of freedm, we can consider more explicitly, by way of conclusion, what he takes authentic freedom (or liberation) to consist in.

St John's declaration that Jesus of Nazareth is self-identical with the divine Logos may be taken as expressing the Church's fundamental conviction that in faith what is manifested in the rational. The foundation of being is Reason: the world is not, therefore, a 'casual side-product' thrown up from the 'ocean of the irrational'.[20] As Ratzinger puts it, since reason is manifested in Christian faith, faith naturally seeks its own reason, and in that reason the very rationality of the real. Conversely, faith entrusts to reason the philosophical task of recognising in faith the condition of possibility for its own activity. Reason must not so press its claims to totality as to deny this. Though such a self-limitation of reason might look at first pre-critical, it provides the heart of the critique of modern European

[20]KÖP. p. 142.

philosophy offered by those entirely un-clerical figures, the Frankfurt School of critical sociology. They pointed out that the Enlightenment contained within itself the seeds of its own downfall.[21] Enlightenment depends on a conviction of the 'absoluteness' or 'divinity' of truth. Should it call into question this pre-supposition of truth, it will end up by justifying the irrational, as has happened in the work of the philosopher–biologist Jacques Monod. Moreover, the more the Enlightenment movement advanced in history, the more it tended to whittle down the concept of reason which was its foundation. The rational becomes the reproducible (in a laboratory). Reason undergoes a positivist fall. People renounce the search for truth and replace it by concern with what can be done with things: a theme to Ratzinger as early as his *Einführung in das Christentum* of 1968.[22] This degeneration of the Enlightenment (which in itself, we should recall, was not anti-Christian or anti-clerical in German-speaking lands) Ratzinger finds reflected in the fate of the Universities and particularly in the student revolt of the later 1960's. Now it is sometimes alleged that the cardinal's objections to liberation theology (in some, at ant rate, of its forms) derive from the trauma induced by the events of May 1968 when he was himself a university professor at Tübingen.[23] In what follows we discover how in fact he sees those events in their wider context.

[21]Notably, T. W. Adorno, *Negative Dialektik* (Frankfurt 1966).

[22]IC pp. 30–39.

[23]However, whilst capable of taking such a serene view, Ratzinger candidly admits that his view of Marxism was deeply affected by suffering the effects of its more rabid student supporters in 1968. See his interview, given via correspondence, in E. J. Dionne Jr., 'The Pope's guardian of orthodoxy', *New York Times Magazine* for 24. 11. 1985. He told that paper: 'I learned that it is impossible to discuss with terror and on terror, as there are no premises for a discussion – and such a discussion becomes collaboration with terror . . . I think that in those years, I learned where discussion must stop because it is turning into a lie, and resistance must begin in order to maintain freedom', art. cit. p. 58.

The origins of the European Universities lie, as well-known, in the mediaeval epoch, when faith declared possible the search for truth. This search eventually extended to all the principal area of human knowledge, thus generating the various academic faculties. All were sustained by common adhesion to the question of truth, whose own possibility was guarded by the faculty of theology. When this Christian context dissolved, a crisis was inevitable. In that the Universities fell under a law of positivism, the accusations of 'irrelevance' hurled by the student radicals of 1968 at their mentors were by no means out of place. The radical resurrection of concern with the 'origin and purpose of the whole' was in itself perfectly legitimate.[24] Unfortunately, in taking the form of Marxism, it walked straight down a cul-de-sac. For, despite appearances, Marxism was a criticism immanent to the system which had brought about the crisis. Like positivism, Marxism rejects the primacy of *logos*. It sees reason as generated 'dialectically' by matter, by the irrational, and must, therefore, regard truth as simply a human postulation.

And just as the degeneration of Enlightenment reason is reproduced in the culture of the Universities, so does it find a final expression in the fate of theology itself. Many academic theologians, Ratzinger complains, hope to acquire parity with their non-theological colleagues by being as good a positivist, methodologically, as the next man (or woman). Rather than seeking truth itself in their authoritative sources, they confine themselves to an historicist re-construction of anoriginal meaning to their texts. Unfortunately, this involves the renouncing of the most distinctive task of theology: the quest for the whole, as something beyond, though not unmanifested in, the various academic disciplines. No wonder, Ratzinger

[24]KÖP p. 145: the term I have paraphrased as 'irrelevance' is *Fachidiotie*: 'specialisation lunacy'.

comments, that students look elsewhere for a truer theology: finding theology in the practical action of an option for a better world-future, on the principle that orthopraxy precedes orthodoxy. Here we see the last bitter fruit of the truth that reason, in subverting faith, undermines its own foundations.

So much for theology. What of the Church's magisterium in this regard? In the affirmations made about reason above, Ratzinger is not pre-supposing a purely abstract reason which works suspended in noetic air. The idea of reason has its own historical and social conditions of emergence and flourishing, and if these are not acknowledged it is vulnerable to the charge of being a 'bourgeois' fiction. Precisely because reason needs such conditions, the community of faith – the Church, with its organs of authority – belongs to the Christian concept of both faith and rationality. In defending the role of the ecclesial magisterium today, one faces, Ratzinger alleges, challenges both from the Left and from the New Right. To the latter, the relationship of Christian understanding to the Church's magisterium is criticised for its isomorphism with that of knowledge under Marxism-Leninism to the determinations of the Communist Party. The magisterium offers a party-line which constricts knowledge in a papal or episcopal bear-hug, forcing science to submit to the higher jurisdiction of an extra-scientific court. To the former, the magisterium provides the nucleus of a reactionary realisation of the Church that is itself locked in a death-struggle with a new Church, wherein Christianity is, in Father Ernesto Cardenal's phrase, 'understood as Marxism'.[25] In the new Church which is coming to be, Christianity becomes an instrument of liberation, stimulated by the humanistic impulses of Marxism, and seeks the new society which it calls the Kingdom of God. Between theology as reflection on the praxis of this transformatory movement, and

[25]Ibid. p. 148.

258

the magisterium which is the protective guardian of the reactionary Church that resists re-birth into the image of the new, there can be no peace.

What answer does Ratzinger give to these criticisms of Left and Right? He responds first to the voices coming from the Right. While there is always a temptation for those who bear the duty of authoritative teaching in the Church to behave like a party, the crucial difference between the party and the magisterium lies in the question of truth, and, more specifically, in the relation of orthodoxy or orthopraxy. Wherever orthodoxy is regarded as the product of orthopraxy, even if it be recognised that some kind of theological reflection necessarily precedes practice, truth will finally depend on the position of the party. But for the Church, man is essentially not the *constructor* of truth but its *receiver*. The Church does not posit truth: she is herself posited by it. Since the whole Church is ordered to the truth, theology and magisterium take the form of irreducibly distinct and mutually necessary kinds of service to that truth. The magisterium traces the boundaries which theology must not transgress if it is to maintain its place in that 'space' of truth which is the Church. Only by obedience to the authentic magisterium can theology preserve the conditions of its own enlightenment. Conversely, the magisterium must allow theology its own freedom by renouncing any attempt to prescribe what should be a theology's content or method – over and above the fundamental structure of faith itself.

Ratzinger's response to critics of the Left is found in the rest of the essay I have been expounding. His reply begins from Matthew 22.21, the saying of Jesus about rendering to God and Caesar what is, respectively, theirs. He sees this as the end of the axiomatic assumption that politics as such is holy. The Roman imperial state tolerated local religions, but only because it regarded itself as the bearer of a higher sacrality. By contrast, the separation of State authority from sacral authority, found *in nuce* in the teaching of Jesus, represents the beginning of the Western idea of freedom. The State no longer carries a religious authority reaching into the most *recherché* corners of the soul. Rather does it point for its ethical foundation to an institution beyond itself. The *Church* is the State's final ethical court of appeal, though it is itself a voluntary association with merely spiritual penalties at its disposal. Although this equilibrium was profoundly disturbed at many points in Christian history, freedom depends on it. Where the State comes to reject the Church as a publically relevant *Instanz*, or court of appeal, it reclaims the foundation of ethics in the form of ideology. Attempts to export the Western recipe for free institutions, for instance, to the Islamic world, come to grief because an idea dependent on the Christian Gospel cannot simply be transplanted to any soil whatever. Or, in Ratzinger's lapidary formula, 'where there is no dualism there is totalitarianism.'[26]

This raises the question of the relation of politics to eschatology, since it is characteristic of liberation theology both to deny the dualism Ratzinger is speaking of, and to propose a new relation of political endeavour to the Christian sense of ultimate concern. Ratzinger considers that the two principal concepts that have informed all attempts to relate Christian faith to political life are eschatology and utopia. The idea of utopia, which emerged explicitly in the Renaissance humanism of More, belongs to a longer tradition of political philosophy uniting Christian and Platonist elements. Its relation to concrete states of affairs can be described as that of mathematical forms to their empirical exemplification. The aim of utopian thinking is the measuring of actual politics by the highest criteria available, rather than the pursuit of ideal aspirations for the future. Such thinking only achieved a connexion with a philosophy of history in the modern period when Ernst Bloch lighted upon it

[26]Ibid. p. 151.

as a possible revolutionary stimulus. Eschatology, on the other hand, is a reflection on the revelation of a divine future for man. Since it concerns man as the receiver of a divine gift, a new earth not made by human hands, it brings in its train a major problem: how can such a divine gift become a practical principle, a source of action, and thus enter into relation with man's *practical* reason, just as in theology faith enters into symbiosis with his *pure*, or speculative, reason?

Ratzinger considers four models of how this is to be done. Two of these, Chiliasm and the theology of evolution found in Teilhard de Chardin, he rejects. Chiliasm, to which he accommodates Marxism, is an essentially irrational attempt to fuse inner-historical and meta-historical categories, the expectation of an inner-historical condition of salvation that transcends the possibilities of political action and yet has to be realised by political means. Teilhardism is a marriage of eschatology with evolution which lacks a political programme, putting in its place a faith in science that assumes 'mythical proportions'.[27] The two other 'models', regarded more benignly by Ratzinger, are what he terms the mainstream union of eschatological and utopian approaches in Church tradition, and, in the microcosmic image of this macrocosm, the monastic community or *civitas*. The eschatological orthodoxy of the Church has found its principal dialogue-partner not in a philosophy of history but in Platonist-Aristotelean ontology. Since Hellenic ethics was above all an exposition of the criteria which should govern life in the polis, it proved capable of complementing Christian eschatology. In the ensuing 'co-ordination', three elements stand out, First, in maintaining the impossibility of any internal fulfilment of the world, eschatology confirms what reason would in any case suggest. For such a fulfilment would ill accord with man's 'open'

[27]Ibid. p. 224.

freedom, which includes openness to failure! Orthodox eschatology accords with Greek ethics in denying that human moral effort can be bypassed in favour of 'the orchestration of plannable mechanisms': this remains the permanently valuable nugget in the Church's rejection of Chiliasm. Secondly, and more positively, orthodox eschatology, in affirming that the possibilities of history will nevertheless be fulfilled meta-historically guarantees the reign of meaning in history. In so doing, it warrants the use of utopian 'model-ideas' for the maximising of human justice, raising such models to the level of genuine works of political reason. Here faith provides the ultimate foundation for practical reason in its political mode, just as Ratzinger has argued, it does for pure reason in its enlightened self-awareness in epistemology and metaphysics. Thirdly and finally, this eschatology finds its own basis not in a particular philosophy of history but in Christian ontology: in the Christian doctrine of God, as taking concrete form in a Christology which has transformed Jewish eschatology by assuming it into itself. The actual effects which this vision of reality can bring about may be seen in miniature in the communities of Christian monasticism at its finest. As Ratzinger approvingly cites the sixth century Palestinian hagiographer Cyril of Scythopolis, the monks have made the desert a *civitas*, and the non-world a world.[28] In this pneumatic revolution, his heroes include, inevitably, St Benedict, but also the early Franciscans whose Third Order ideal enabled the monastic 'city' to embrace those engaged in professional or other secular avocations in the wider world.

Today, Ratzinger considers, we are halfway between an irrationalistic Chiliasm (namely, Marxism) and a hopeless positivism. In this situation, the Church's main task will be a repristinisation of the functioning of the Platonist-Christian-

[28]Cyril of Scythopolis, *Vita Sabae* c. 15, cited KÖP, p. 222.

Humanist utopia. By expanding the concept of reason in this context, the Church can encourage governors and governed to put the right questions about the values that are to regulate the empirical realm.

This relation between the grid of values which utopian thought highlights, and the messy day-to-day pressures in which political life is embedded leads on naturally to Ratzinger's discussion of conscience. He reminds us of Hitler's notorious promise, issued to the president of the senate of the *Freistadt* Danzig, Hermann Rauschning, that National Socialism will liberate man from conscience.[29] For Ratzinger, the affirmation of the 'absoluteness' of conscience is the true antidote to tyranny. The enslavement of man on the pretext of his liberation is an ever-recurring danger. Thus the anatomy of totalitarianism and its cures is a perennial need. Ratzinger sees numerous similarities between the present period and the years which witnessed the rise of Nazism, for in both revolution has been held to be in itself salvation, and the negation of order is sought for its own sake. This makes our age an hour where conscience is especially needed, and justifies looking for inspiration to those classics which have registered its significance.

Ratzinger thus turns to the German man of letters, Reinhold Schneider.[30] Schneider defined conscience as the awareness of our responsibility before the whole of creation and him who created it. It is a concept in need of constant purification. It can be twisted into that of the super-ego, or the reflection of social convention. It can be made an alibi for obstinacy and egoism.

---

[29]T. Schieder, *Hermann Rauschnings 'Gespräche mit Hitler'* als *Geschichtsquelle* (Opladen 1972), p. 19, cited KÖP, p. 153.

[30]On Schneider, whose writing was banned under the Third Reich, one might consult H. U. von Balthasar's study, *Reinhold Schneider. Sein Weg und sein Werk* (Cologne 1953). Cf. also J. M. Ritchie, *German Literature under National Socialism* (London 1983), pp. 122–123.

But these manifold ways of abusing the concept of conscience cannot annul its greatness. In his novel based on the life of the Spanish Dominican defender of the Indians, Bartolomeo de Las Casas, Schneider presents conscience in three forms.[31] In Las Casas himself, we see 'prophetic conscience'. Though the *Brevissima Relación de la destrucción de las Indias Occidentales* was partial and exaggerated, nevertheless the crimes committed against the native population of the Americas were horrific enough. Prophetic conscience is conscience gone missionary. Such conscience 'locates itself with serenity among thrones', and never ceases to disturb the peace of those whose power is exercised at the expense of the rights of others. That such conscience had its effect may be seen in the modification of the laws of the Indies, as between the first laws of Isabella la Católica and the 'New Laws' of 1542. Indeed, for Schneider, prophetic conscience must awaken a second mode of conscience, 'governing conscience', which in his novel is embodied in the emperor Charles V. This is the conscience of one who is entrusted with power and must exercise it responsibly. Ratzinger sees it exemplified in De Gaulle's decision to let Algeria go, as described by the writer-minister André Malraux. Nevertheless, for Schneider, as echoed by Ratzinger, the supreme form of conscience is 'suffering conscience', represented in the Las Casas story by a nameless girl of the Lucayos tribe. In the last analysis, injustice can be rooted out of the human heart only by the cathartic perception of the voluntary suffering of those who are faithful to conscience. Only as the vehicle for the power of the Cross does conscience redeem.

From the role of the Church in the Spanish America of the *conquistadores* to her role in the pluralist democracies of today. After the war, Ratzinger points out, the advent of democracy

[31]Schneider's drama of 1938 (a significant date!) was entitled *Las Casas vor Karl V. Szenen aus der Konquitadorenzeit.*

was greeted with a quasi-religious enthusiasm in liberated Europe and elsewhere. Today the position is much more ambiguous. Characteristically, Third World countries with Marxist governments are regarded as having reached a condition of order which should not be disturbed, whereas those that vacillate between dictatorship and democracy are recommended Marxian ideals of liberation. In this uncertainty of political judgment on the affairs of other peoples we can see, Ratzinger suggests, our more painful and intimate uncertainty about our own. Frankly, pluralist democracy has not shown itself capable of uniting citizens in a deep-rooted adhesion to a common form of life. Economic crises bring it to a precipice; shifts in the life of the spirit threaten to remove the ground from beneath its feet. Ratzinger finds that the menace to democracy lies chiefly in an unwillingness to accept the intrinsic imperfection of everything human. Prominent among the (perhaps unwitting) enemies of democracy are those who hold that, in a liberated society, the good will be irrevocably sustained by structures. For those who think thus, a State supported merely by ethics is likely to be imperfect and so must be rejected. Ratzinger sees in this approach the very essence of materialism, itself more an anthropological programme than the denial of a non-material sphere of reality for its own sake. A 'liberation' founded on the marginalisation of ethics, and so of responsibility and conscience, involves a perfectionism of an intrinsically immoral kind. Moreover, this attempt to render the ethical dimension of superfluous by resort to a quasi-mechanical guarantee of social justice reflects that truncated concept of reason which Bacon and Comte bequeathed to European thought. In a human physics, ethics is reduced to a calculation of advantages and disadvantages, and the good *in se* is lost to view. Ratzinger mentions a recent civil case in Bavaria where charges of sacrilege were dismissed on the grounds that they constituted no threat to the public peace. Here a good which law should protect is laid aside by a judicial practice that simply seeks to avoid clashes between opposed interests. For the survival of society and the State, some deeper moral consensus than this must be reconstructed. The third and final source of the acid corroding pluralist democracy that Ratzinger identifies is flight from transcendence. Where the possibilities of life in this world are taken to be the totality of life, they come to seem vacuous. Marx taught that we must eradicate the sense of transcendence so that man, once cured of false consolations, may construct a perfect world. Today, we know that man needs transcendence so that he can build up a necessarily imperfect world in a way which will enable people to live together in a humane fashion.

Ratzinger concludes that a pluralist democracy for its own survival and flourishing must draw on sources of spiritual power beyond itself. Might Christianity be such a potential aid? *Prima facie*, the suggestion is not plausible given the Church's track record which reveals: messianic perfectionism, leading to an anarchistic approach to the State; the denial of the relevance of the works of justice to grace-sustained righteousness, manifested in Augustine's almost demonic concept of the *civitas terrena*; and the tendency of Christian monotheism, with its claims to an exclusive truth, to breed political intolerance. Nevertheless, Ratzinger believes that the Christian Church can and must be the kind of resource for the State which he deems needful. The foundational act in the development of society is moral education. In the West, ethics lives through the posthumous influence of Christendom which gave it the basis of its rationality and internal structure. When Christian revelation is relegated to the status of what a man does with his solitude, being inserted into the 'pantheon of all possible value-systems' the ethos which that revelation sustained begins to de-

[32]KÖP p. 195.

compose.[32] Thus, for instance, the denial of the bond of marriage as the fundamental form of relations between the sexes leads to a degradation of sexual life, to a struggle of the sexes, and the generations, with each other, and a rupture between spirit and matter. The churches, in preferring to see themselves simply as 'social forces' are guilty of retracting those claims to a wider truth which should render them precious to the State. In effect, Ratzinger presents an *aporia*: if the Church renounces her claim to teach both truth and values with authority then she ceases to be able to offer to the State what the State needs from her. If, on the other hand, the State accepts her claim in an unconditional fashion, it eliminates itself as a pluralist reality and even as a reality distinct from the Church. Today, however, the second danger is so minimal that it can safely be ignored. The State must recognise once again in the Church a fount of value and truth which can render consensus possible.

Looking at Europe in particular, Ratzinger hopes that the idea of Europe can offer a viable synthesis of political reality and moral idealism. He points out the Christian significance of the concept of Europe: the very word entered the popular vernaculars in the early modern period not just because of the influence of classical humanistic thought but via reaction to the threat from Islam in the shape of the Turks. However, the spiritual capital of the concept of Europe has been squandered. In the Great Revolution of the West, God was dethroned as the public *summum bonum* and replaced by the nation. After 1848, the socialist tradition replaced the nation here by the proletarian revolution. Meanwhile, its capitalist alternative found yet another idol, creating the consumerist dystopia in which 'their God is their stomach'. The retrieval of the idea of Europe will involve drawing on both the classical and the Christian heritage. From the Greek background, we must recover the relation between government and *eunomia*: a justice that cannot be manipulated for it stands over power, limiting and controlling it, and preserving its 'transparency' to value. But this fundamental connexion of law with moral norms that are both common and binding for all citizens cannot be re-established without appeal to the supernatural, to the lost *summum bonum* of Christendom. Though the *Lebensraum* of non-believers must be at all times zealously preserved, Europe can be saved from the fissiparous forces of nationalism and from an international economic and administrative technocracy careless of the cry of the world's poor at its gates, only by restoring the public relevance of Christian doctrine. It is here that, for Ratzinger, ecumenism has its greatest relevance, since Catholic, Orthodox, Anglican, Lutheran and Reformed could work together for the re-creation of a 'eunomic' Europe from the Atlantic to the Urals.

Ratzinger's reflections come to their climax in his account of freedom, a term which entered into the titles of both the 'negative' and the 'positive' documents on liberation theology issued by his Congregation. He points out the curious tendency of the pursuit of freedom to throw up fresh forms of constriction – something illustrated, as we have noted, by the history of his own Bavaria in the Napoleonic age. The revolutions of the past transferred power from persons to institutions so as to secure objectivity in the exercise of power but they all too often produce a grey bureaucratic uniformity of the sort described in Kafka's novels. The Enlightenment set aside the multiple organic forms of traditional society (which themselves enshrined inherited liberties of various limited kinds) in the name of the uniquely binding force of reason. But since all men are not, in practice, reasonable, it found itself obliged to make the absolute monarch into the organ of a higher liberty. And so forth. From the ambiguous concept of freedom in the *Aufklärungszeit*, there come down to us two lines of development: one finds freedom through the apparatus of the democratic State, the other through the 'logic of history'. The former sub-tradition, which we can label 'Rousseauesque', conceives of citizens as passing from a state of heterodetermination to one of autodetermination through democratic participation. But it leaves unresolved the problem of whether a majority voice must necessarily incarnate a higher reason. The alternative sub-tradition, that which passes through Hegel, understands all history as a history of freedom which advances not least through the challenges offered by what is opposed to freedom. But here freedom becomes lost in a sea of infinitude: a man emancipated not only from tradition and authority but from his own created essence, enters a 'vacuum without meaning and without light'.[33]

In each case, what is omitted is the central fact that man is the bearer of rights, and that his freedom exists only where these rights are fostered by the rule of law. Freedom is a condition of being where the nexus of rights that reflect man's essence with all its inherent possibilities is efficaciously defended. The Exodus, a *topos* dear to liberation-theological exegesis, cannot be sundered from the gift of the Torah on Sinai: liberating ordinances which provide an orientation for the life-pattern of a community. Though this community, now universalised in the Church of Christ, is not a State-community, the Word of God it bears within it offers an ethical direction for the State to follow. If we follow the cue of liberation theology at its best, and re-integrate the tradition of Catholic social doctrine in dogmatics as a whole, we find that every attempt to establish an arbitrary absolute power, whether that of a majority or that of a party, is contradicted by the fundamental Christian revelation of God. Its God of absolute power is an idol; whereas the true God, being in himself the relationality of triune love, is perfect freedom. Here, Ratzinger implies in conclusion this collection,

---

[33]Cited after the simultaneously published Italian version, *Chiesa, ecumenismo e politica* (Milan 1987), p. 180.

the future of a purified liberation theology must be found: in the working out of the Trinitarian and Christological preconditions of Catholic social doctrine, which work will give those who seek to realise that doctrine new inspiration and motivating power.

Ecumenism

Such a purified liberation theology, taking up the permanently valuable element in *Gaudium et Spes*, should not however, absorb all energies to the detriment of, for instance, the concern with the Church's unity expressed in the Decree on Ecumenism, *Unitatis redintegratio*. What, according to the mature Ratzinger, is the ultimate aim of Catholic ecumenical endeavour?[34] It is the transformation of the separated confessional churches as currently existing into authentic 'particular' churches, each of which would be a concrete embodiment of the single *Catholica*. To this desired aim, the Second Vatican Council made a unique, yet in one sense a misleading, contribution. It canonised the research into common Christian sources which Catholic scholars had perforce pursued privately in the pre-Conciliar period. Catholic ecumenism thus became respectable, indeed *de rigueur*, almost overnight. This meteoric rise to fame and fortune produced, unfortunately, quite unrealistic expectations on the part of non-specialists who thought that Christian divisions were about to disappear for ever before their very eyes. In the inevitable disillusion which followed, some ecumenists were encouraged to seek what for Catholic ecclesiology could only be called desperate solutions.

Ratzinger describes *three* such unacceptable short-cuts. One solution was to appeal for a restoration of unity purely *from*

---

[34]See section II of KÖP, 'Ökumenische Probleme'.

below. In this strategy, the ecumenist borrows from the poliltical theorist a distinction between the State, whose authority is formal, static and in the last analysis parasitic, and society, which is the real bearer of values and creativity. Applied to the Church, such an analysis allows one to bypass the ordained leadership and appeal directly to the mass of the laity, in the hope that a new, 'progressive' world-church could be created by popular union from among the rank-and-file of the ancient historic churches. Such a 'solution' soon lost favour, however, because it became clear that a world-church defined solely by its willingness to engage in 'advanced' temporal projects would be too fluid an entity to enjoy any significant unity anyhow. A second deviant solution, canvassed more recently, takes the opposite tack of appealing for the restoration of unity exclusively *from above*. Here the idea is that Church authority could, by virtue of its own ministerial mandate, suspend the normal pre-conditions for entry into Catholic unity, in the hope that, once schismatics found themselves in the mainstream of the Church's life, their objections to particular Catholic doctrines would subsequently wither away. This 'solution', associated with the names of Heinrich Fries and the late Karl Rahner, is rejected by Ratzinger as dependent on a gross exaggeration of the scope of papal and episcopal authority.[35] That authority is bound by the apostolic deposit whose integrity it serves: pope and bishops cannot dream up any idea they like ('illuminism') and decide to put it into practice ('voluntarism'). Such ecumenism from above is a caricature of the Catholic view of the ministerial priesthood, just as ecumenism from below is a caricature of the Protestant view of the priesthood of the laity. Finally, a third unacceptable solution consists in a false egalitarianism, whereby the existing traditions of thought and

[35] I have myself offered an evaluation of this controversy in '*Einigung der Kirchen*: an ecumenical controversy', *One in Christ* XXI. 2 (1985), pp. 139–166.

practice in various Christian confessions are considered neutrally as *de facto* 'traditions', without reference to their grounding, or lack of it, in Scripture and (apostolic) Tradition. In such *horizontal* ecumenism, the common search for evangelical truth is replaced by an attempt to render all inherited religious patterns mutually compatible for the sake of reunion all round.

Over against the claims of such ecumenism 'from above', 'from below', and 'from the side', Ratzinger proposes a proper shape for ecumenical endeavour. This involves an inter-action between three elements: the faith-experience of the people of God; the careful study of theologians; the doctrinal preaching of the bishops. Here Ratzinger comes close to the portrait of Church life painted by John Henry Newman in the celebrated 1877 'Preface' to his *Via Media*. The sacerdotal office of the parish priest with his flock; the prophetic office of the theologian in the schools; the regal office of the Pope in his curia: it is from all of these *together* that insights reconstructive of Christian unity emerge and mature.[36]

Of its nature, this is a slow process. Ratzinger thinks it unlikely that the 'reconciling' of the 'diversities' of the existing churches will happen in the lifetime of those alive today. A vital precondition of successful ecumenism is waiting on God's will, a readiness *not* to act before the hour of his, rather than our, choosing. Meanwhile, there is much we can do together: Catholics and non-Catholics can co-operate in charitable and social work, in common moral witness (at least on many issues) and in the shared experience of fundamental Christian existence.

---

[36]J. H. Newman, *The Via Media of the Anglican Church* (London 1877) pp. xv–xciv. The importance of this lengthy passage is underlined by N. Lash, 'Catholic Theology and the crisis of classicism', *New Blackfriars* 66. 780 (June 1985), pp. 279–287. However, as already indicated in the context of Chapter 9 above, agreement that all three elements, offices or functions need to be recognised and inter-related may co-exist with disagreement on *how* this is to be done.

Indeed, Ratzinger goes so far as to say that, in recognising the non-Catholic 'other' precisely in his 'otherness', we are ourselves enriched. Though Christian division is in itself an evil, it has been a divinely permitted means of producing good since the various confessions have developed distinctive and precious Gospel emphases of their own. He means, presumably, that whilst the totality of elements that make up the *esse* of the Church subsists only in the (Roman) Catholic communion, elements necessary for the Church's *plene esse*, her plenary flowering, may have to be sought, at least in certain periods and places, from beyond her visible boundaries.

Granted the many 'bilateral' negotiations in which the Catholic Church is currently involved, ranging as these do from the Non-Chalcedonian Orthodox to the Baptists, Ratzinger might have chosen to illustrate these fundamental themes from relations with a wide range of churches. In fact, he concentrates on two: those of Canterbury and Wittenberg. With regard to Anglicanism, it may be said that, generally speaking, only the English can understand it. Catholics of, for instance, Irish, Italian or Slavonic descent, though born and educated in England, may be found struggling to comprehend it. English Anglicans, forgetful that, for over a century, they have constituted part of a world-wide Anglican Communion, are notorious for treating the goings-on of Anglicans overseas as less than fully serious. It was, then, somewhat audacious of Ratzinger to have responded to the invitation of the parson-editor of a newly-founded journal to record his reflections on the Anglican–Roman Catholic conversations.

He correctly identifies a principal difficulty in ecumenical negotiations with Anglicans: though their communion appears to be an episcopally ordered church on the same model as those of Orthodoxy and the Old Catholics – and the High Church party has always defined itself by the affirmation that this is so – in practice Anglicanism operates on a principle of 'dispersed authority' whereby no institution or person can speak for Anglicans at large. The idea of dispersed authority is, in fact, the making into a virtue of what came to be by historical necessity. For, as a senior Anglican theologian, Stephen Sykes, has pointed out, there co-exist within the Anglican bosom those who see Anglicanism as a form of 'undifferentiated Catholicism', appealing for authority to the beliefs and structures of the primitive Church; those who regard the English Reformation as re-constituting the mediaeval *ecclesia anglicana* on the basis of pure apostolic doctrine, according primacy of place to the *norma normans et non normata* of the Bible; and, finally, those who

> regard Anglicans as simply Englishmen (and honorary Englishmen in other countries) going about their religious business as seems right and proper from time to time.[37]

More recently, it is true, some Anglicans are wondering whether the principle of dispersed authority is really a virtue at all, as they experience the fissiparous force of the attempt to ordain women to – above all – the historic episcopate. This is serious because it imperils agreement about the proper mode of transmission of a form of Christianity on whose content Anglicans have in any case always disagreed. It is for this reason that many thoughtful Anglicans at the present time are seeking a stronger primatial rôle for the see of Canterbury: the idea of an 'Anglican Pope'. But as Sykes ends a review of the story of Anglican ecclesiology:

> There seems nothing to protect us from the conclusion that Anglicanism as it now exists is founded on an incoherent doctrine of the Church; and that its attempts to resolve or

[37]S. W. Sykes, 'Anglicanism and Protestantism', in idem. (ed.), *England and Germany. Studies in Theological Diplomacy* (Frankfurt and Berne 1982), pp. 113–130, and here at p. 293.

conceal this gross internal antinomy has repeatedly led it into a series of chronic conflicts from which it barely escapes with any integrity.[38]

Ratzinger approaches these Anglican difficulties, very properly, not in terms of mere Church politics – how to paper over cracks in the plaster – but in terms of the mystery of the Church as bearer of the Gospel. The question of authority, he points out, is fundamentally identical with that of Tradition. The supreme authority for the Church is Scripture-read-in-Tradition, but this raises the question of where that common 'traditional' life may be found which is truly an adequate meidum for the interpretation of Scripture. The Catholic response is that the universal Church provides such a medium. The apparent inability of Anglicans to echo this response, except in some vague or ideal sense, causes them to reject the notion of the inherent inerrancy of ecumenical Councils, and has led also to a mutation in the character of the episcopal office in their communion. For the Anglican signatories to the Agreed Statements, ecumenical councils are only intrinsically authoritative if their teaching is manifestly that of Scripture. But Ratzinger points out that, should observers external to a Council be able to gauge the manifest sense of Scripture, Councils would be superfluous anyway.

Moreover, since a bishop is only a pastor-with-authority insofar as he represents in himself the universal Church, the rupture – even if only partial – with that Church must necessarily alter his status. As the universal Church is not simply the sum-total of particular churches but a mystery of communion which enters into those churches to make them what they are, the Tudor sundering of the *Ecclesia anglicana* from the rest of Catholic Christendom by the 1534 Act of Supremacy could not but modify the manner in which the

---

[38]Ibid. p. 127.

Anglican church was episcopal. Thus prescinding from the vexed question of Anglican Orders, Ratzinger offers a comment on the Anglican position which would apply as well to Henrician Catholicism as to the church of Edward VI or the Elizabethan Settlement.

The most obvious consequence of these *lacunae* may be found, for Ratzinger, in those passages of the Agreed Statements where, to Anglicans, 'tradition' means the texts inherited from Christian antiquity – Fathers, liturgies, credal confessions, canons – whereas, to Catholics, it must mean the living voice of the Church today bringing the resources of the past to bear on the questions of the present. In the last analysis, the Church teaches in the same manner as her Master: 'with authority, and not as the scribes'.[39]

Ratzinger's comments on the parallel dialogue with Lutheranism concern chiefly the controverted figure of Luther himself. He remarks that changing fashions in Catholic Luther-research have given us a very diverse gallery of images of Luther. He himself finds two figures within the Wittenberg Reformer. First, there is the Luther of the Catechisms, the hymns and the liturgical reforms: and this Luther can be received by Catholics whose own biblical and liturgical revivals in this century reproduce many of Luther's own criticisms of the late mediaeval Church. But besides this Luther there is also another: the radical theologian and polemicist whose particular version of the doctrine of justification by faith is incompatible with the Catholic understanding of faith as a co-believing with the whole Church, within a Christian existence composed equally by faith, hope and charity.

It is certainly the case that the Catholic image of Luther has

[39]One should note that the German version of Ratzinger's *Insight* essay has an appendix devoted to the reply of a group of ecumenists, also in *Insight* but in I. 4 (November 1983), as well as to contributions from J. M. R. Tillard OP in *The Tablet* for 7.1. 1984 and 14.1. 1984.

rarely been stable – not least because of the ambivalence in Luther's own personality and religious aims. As the Jesuit historian Hartmann Grisar wrote as long ago as 1926, 'the Catholic opponents of Luther have never agreed on many points'.[40] And in a contemporary study of *das moderne katholische Lutherbild*, the author asks, '*The* modern Catholic image of Luther? *Is* there among Catholics *an* image of Luther?'.[41] Ratzinger's notion of the 'two Luthers' was anticipated, as he himself notes, by Harnack. Essentially, Ratzinger follows the lead given by the Luther specialist Paul Hacker in seeing the fundamental difference between the Wittenberg doctor and the Catholic Church as consisting in the peculiar Lutheran version of justification by faith, derived as this was from Luther's personal religious experience, and notably the *Turmerlebnis* or 'tower-experience' of 1518.[42] The bitter and extreme anguish of sinful man before the just God requires, according to Luther, personal certitude of salvation if it is ever to be assuaged. In this Luther upset the applecart of Christian existence whose formula is ever found in the union of the three theological virtues. From this flows his extraordinarily harsh abuse of the claims of *maledicta caritas*, 'that accursed charity', to a constitutive role in our justification.

Ratzinger fears that, while in the present climate of theological pluralism, Catholic and Lutheran exegetes and scholars have indeed attained a happy unity on various aspects of the Gospel-in-tradition, such concord is, of its nature, a partial and brittle instrument. It covers only segments of Christian

[40]H. Grisar S.J., *Martin Luther. His Life and Work* (St Louis, Mo. and London 1930), p. iii.

[41]W. Beyna, *Das moderne katholische Lutherbild* (Essen 1969), p. 8.

[42]P. Hacker, *Das Ich im Glauben bei Martin Luther* (Salzburg 1966). For Ratzinger's evaluation of Lutheranism, see also his 'Theologische Aufgaben und Fragen bei der Begegnung lutherischer und katholischer Theologie nach dem Konzil', *Oecumenica* (Gütersloh 1969), pp. 251–270.

believing, and that in a way which is very probably subject to shifts in intellectual style. The making of such a *wissenschaftlich* consensus cannot, in and of itself, ground the faith of a re-united Church. Unity will be forged not through somewhat artificial attempts to draw non-contradiction from the opposed positions of the past, but by taking 'new steps' in the future. Though grateful for the work of participants in the formal dialogues, he does not seem to regard documents like the inter-Church Agreed Statements as exemplifying such advance. They are too donnish; and too redolent of the scissors-and-paste of committees. Despite such patristic precedents as the Formula of Reunion achieved between the Alexandrian and Antiochene parties after the Council of Ephesus, Ratzinger looks elsewhere for signs of hope.

We may perhaps see one such step in Ratzinger's list of *desiderata* for candidates to the papal office, which he describes elsewhere in the writings of his prefecture with reference to the theology of the Petrine office found in the teaching of Reginald Pole, the last Catholic archbishop of Canterbury.[43] Pole, in controversy with Anglicans, saw in the papal power not a grotesque hyperinflation of ministerial authority, but its exact opposite. By identifying the confession of Peter with Peter himself, and the universal primatial office with the person of its office holder, the Catholic Church – or so Pole throught – binds the Pope to the most complete obedience to Jesus Christ and his Cross. That bishop whose church rests on the witness, the martyrdom, of Peter must be himself a witness or martyr *par. excellence*. Many members of non-Catholic churches, though they cannot accept the universal primacy of the Pope in teaching and jurisdiction, find themselves attracted to the present successor of Peter as he brings the message and power of the Gospel into diverse situations across the globe. Through

[43]KÖP pp. 41–47

such evangelical living of office, divine grace can draw towards unity those who, though separated from each other, are not separated from the Spirit of God.

The unity and plurality of Christian wisdom

The unity of the Church was not, however, the only form of unity which interested Ratzinger. The unity of Christian wisdom was also a central preoccupation. Ratzinger held up as an ideal for all those concerned with the Church's intellectual life that unity of philosophy and theology found in early Christianity.[44] Since the Christian Gospel offers its truth as an answer to the basic questions of both life and death, Justin Martyr, writing in the early second century, could call Christianity the 'true philosophy'.[45] Today, as in the world of late antiquity, the anxiety and sense of meaninglessness which prevade culture mean that

> sooner or later, the professional philosopher and the professional theologian will be forced to realise what it is that people expect of them. This expectation far surpasses the external trappings of scholarship. People expect answers to the great questions of life: deep down, what does it mean to be a human being?[46]

According to Ratzinger, it is by keeping this appeal in mind that we can grasp the rational claims of both philosophy and theology, and their mutual relationship.

[44]For the early Christian account of the Gospel as 'philosophy', Ratzinger draws on O. Michel, ThWNT IX, col. 185, and on H. U. von Balthasar, 'Philosophie, Christentum, Mönchtum', *Sponsa Verbi* (Einsiedeln 1961), pp. 349–387.

[45]J. Ratzinger, 'Faith, Philosophy and Theology', in *The College of St Thomas Centenial Lectures* (St Paul, Minnesota 1985), pp. 10–13; = 'Glaube, Philosophie und Theologie', *Kritik und Bericht* (1986), pp. 56–66. Cited below as FPT.

[46]FPT p. 10.

The somewhat ambiguous attitude which Ratzinger assumed towards the Thomist movement of the thirteenth century in connexion with his study of Bonaventure now re-emerges. Or, more precisely, Ratzinger believes that the sharp distinction between philosophy and theology, as respectively the reflective tasks of natural reason and supernaturalised understanding, presses the classic Thomist texts beyond what they can, or should, bear.[47] And once, as in some circles of the Neo-Thomist revival, philosophy is assigned to the sphere of pure reason, and theology to that of revelation, the methodological relation of the two becomes exceedingly problematic. For such philosophers as Martin Heidegger or Karl Jaspers, theology destroys philosophy: the 'open movement of the transcendent is shattered in favour of an imagined certainty'.[48] But Ratzinger insists that, far from bringing the journey of thought to a premature and spurious end, Christian belief extends it, facilitates it, and gives it bearings.

> Might it not be that such answers give the ultimate questions of life and death their real depth, and their dramatic character? Could it not be said that such answers actually give radical form to both the thought and the questions themselves. Might they not indeed open the way, rather than block it off?[49]

Need philosophy defend itself against that *a priori* of thought which is faith? Must its purity and freedom be threatened by faith? Again, the same problem recurs from the side of theology for many people. The rejection of philosophy as a corrosive of

[47]For the historical question, Ratzinger refers his reader: to F. van Steenberghen, *Die Philosophie im 13. Jahrhundert (Munich-Paderborn 1977)*; E. Gilson, *Le Thomisme* (Paris 1945[5]); A. Hayen, *Thomas von Aquin gestern und heute* (Frankfurt 1953).

[48]FPT p. 11. CF. J. Pieper, *Verteidigungsrede für die Philosophie* (Munich 1966), p. 128.

[49]FPT p. 11.

theology is as ancient as Tertullian. Luther's *sola scriptura* was not only an attack on the classic presentation of Scripture through tradition and the Church's teaching office. It was also a 'declaration of war against the presence of Aristotle and Plato in the theology of the Scholastics'.

> Bringing philosophy into theology for Luther meant the destruction of the message of grace, which is the ruin of the Gospel at its very core. For him, philosophy is the expression of the man who knows nothing of grace, and who attempts to build his own wisdom and justice by himself. The opposition between justification by works and justification by grace, which in turn distinguishes the real Christian from the anti-Christian, becomes identical with the opposition between philosophy and the form of thought which comes from the words of Scripture.[50]

This Lutheran 'no!' to philosophy was revived in our own time by Karl Barth. Barth saw the principle of the 'analogy of being', used in Catholic philosophical theology, as the only – and yet perfectly adequate – reason for not becoming a Catholic. And, when he spoke of the analogy of being, what he had in mind was:

> the ontological option of Catholic theology for the synthesis it permits between the idea of being in philosophy and the idea of God in the Gospel.[51]

To Barth, as Ratzinger reminds us, this is idolatry: faith must expose as idols all the images of God which derive from human thinking. Faith lives by paradox, not by making links with finite reality as viewed by un-faith. Here again, therefore, we enter a

[50]Ibid. Ratzinger uses here B. Lohse, *Martin Luther. Eine Einführung in sein Leben und sein Werk* (Munich 1981), pp. 166ff.
[51]FPT p. 11. Cf. H. U. von Balthasar, *Karl Barth. Darstellung und Deutung seiner Theologie* (Cologne 1951).

cul-de-sac. Theology too, it seems, must defend itself against the *a priori* of philosophical knowledge, something which menaces the integrity, and novelty, of faith.

What can be done to overcome this impasse and restore the unity of Christian wisdom as a total reflection on the total man in his total context? Ratzinger suggests that, as a matter of principle, philosophy and theology are vital to each other. Philosophical thought cannot be set in motion without some *a priori* concepts. It must be fed; it cannot gyrate in a void, as reflection on reflection on reflection. . . . Since the time of Plato, philosophy has always thrived on critical dialogue with religious tradition. The priorities of that tradition have been its starting-points in seeking truth. Similarly, theology cannot avoid drawing on philosophical concepts. If it is to do more than simply repeat the words of Scripture, or gather up the data of the historian – if it is truly to *understand*, then it must engage in philosophical reflection. Neither Luther nor Barth were able to shake off philosophical ideas completely. Indeed, Ratzinger hazards, the history of Protestant theology has been quite as much influenced by philosophy as has that of Catholic. And where ontology, in particular, is abandoned, as it was in nineteenth century German Protestantism, the idea of God itself collapses. The only alternative to ontology is to present the thought of God as sheer paradox, in the manner of Barth. But the strain of this is too great: people cannot live with pure contradiction. And, looking at the same issue from the other side:

> the true philosopher, if he wishes to reach the ultimate questions, cannot free himself from the question of God, the question about the foundation and end of being itself.[52]

Ratzinger proposes that faith and philosophy are related on

[52]FPT p. 12.

three levels. First, they share a common orientation to those fundamental questions about man which are posed by the phenomenon of death – itself the most radical form of the more general question of how one ought to live. Stimulated by this 'metaphysical thorn in the side of man', faith seeks to relate its own answer in itnelligible fashion to the original question, a question that belongs to philosophical thought. Secondly, in confessing the existence of God as One who has power over reality in its totality, the faith of Israel gave rise to a universal claim whose universality is inseparable from its rationality.

> Thus within Israel herself, the synthesis between Greek and biblical thought was already prepared, the same synthesis which the Fathers of the Church struggled to achieve.[53]

A faith which abandons its claim to rationality loses one of its own fundamental traits. Thirdly and finally, the relation of philosophy and faith comes about because, as First Peter reminds us, when anyone asks him about the *logos* of hope, the believer must offer him an *apo-logia*.[54] By means of Christians, the *Logos* becomes an answer to human questioning. At its deepest, this apologetic presentation of theology is a missionary enterprise, and moreover:

> it can only be missionary when it really goes beyond all traditions, and becomes an appeal to reason itself, in complete openness to truth.[55]

And Ratzinger links the waning of the missionary imperative in some circles of the Church today with the loss of philosophy in some contemporary theology.

[53]Ibid.
[54]I Peter 3, 15.
[55]FPT p. 13.

Here we find Ratzinger concerned with the *unity* of Christian wisdom in its two essential modalities, philosophical and theological. But his prefecture saw him no less interested in its complementary *pluralism* and, more specifically, in the issues raised by the plurality of theologies existing side by side in the contemporary Catholic Church.[56] Apparently, the term 'pluralism' was coined in England at the turn of the century in the context of political theory.[57] In opposition to a doctrine of sovereignty for which isolated individuals stand over against the State with its supreme powers, 'pluralism' affirms that each individual lives within a multiplicity of social groupings. The State cannot exercise authority in an absolute manner: it may only impose its obligations as one set among others. Man is always greater than any of his social roles, including that of citizen. The fact that a variety of *dirigeants* share among them the making of the social fabric prevents undue concentration of power and assures a space of liberty to the personality.

Such conceptions, firmly opposed as they were to the idea of the State found in the thinkers of the Enlightenment, derived from late Victorian research into the 'corporative' life of the mediaeval period and so belonged within the Christian tradition of social and political ideas. They bore a distinct family resemblance to the emerging Catholic social doctrine of the papacy of Leo XIII. There too, the limitation of the competence of the State and the stress on social units which the State could only presuppose and must therefore respect were vital aspects of the search for a just social order.[58]

---

[56]J. Ratzinger, 'Le pluralisme: problème posé à l'Eglise et à la théologie', *Studia Moralia* 24 (1986), pp. 299–318. Cited below as PPPET.

[57]See P. Henrici, 'Kirche und Pluralismus', *Internationale Katholische Zeitung* 12 (1983), pp. 97–100.

[58]PPPET pp. 299–300. See also J. Höffner, *Christliche Gesellschaftslehre* (Cologne 1975); R. Ruhnau, *Der Katholizismus in der sozialen Bewährung* (Paderborn 1980).

THE PREFECT

However, the internal logic of these ideas raised a question for the Church. If each social body has only a relative value, will this not apply to the Church also? Should not the Church confine itself to religious needs and interests? If, though, a 'religious need' or 'interest' is the expression of an ultimate ligature (compare 're-*lig*-ion') or bond whereby man acts as what he definitively is, then a community ordered to this ultimate need will surely transcend other communities, being of a different nature from them. While in the 1920's the founder of political theology in the Protestant domain, Carl Schmitt, criticised the pluralist idea as a source of social decomposition,[59] the abuse of authority in the totalitarian systems of central Europe in succeeding decades restored it to general favour. From a juridical and social standpoint, the Church in the modern world tends to be seen as a particular kind of association. This being so, people have difficulty in grasping why its moral imperatives should receive greater attention from legislators than those of any other interest group. Such a view of the Church as a free association is sometimes also made the theoretical basis of liberty of teaching within her. Those who adopt this approach might bear in mind, Ratzinger suggests, that

> no party or interest group could tolerate in regard to its internal positions the pluralism of opinions that currently exists in the Church. All common defence of its interests would become illusory.[60]

In a situation where the Catholic selects the opinions he prefers from the bar's gantry and mixes them in the cocktail of his choice, the Church's magisterium becomes an absurdity and a usurpation, and its interventions are met with an unprecedented vehemence of opposition.

[59]C. Schmitt, *Staatsethik und pluralistische Staat* (= *Kantstudien* 35; 1930), pp. 28–42.
[60]PPPET p. 301.

285

But this is not to say that the model of political pluralism is wholly inapplicable to the Catholic case. The Christian faith has always sought to illuminate man's link with divine truth. In this, the religion, *Ver-bindung*, which arises from faith is distinct from all other forms of associational link, *Verbänden*. But because faith gives man a new orientation in his profoundest depths, it acts as liberation in all other domains of living. It does not prescribe for man the details of his social role: the Christian can live under different types of State and in various associations. This does not entail disengagement from social responsibility and retreat into pure interiority. There are certain options imposed upon us by the Decalogue as re-interpreted in the New Testament, and they may well draw the Church and the individual Christian into conflict with the powers of this world. Yet the particular 're-groupings' which the determined pursuit of such goals (the defence of the family and conjugal fidelity; of the victims of injustice; of the unborn; and of human rights wherever they are in jeopardy) may necessitate can never receive any general or permanent mandate from the Church. Since Christian eschatology locates theocracy only at the end of time, the Gospel of which that eschatology is a crucial part must imply the relativity of all political and social schemes. Indeed, Ratzinger goes so far as to call the recognition of such pluralism something 'constitutive of Christianity'.[61] The believing community does not find its unity in social or political praxis, but in the obliging power of the truth.

So much for the pluralism which should be found in the Church's relations with civil society. What, then, of pluralism in the domain of theology itself? When we have done justice to the factor of unity, recognising that, in the inn of the Church the menu is *table d'hôte*, a determinate faith to be shared by those who can and wish to accept it, what scope remains for the factor

[61] Ibid. p. 306.

of plurality? Is the life of the Church to be reduced to a monolith, a uniformed army of look-alikes on the march? By no means. Ratzigner points out that this question was already answered by the primitive Church which spoke of *symphonia* in order to express its perception of the 'synthesis between unity and multiplicity' which is found within the ecclesial community.[62]

This *symphonia* may be thought of on four levels. First, there is the level of the Bible itself, which knows the plurality of 'prophets and apostles': the Old and New Testaments, and the internal diversity which characterises each of those two collections. Appealing to texts of Clement of Alexandria, Methodius of Olympus and Eusebius, Ratzinger holds that this is a matter of the

> fundamental form of the expression of truth in the Church, resting as this truth does on a complex *ensemble*, rich in tensions. The voice of the faith is not heard as mono-phony, but as symphony; not as a monophonic chant but as a composition in polyphony, with many notes which seem dissonant.... To lay aside one of the themes of this symphony is to impoverish the whole. The Fathers called this attitude 'heresy': that is, a simplificatory choice, for only in the totality with its tensions is the truth to be found.[63]

Secondly, there is the *symphonia* of Christians among themselves. The Church's own kind of unity reflects the expressive form of revealed truth. No empirical element can give this Church of so diverse a humanity its unity: that unity is the gift of a non-empirical reality – the Holy Spirit. And Athanasius, whose *Contra Arianos* Ratzinger appeals to in this connexion, also provided the reference cited in support of a

[62]Ibid. p. 307.
[63]Ibid.; Clement of Alexandria, *Stromateis* 6, 15; Methodius of Olympus, *De libero arbitrio* 1; Eusebius, *Historia ecclesiastica* VI. 31, 3.

third variety of *symphonia*, that between man and God which brings with it the unity of creation and Creator.[64] For the greater unity to which faith tends is not just that of socialisation in the fellowship of a group, but that profounder socialisation which consists in our communion with the divine. Finally, we must bear in mind that, as a fragment of Theodore of Heraclea's commentary on John's Gospel has it, man himself is a plural being who is in search of the integration of the 'contrasting forces of his own "I".'[65] The harmony which he receives from God as redemption may also be conceived as a symphony which does not suppress the multiple aspects of what it is to be human but draws them out of division into unity.

With this rich concept of *symphonia* as inspiration, then, what does Ratzinger have to say about the plurality of theologies as such? Until recently, the *noyau essentiel* of all theologies was located in the Creeds, and the conciliar dogmas and decisions. But today this claim is contested, on the grounds of the cultural conditioning of all human discourse. Such critics are not, Ratzinger remarks, distinguished for their logic:

> Either there is no possibility of the non-temporal understanding of language, in which case noone can forge new formulas of an adequate sort. Or there is such a possibility, in which case an interpretation that corresponds to the word of Scripture, leading back to that word rather than forsaking it, will suffice.[66]

Not for the first time, Ratzinger looks to the example of Guardini, who set his face against all historicism and pragmatism, affirming man's aptitude for truth, which aptitude confers on man his dignity, and makes his suffering supportable, and even great.

[64]Athanasius, *Adversus Arianos* 3, 23; *Epistola de synodis Arimini et Seleuciae* 48.
[65]Theodore of Heraclea, *Fragmenta in Joannem* 14, 27.
[66]PPPET p. 312.

The Church must have a voice, able to express herself as Church and to separate erroneous faith from true. That is: faith and theology are not identical; each has its own voice, but the voice of theology depends on faith and is ordered to it. Theology is, and must remain, explication of the faith. If it ceases to expound, but, finding fault with the substance of faith, changes it, giving itself a new text to comment, why, then it ceases to exist as theology.[67]

Faith and theology differ as a text and its explication. Unity is the domain of faith; pluralism that of theology. The permanence of the reference-points of faith is what makes possible plurality in theology. What Ratzinger terms 'fruitful pluralism' occurs wherever people bring together in one the multiple forms which the historic expression of the faith has taken, and do so:

without stifling this plurality, but giving it proper recognition in the organic inter-connectedness of that truth which transcends man[68]

Ratzinger confesses that he long had the impression that, as thinkers, heretics were a good deal more interesting than the Church's divines, at least in recent centuries. Yet, he goes on, still in personal vein:

When I consider the great theologians, from Möhler to Newman and Scheeben, from Rosmini to Guardini, or in our own epoch, de Lubac, Congar, Balthasar, how much richer and more truly contemporary is their message than that of those for whom the Church's fellowship has ceased to be. In these writers,

[67]Ibid. p. 314.
[68]Ibid. p. 316. On the seventh centenary of the death of St Thomas in 1974, Ratzinger had already praised the pluralism of mediaeval theology, as exemplified in the contrasting figures of Bonaventure and Thomas: see J. Ratzinger (ed.), *Aktualität der Scholastik* (Regensburg 1975), p. 77.

there is something else, too, that stands out: with them, pluralism happens not because it is willed, but because each of them, equipped in his own time with his own powers, seeks for nothing other than the truth. Wanting the truth: that involves not making oneself its measure but, instead, welcoming as the voice and highway of truth the immense perspectives that the faith of the Church offers.[69]

Writing in French, Ratzinger takes the obvious example: the greatness of French theology did not derive from its desire to do something French, but from its commitment to finding the truth and expressing it as well as possible. 'Only that pluralism is great which is directed towards unity'.[70] Or, as Professor Nicholas Lash has put it: 'The many theologies exist at the service of a common tradition'.[71]

By contrast to this 'fruitful pluralism' there is, however, a 'ruinous pluralism': a distinction obviously cognate with that offered by the fathers of the Extraordinary Synod of late autumn 1985 on the reception of the Second Vatican Council. In its 'Final Report' the Synod delcared:

> Pluriformity is a genuine richness and involves a completion, it is true catholicity; but the pluralism of deeply opposed positions leads to dissolution and destruction and the loss of identity.[72]

According to Ratzinger, such 'ruinous pluralism' is born when people have 'lost the ability to re-unite the great tensions

---

[69]PPPET p. 317.

[70]Ibid. p. 318.

[71]N. Lash, 'Theologies at the service of a common tradition', in C. Geffré et al. (ed.), *Different Theologies, Common Responsibility: Babel or Pentecost* (= *Concilium* 171; Edinburgh 1984), p. 82.

[72]*Final Report* II. C. 2.; = *Synod Report. The Final Report and Message to the People of God of the Extraordinary General Assembly of the Synod of Bishops. Rome, 24 November–8 December 1985 on the theme; The Second Vatican Council. A celebration, reaffirmation and a carrying forward of its work* (London 1986), p. 16.

internal to the totality of the faith'.[73] His own expression of the distinction is indebted to an ecclesiology of the Church as the corporate subject of her own Tradition. For believers, the Church is not simply a sociological phenomenon, but a unique subject, raised into being by the Holy Spirit and so transcending the otherwise insurmountable limitations of human subjectivity by placing history in touch with the source of reality itself. If one effaces the connexion with a subject traversing historically all history yet remaining self-identical through all its changes, there remains only 'contradictory and disordered linguistic fragments'.

> For the internal plurality of the symphony of faith there is substituted the dislocated pluralism of a home-made Christianity.[74]

The only 'home' in which Christianity can be made is that which God himself has established for it: the single, world-wide household of faith.

[73]PPPFT p. 316.
[74]Ibid.

CONCLUSION

The strength of the theology studied in this book lies principally in its combination of (1) a sense of the supreme *objectivity* of Christian revelation and of the patterns of life and thought which flow from it; (2) an awareness of *historicity*, of the importance of the historical medium via which both the once-for-all, unrepeatable origin and its mediation in tradition enter within our grasp; and (3) a conviction of the power of this revelation, duly received, to satisfy the deepest needs of human *subjectivity*. Naturally, it is quite possible that the strengths of this theology are only personal in part, otherwise deriving their merits from the wider theological culture in which a personal enterprise is embedded. In a long-sighted historical perspective, it may be pointed out that the German Enlightenment provided German-language theology, both Protestant and Catholic, with a philosophical culture that was far less rebarbatively unsympathetic to the theological task than was its counterpart in England. For the late German Enlightenment in particular:

> the starting-point of knowledge is experience – but not experience reducible to sensation. Thus the deeper sense of historical reality and of the historical evolution of religion (Lessing), and appeal to a doctrine of the whole man (Hamann), the intellectual intuition of faith in God (Jacobi), and the integration of monism and individuality leading to a view of history as the intelligible expression of nature and God (Herder), served to reinforce and enrich, rather than to contradict, the tendencies of the *Aufklärung*, bringing philosophy, religion and historiography together in powerful combination.

More particularly, the positive aspect of the German Enlightenment did two things of great value for theology. First,

292

it gave a strong impulse to the recognition that man is a being set within an historical world, so that

> all theological assertions about man must locate transcendental claims in the context of human historicity.

Secondly, and complementing the above:

> the view of productive reason derived from the German Enlightenment gave to theology an understanding of its task as constructive, revealing the theologian less as a reflector and analyst of a past tradition, but as the builder of a continuing tradition.[1]

Nevertheless, as the writer here cited, A. O. Dyson, stresses, the same heritage was also a flawed one. The Enlightenment's impulse towards the recognition of human historicity contained an underlying tendency towards relativism and nihilism. Moreover, German theology's character as a public discipline, deeply indebted to the presuppositions of culture, has rendered it vulnerable to domination by changing philosophical and other fashions. Finally, the same factor has led to a sharp tension between Church and theology, and in particular between 'the certitude of faith and the variability of critical findings'.[2] If this is so, then it says much for the integrity of Ratzinger's approach that he preserves the strengths of German theology, as here evoked by an English writer, and avoids its characteristic pitfalls.

While I hope that this book may have made a modest contribution to appreciation of the vigour and breadth of Ratzinger's thought, it is perhaps inevitable that to historians of the contemporary Church his name will remain linked to a

---

[1] A. O. Dyson, 'Theological legacies of the Enlightenment: England and Germany', in S. W. Sykes (ed.), England and Germany. Studies in Theological Diplomacy op cit., p. 60.
[2] Ibid. p. 61.

single issue: that of the reception of the Second Vatican Council in that communion of churches which constitutes the Roman Catholic Church throughout the world. The effect of Ratzinger's much publicised intervention, in an interview given to *Jesus*, an Italian monthly devoted to 'cultura e attualitá cristianà', later published in book form, was to encourage greater frankness about the shadow-side of the post-conciliar Church.[3] However, Ratzinger's criticisms were not made from the stand-point of a latter-day Ottaviani, lamenting in sackcloth and ashes his own 'progressive' role which had helped to undermine in the years of the Council the old *curiales* inherited from the Church of Pius XII. If he considered that in some ways what he termed the 'evil spirit of a narrow Scholastic orthodoxy' had been swept from the Christian household only to be replaced by seven spirits worse than the first,[4] he did not consider that this state of affairs had come about through excessive zeal for the Council's decisions but through their misapplication, not least by way of an inappropriately unilateral concentration of interest on *Gaudium et Spes*. The Extraordinary Synod of 1985, which set itself to consider the picture both as a whole and in detail, concurred with the judgment that it was a canvas in *chiaroscuro*, with light and shade in different areas.[5] The synodal fathers' Final Report was, however, more optimistic in tone than Ratzinger: Caravaggio to his Goya. But perhaps the difference is more one of genre than of substance. An individual may judge it timely to offer a prophecy of woe; a solemn gathering of the episcopate must bear in mind their duty not to undermine the theological virtue of hope.

The major constructive achievement of the Council was the

---

[3] V. Messori, 'A colloquio con il cardinale Joseph Raztinger: Ecco perché la fede è in crisi', art. cit.; idem., *A colloquio con il cardinale Joseph Ratzinger. Rapporto sulla fede* op. cit.
[4] PPPFT p. 31.
[5] *Final Report* I.3; = *Synod Report*, op. cit. p. 7.

recovery of the tradition of the pre-Tridentine Church, and notably of tradition in its crucial patristic phase when the Christian religion took on its classic form. It was a Council of patristic (and biblical) *ressourcement*, intended to usher Catholics into a larger room than that of the last few centuries. Moreover, the same theologians who forged this neo-patristic synthesis – essentially, the French and German language divines of the inter-war period – were convinced that it would provide a new basis on which to address the world of today and its problems. Its greater anthropological depth would enable the Church to be more human without becoming less divine.

Wholly admirable in itself, this programme turned out to have two flaws. First, though the Conciliar majority rightly perceived that 'traditional Catholicism' of the kind now represented by Archbishop Marcel Lefebvre and his followers was really little more ancient than their grandmothers, they underestimated the disorienting effect of its supplanting.

In depriving Catholics of the language in which they had habitually ordered their religious universe and through which they had come to their own self-understanding, the displacement of the immediately pre-conciliar tradition, essentially the product of the sixteenth century Catholic Reformation and the Catholic revival of the nineteenth century, generated a sense of *anomie*, an obscuring of corporate and personal identity. Though to some degree, this was inevitable once the Conciliar project was launched, had there been greater care and less iconoclasm the Church at large:

> might ... have endured (its) dislocation and diminishment less convulsively, more gracefully and with greater wisdom.[6]

Secondly, the unity of the Council's twin imperatives of

[6] R. B. Imbelli, 'Vatican II: twenty years later', *Commonweal* CIX. 17 (8 October 1982), p. 524.

ressourcement and *aggiornamento*, founded as this was on the theological anthropology of the Fathers, proved more fragile than had been expected. Once *aggiornamento* had parted company from *ressourcement*, adaptation could degenerate into mere accommodation to habits of mind and behaviour in secular culture. Using the excuse of pastoral necessity, *insouciance* towards the tradition as a whole might be justified or even obligatory in an effort to relate the hypothetically re-constructed Christian origin to contemporary needs and expectations. Many of those needs and expectations must, indeed, be taken with great seriousness. However, the manner in which the Christian origin ('the Gospel') is related ('relevant') to them cannot be determined by overshooting the past: that is what 'Tradition' means. The task today is to take forward the constructive moment of the Council's achievement: the binding of tradition and contemporaneity in a living unity. For this, the work of both historical and systematic theologians will play a part. The historical theologian echoes the words of Jesus in St John's Gospel:

Gather up the fragments left over, that nothing may be lost.[7]

The systematic theologian forges the language in which the meaning of Tradition may be received anew, in response to the concerns of the present-day, but also challenging, complementing and transforming those concerns by the divine power which Tradition holds. It is in its positive contribution to this two-fold project that the theology of Joseph Ratzinger must be judged.

[7]John 6, 12.

BIBLIOGRAPHY

This Bibliography is based on that assembled by H. Höfl in W. Baier et al. (ed.) *Weisheit Gottes – Weisheit der Welt. Festschrift für Joseph Kardinal Ratzinger zum 60. Geburtstag* (Sankt Ottilien 1987) pp 3*–77*. Thanks are due to the publishers EOS-Verlag, Erzabtei St Ottilien, D-8917, St Ottilien, West Germany.

A. Books

1. *Volk und Haus Gottes in Augustins Lehre von der Kirche* (Munich 1954).
2. *Die Geschichtstheologie des heiligen Bonaventura* (Munich 1959). E.T. *The Theology of History in St Bonaventure* (Chicago 1971).
3. *Die christliche Brüderlichkeit* (Munich 1960). E.T. *Christian Brotherhood* (London 1966).
4. *Der Gott des Glaubens und der Gott der Philosophen* (Munich 1960).
5. (With K. Rahner) *Episkopat und Primat* (Freiburg 1961). E.T. *The Episcopate and the Primacy* (London-Edinburgh-New York 1962).
6. *Die erste Sitzungsperiode des 2. Vatikanischen Konzils. Ein Rückblick* (Cologne 1963).
7. *Das Konzil auf dem Weg. Rückblick auf die zweite Sitzungsperiode* (Cologne 1964).
8. *Der gegenwärtige Stand der Arbeiten des Zweiten Vatikanischen Konzils* (Bonn 1964).
9. *Ergebnisse und Probleme der dritten Konzilsperiode* (Cologne 1965).
10. (With K. Rahner) *Offenbarung und Überlieferung* (Freiburg 1965). E.T. *Revelation and Tradition* (New York-London 1966).

11. *Probleme der vierten Konzilsperiode* (Bonn 1965).
12. *Vom Sinn des Christseins. Drei Adventspredigten* (Munich 1965). E.T. *Being Christian* (Chicago 1970).
13. *Die letzte Sitzungsperiode des Konzils* (Cologne 1966).
14. *Das Problem der Dogmengeschichte in der Sicht der katholischen Theologie* (Cologne-Opladen 1966).
15. *Die sakramentale Begründung christlicher Existenz* (Meitingen/Freising 1966).
16. *Theological Highlights of Vatican II* (New York 1966). [E.T. of 6, 7, 9, 13 above].
17. *Einführung in das Christentum. Vorlesungen über das Apostolische Glaubensbekenntnis* (Munich 1968). E.T. *Introduction to Christianity* (London 1969).
18. *Meditationen zur Karwoche* (Meitingen/Freising 1969).
19. *Das neue Volk Gottes. Entwürfe zur Ekklesiologie* (Düsseldorf 1969).
20. (With H. Maier) *Demokratie in der Kirche. Möglichkeiten, Grenzen, Gefahren* (Limburg 1970).
21. *Glaube und Zukunft* (Munich 1970). E.T. *Faith and Future* (Chicago 1971).
22. *Die Situation der Kirche heute. Hoffnungen und Gefahren* [with Cardinal J. Höffner] (Cologne 1970).
23. *Die Einheit der Nationen. Eine Vision der Kirchenväter* (Salzburg-Munich 1971).
24. (With H. U. v. Balthasar) *Zwei Plädoyers. Warum ich noch ein Christ bin. Warum ich noch in der Kirche bin* (Munich 1971). E.T. *Two Say Why. Why I am still a Christian. Why I am still in the Church* (Chicago-London 1971).
25. *Storia e dogma* (Milan 1971).
26. *Dogma und Verkündigung* (Munich 1973). E.T. *Dogma and Preaching* (Chicago 1983).
27. *Die Hoffnung des Senfkorns. Betrachtungen zu den 12 Monaten des Jahres* (Meitingen/Freising 1973).

28. (With U. Hommes) *Das Heil des Menschen. Innerweltlich-christlich* (Munich 1975).

29. *Der Gott Jesu Christi. Betrachtungen über den Dreieinigen Gott* (Munich 1976). E.T. *The God of Jesus Christ. Meditations on God the Trinity* (Chicago 1978).

30. *Erlösung, mehr als eine Phrase?* (Steinfeld 1977).

31. *Eschatologie – Tod und ewiges Leben* (Regensburg 1977). E.T. *Eschatology, Death and Eternal Life* (Washington 1988).

32. (With K. Lehmann) *Mit der Kirche leben* (Freiburg 1977). E.T. *Living with the Church* (Chicago 1978).

33. *Die Tochter Zion. Betrachtungen über den Marienglauben der Kirche* (Einsiedeln 1977). E.T. *Daughter Zion* (San Francisco 1983).

34. *Eucharistie – Mitte der Kirche. Vier Predigten* (Munich 1978).

35. *Gottes Angesicht suchen. Betrachtungen im Kirchenjahr* (Freising 1978). E.T. *Seeking God's Face* (Chicago 1982).

36. *Licht, das uns leuchtet. Besinnungen zu Advent und Weihnachten* (Freiburg 1978).

37. *'Ich glaube.' Strukturen des Christlichen* ed. W. Kraning (Leipzig 1979) [a selection from various works].

38. *Mitarbeiter der Wahrheit. Gedanken für jeden Tag* ed. I. Grassl (with images by R. Seewald) (Munich 1979).

39. *A Mustármag remény* (Eisenstadt 1979) [a selection from various works].

40. *Zum Begriff des Sakramentes* (Munich 1979).

41. *Konsequenzen des Schöpfungsglaubens* (Salzburg 1980).

42. (With H. U. v. Balthasar) *Maria – Kirche im Ursprung* (Freiburg 1980).

43. *Christlicher Glaube und Europa. 12 Predigten* (Munich 1981).

44. *Das Fest des Glaubens. Versuche zur Theologie des Gottesdienstes* (Einsiedeln 1981). E.T. *The Feast of Faith* (San Francisco 1986).

45. *Glaube – Erneuerung – Hoffnung. Theologisches Nachdenken über die heutige Situation der Kirche* ed. W. Kraning (Leipzig

1981) [a selection from various works].

46. *Umkehr zur Mitte. Meditationen eines Theologen* ed. G. Nachtwei (Leipzig 1981).

47. (With H. Schlier) *Lob der Weihnacht* (Freiburg 1982).

48. *Theologische Prinzipienlehre. Bausteine zur Fundamental-theologie* (Munich 1982). E.T. *Principles of Catholic Theology* (San Francisco 1987).

49. *Zeitfragen und christlicher Glaube. Acht Predigten aus den Münchner Jahren* (Würzburg 1982).

50. (With D. J. Ryan, G. Daneels, F. Macharski) *Die Krise der Katechese und ihre Überwindung. Rede in Frankreich* (Einsiedeln 1983).

51. *Demokratie, Pluralismus, Christentum* (Leutesdorf 1984).

52. *Schauen auf den Durchbohrten. Versuche zu einer spirituellen Christologie* (Einsiedeln 1984). E.T. *Behold the Pierced One* (San Francisco 1986).

53. *Il cammino pasquale* (Milan 1985). E.T. *Journey towards Easter* (Middlegreen 1987).

54. *Suchen, was droben ist. Meditationen das Jahr hindurch* (Freiburg 1985). E.T. *Seek that which is above* (San Francisco 1986).

55. *Rapporto sulla fede. Vittorio Messori a colloquio con Joseph Ratzinger* (Turin 1985). E.T. *The Ratzinger Report* (San Francisco 1985).

56. *Iglesia Comunicadora de Vida. Conferencias y Homilías pronunciadas en su visita al Perú* (Lima 1986).

57. *La devozione al Cuore di Gesù* (Casale Monferrato 1986).

58. *Im Anfang schuf Gott. Vier Münchener Fastenpredigten über Schöpfung und Fall* (Munich 1986).

59. *Politik und Erlösung. Zum Verhältnis von Glaube, Rationalität und Irrationalem in der sogenannten Theologie der Befreiung* (Opladen 1986).

60. *Kirche, Ökumene und Politik* (Einsiedeln 1987).

B. Articles

1954

1. 'Herkunft und Sinn der Civitas-Lehre Augustins' *Augustinus Magister* II (Paris 1954) pp 965–979; also in W. Lammers (ed.) *Geschichtsdenken und Geschichtsbild im Mittelalter* (Darmstadt 1961) pp 55–75.

1956

2. 'Beobachtungen zum Kirchenbegriff des Tyconius im "Liber regularum"' *Revue des études augustiniennes* 2 (1956) pp 173–185; also in *Das neue Volk Gottes* pp 11–23.
3. 'Das Konzil von Chalkedon' *Theologische Revue* 52 (1956) pp 103–122.
4. 'Die Kirche als Geheimnis des Glaubens' *Lebendiges Zeugnis* 4 (1956/57) pp 19–34; also as 'Vom Ursprung und vom Wesen der Kirche' in *Das neue Volk Gottes* pp 75–89.

1957

5. 'Der Einfluss des Bettelordensstreites auf die Entwicklung der Lehre vom päpstlichen Universalprimat' in *Theologie in Geschichte und Gegenwart. Festgabe für f. Michael Schmaus zum 60. Geburtstag* ed. J. Auer (Munich 1957) pp 697–724; also as 'Zum Einfluss des Bettelordensstreites auf die Entwicklung der Primatslehre', in *Das neue Volk Gottes* pp 49–71.
6. 'Originalität und Überlieferung in Augustins Begriff der Confessio' *Revue des études augustiniennes* 3 (1957) pp 375–392.

1958

7. 'Gedanken zur Krise der Verkündigung' *Klerusblatt* 38 (1958) pp 211f, 235ff.
8. 'Die neuen Heiden und die Kirche' *Hochland* 51 (1958/59) pp 1–11; also *Das neue Volk Gottes* pp 325–338.

9. 'Offenbarung – Schrift – Überlieferung. Ein Text des hl. Bonaventura und seine Bedeutung für die gegenwärtige Theologie' *Trierer Theologische Zeitschrift* 67 (1958) pp 13–27.
10. 'Vom Sinn des Advents' *Klerusblatt* 38 (1958) pp 418–420; also in *Dogma und Verkündigung* pp 373–382.

1959
11. 'Auferstehung und ewiges Leben' in T. Bogler (ed.) *Tod und Leben von den Letzten Dingen* (Maria Laach 1959) pp 92–103; also in *Dogma und Verkündigung* pp 301–314.
12. 'Paulinisches Christentum? Zu G. Schneider: Kernprobleme des Christentums. Studie zu Paulus, Evangelium und Paulinismus, Stuttgart 1959' *Hochland* 52 (1959/60) pp 367–375.
13. 'Primat, Episkopat und successio apostolica' *Catholica* 13 (1959) pp 260–277; also in *Theologisches Jahrbuch* 1962, pp 118–133.
14. 'Tod und Auferstehung. Erwägungen zum christlichen Verständnis des Todes' *Klerusblatt* 39 (1959) pp 366–370; also as 'Zur Theologie des Todes' in *Dogma und Verkündigung* pp 281–294.
15. 'Das unbesiegte Licht. Eine Ansprache' *Hochland* 52 (1959/60) pp 97–100; also as 'Drei Weihnachtsbetrachtungen' in *Dogma und Verkündigung* pp 383–399.
16. 'Das Geheimnis der Osternacht' *Klerusblatt* 39 (1959) pp 101f; also in *Dogma und Verkündigung* pp 341–347.

1960
17. 'Grundgedanken der eucharistischen Erneuerung des 20.Jahrhunderts' *Klernsblatt* 40 (1960) pp 208–211.
18. 'Licht und Erleuchtung. Erwägungen zu Stellung und Entwicklung des Themas in der abendländischen Geistesgeschichte' *Studium Generale* 13 (1960) pp 368–378.
19. 'Der Mensch und die Zeit im Denken des hl. Bonaventura'

in *L'homme et son destin d'après les penseurs du moyen âge* (Louvain-Paris 1960) pp 473–483.

20. 'Theologia perennis? Über Zeitgemäßheit und Zeitlosigkeit in der Theologie' *Wort und Wahrheit* 15 (1960) 179–188; E.T. 'The changeable and unchangeable in Theology' in *Theological Digest* 10 (1962) pp 71–76 [résumé].

21. 'Wesen und Weisen der auctoritas im Werk des hl. Bonaventura' in *Die Kirche und ihre Ämter und Stände. Festgabe für Kardinal Joseph Frings zum Goldenen Priesterjubiläum* ed. W. Corsten – A. Frotz – P. Linden (Cologne 1960) pp 58–72.

22. 'Zum Problem der Entmythologisierung des Neuen Testamentes' *Religionsunterricht an höheren Schulen* 3 (1960) pp 2–11.

1961

23. 'Bewußtsein und Wissen Christi. Zu E. Gutwengers gleichnamigem Buch' *Münchener Theologische Zeitschrift* (1961) pp 78–81.

24. 'Christlicher Universalismus. Zum Aufsatzwerk H. U. v. Balthasars' *Hochland* 54 (1961/62) pp 68–76.

25. 'Christozentrik in der Verkündigung' *Trierer Theologische Zeitschrift* 70 (1961) pp 1–14; *Katechetische Blätter* 86 (1961) pp 299–310; *Theologisches Jahrbuch* 1962, 437–449, also (in revised form) in *Dogma und Verkündigung* pp 43–64.

26. 'Eine Theologie über Fatima. Zu Virgil Marions gleichnamigem Buch' *Münchener Theologische Zeitschrift* 12 (1961) pp 305–307.

27. 'Der Eucharistische Weltkongreß im Spiegel der Kritik' *Statio orbis* 1, ed. R. Egenter, O. Pirner, H. Hofbauer (Munich 1961) pp 227–242.

28. 'Die Kirche in der Frömmigkeit des hl. Augustinus' *Sentire ecclesiam. Das Bewußtsein von der Kirche als gestaltende Kraft der Frömmigkeit. Festschrift für Hugo Rahner zum 60. Geburtstag,* ed. J. Daniélou – H. Vorgrimler (Freiburg 1961) pp 152–175;

also in *Das neue Volk Gottes* pp 24–48.

29. 'Menschheit und Staatenbau in der Sicht der frühen Kirche' *Studium Generale* 14 (1961) pp 664–682.

30. 'Der Tod und das Ende der Zeiten' *Die Kirche und die Mächte der Welt. Seelsorge für morgen* ed. K. Rudolf (Vienna 1961) pp 97–107.

31. '"Wiedervereinigung im Glauben" in katholischer Sicht' *Klerusblatt* 41 (1961) pp 25–28.

32. 'Zur Theologie des Konzils' *Militärseelsorge* 4 (1961/62) pp 8–23; *Catholica* 15 (1961), pp 292–304; *Vatikanum Secundum I, Die erste Konzilsperiode*, ed. O. Müller (Leipzig 1963) pp 29–39; also (in revised form) in *Das neue Volk Gottes* pp 147–170.

1962

33. 'Freimut und Gehorsam. Das Verhältnis des Christen zu seiner Kirche, *Wort und Wahrheit* 17 (1962) pp 409–421; also in *Das neue Volk Gottes* pp 249–266. E.T. A. LaPierre (ed.) *The Church. Readings in Theology* (New York 1963) pp 194–217; 'Frank witness and docile obedience' in *Theological Digest* 13 (1965) 101–106 [résumé].

34. 'Gratia praesupponit naturam. Erwägungen über Sinn und Grenze eines scholastischen Axioms' in *Einsicht und Glaube. Festschrift für Gottlieb Söhngen zum 70 Geburtstag*, ed. H. Fries – J. Ratzinger (Freiburg 1962) pp 135–149; also in *Dogma und Verkundigung* pp 161–181.

35. 'Kritik an der Kirche? Dogmatische Bemerkungen. Kirche der Heiligen – Kirche der Sünder' *Test. Zeugnisse studentischer Sozialarbeit* 3 (1962) pp. 22–25.

36. 'Mariä Heimsuchung. Eine Homilie' *Bibel und Leben* 3 (1962) pp 138–140; also in *Dogma und Verkündigung* pp 411–414.

37. 'Der Stammbaum Jesu. Eine Homilie' *Bibel und Leben* 3 (1962) pp 275–278; also in *Dogma und Verkündigung* pp 317–321.

38. 'Vom Geist der Brüderlichkeit' *Horizonte* 1 (1962) 1f; also in *Dogma und Verkündigung* pp 235–237.

39. 'Vom Ursprung und Wesen der Kirche' in *Humanitas christiana. Werkblatt für das Erzbischöfliche Abendgymnasium Collegium Marianum Neuss* 6 (1962) pp 2–11; *Das neue Volk Gottes* pp 75–89; also as 'Die Kirche als Geheimnis des Glaubens' in *Lebendiges Zeugnis* 4 (1956/57), pp 19–34.

1963

40. 'Debatte über das Offenbarungsschema' *Klerusblatt* 43 (1963) pp 209f. E.T. 'The Second Vatican Council. The First Session' in *The Furrow* 14 (1963) 267–288.

41. 'Eine deutsche Ausgabe der Franziskuslegende Bonaventuras' *Wissenschaft und Weisheit* 26 (1963) pp 87–93.

42. 'Erwägungen zur dogmatischen und aszetischen Bedeutung der christlichen Brüderlichkeit' *Korrespondenzblatt des Collegium Canisianum* 97 (1963) pp 2–14; also as 'Bruderschaft und Brüderlichkeit' in *Pastoralkatechetische Hefte* 22 (1964) pp 9–35.

43. 'Das geistliche Amt und die Einheit der Kirche' *Catholica* 17 (1963) pp 165–179; also in J. C. Hampe (ed.) *Die Autorität der Freiheit* II (Munich 1967) pp 417–433; *Theologische Jahrbuch* 1969, pp 405–418; *Das neue Volk Gottes* pp 105–120. E.T. in *Journal of Ecumenical Studies* 1 (1964) pp 42–57; 'Office and Unity of the Church' in *Theological Digest* 14 (1966) pp 95–100.

44. 'Die Heilige Schrift und die Tradition' *Theologische-praktische Quartalschrift* III (1963) pp 224–227.

45. 'Sentire ecclesiam' *Geist und Leben* 36 (1963) pp 321–326.

46. 'Theologische Fragen auf dem II. Vaikanischen Konzil' *Protokoll der Dechanten-Konferenz vom 4.-6.6.1963* (Münster 1963) pp 10–15.

47. 'Die Vision der Väter von der Einheit der Völker' *Katholische Gedanke* 19 (1963) pp 1–9.

48. 'Wesen und Grenzen der Kirche' in *Das Zweite Vatikanische Konzil* ed. K. Forster (Würzburg 1963) pp 47–68; also as 'Der Kirchenbegriff und die Frage nach der Gliedschaft der Kirche' in *Das neue Volk Gottes* pp 90–104.

49. 'Der Wortgebrauch von natura und die beginnende Verselbständigung der Metaphysik bei Bonaventura' in P. Wilpert (ed.) *Die Metaphysik im Mitelalter* (Berlin 1963) pp 483–498.

1964

50. 'Atheismus' *Religionsunterricht an höheren Schulen* 7 (1964) pp 1–6; also in M. Schmaus – A. Läpple (ed.) *Wahrheit und Zeugnis* (Düsseldorf 1964) pp 94–100.

51. 'Der christliche Glaube und die Weltreligionen' in *Gott in Welt II. Festgabe für Karl Rahner zum 60. Geburtstag* ed. J. B. Metz et al. (Freiburg 1964) pp 287–305.

52. 'Ekklesiologische Bemerkungen zum Schema "de episcopis"' *Documentation Catholique* (1964) Nr. 135 pp 1–9.

53. 'Glückwünsche für K. Rahner' *Der Christliche Sonntag* 16 (1964) pp 75f.

54. 'Die Kirche und die Kirchen' *Reformatio* 13 (1964) pp 85–108.

55. 'Naturrecht, Evangelium und Ideologie in der katholischen Soziallehre; in *Christlicher Glaube und Ideologie* ed. K. v. Bismarck – W. Dirks (Berlin-Mainz 1964) pp 24–30.

56. 'Papst, Patriarch, Bischof' in J. C. Hampe (ed.) *Ende der Gegenreformation? Das Konzil. Dokumente und Deutung* (Stuttgart-Berlin-Mainz 1964) pp 155–163.

57. 'Zeichen unter den Völkern' in M. Schmaus – A. Läppe (ed.) *Wahrheit und Zeugnis* (Düsseldorf 1964) pp 456–466.

58. 'Zur Katechismuslehre von Schrift und Tradition' *Theologische Revue* 60 (1964) pp 217–224.

59. 'Zur Konzilsdiskussion über das Verhältnis von Schrift und Überlieferung' in F. Buschmann (ed.) *Das Zweite Vatikanum,*

Dritte Konzilsphase (Giessen 1964) pp 147–155.

60. 'Zurück zur Ordnung der Alten Kirche' in J. C. Hampe (ed.), *Ende der Gegenreformation? Das Konzil. Dokumente und Deutung* (Stuttgart-Berlin-Mainz 1964) pp 183f.

1965

61. 'Angesichts der Welt von heute. Überlegungen zur Konfrontation mit der Kirche im Schema XIII' *Wort und Wahrheit* 20 (1965) pp 493–504. Expanded version: 'Der Christ und die Welt von heute. Überlegungen zum sogenannten Schema XIII des Zweiten Vatikanischen Konzils' in J. B. Metz (ed.) *Weltverständnis im Glauben* (Mainz 1965) pp 143–160. Further revised as 'Der Christ und die Welt von heute' in *Dogma und Verkündigung* pp 183–204.

62. 'Das Geschick Jesu und die Kirche' in Y. Congar et al. *Kirche heute* (Bergen-Enkheim 1965) pp 7–18. E.T. *Church today* (Chicago 1968).

63. 'Nachfolge Christi' *Klerusblatt* 45 (1965) pp 140f. *Die Funkpostille* 1964/65, pp 99–104; also as 'Nachfolge' in *Dogma und Verkündigung* pp 141–145.

64. 'Over het Kerkbegrip der Vaders' *Documentation catholique dossiers* 4. *Veranderd Kerkbewustzijn* (Hilversum 1965) pp 18–30.

65. 'Die pastoralen Implikationen der Lehre von der Kollegialität der Bischöfe' *Concilium* (German edition) 1 (1965) pp 16–29; also in *Das neue Volk Gottes* pp 201–224.

66. 'Das Problem der Mariologie. Überlegungen zu einigen Neuerscheinungen' *Theologische Revue* 61 (1965) pp 73–82.

67. 'Die sakramentale Begründung christlicher Existenz' *'Blätter' Zeitschrift für Studierende* (Vienna) 20 (1965/66) pp 22–27; *Der grosse Entschluss. Monatsschrift für lebendiges Christentum* Vienna 21 (1966) pp 392–397.

68. 'Salus extra Ecclesiam nulla est' *Documentation catholique dossiers* 4. *Veranderd Kerkbewustzijn* (Hilversum 1965)

pp 42–50; revised as 'Kein Heil außerhalb der Kirche?' in *Das neue Volk Gottes* pp 339–361.

1966

69. 'Die bischöfliche Kollegialität. Theologische Entfaltung' in G. Barauna *De Ecclesia* II (Freiburg-Frankfurt 1966) pp 44–70.

70. 'Der Katholizismus nach dem Konzil – Katholische Sicht' in *Auf Dein Wort hin. 81. Deutscher Katholikentag* (Paderborn 1966) pp 245–266; *Klerusblatt* 46 (1966) pp 279–285; in expanded form 'Der Katholizismus nach dem Konzil' in *Das neue Volk Gottes* pp 302–321. E.T. in *The Furrow* 18 (1967) pp 3–23.

71. 'Vorwort' in P. Hacker *Das Ich im Glauben bei Martin Luther* (Graz 1966) pp 7–9.

72. 'Was heißt Erneuerung der Kirche?' *Diakonia* 1 (1966) pp 303–316; also in *Das neue Volk Gottes* pp 267–281.

73. 'Weltoffene Kirche? Überlegungen zur Struktur des Zweiten Vatikanischen Konzils' T. Filthaut (ed.) *Umkehr und Erneuerung. Kirche nach dem Konzil* (Mainz 1966) pp 273–291; also in *Das neue Volk Gottes* pp 281–301.

74. 'Zum Personverständnis der Dogmatik' in J. Speck (ed.), *Das Personverständnis in der Pädagogik und ihren Nachbarwissenschaften* (Münster 1966) pp 157–171. Also (in revised form) 'Zum Personverständnis in der Theologie', in: *Dogma und Verkündigung* pp 205–223.

1967

75. 'Christi Himmelfahrt' *Geist und Leben* 40 (1967) pp 81–84; also in *Dogma und Verkündigung* pp 361–366.

76. 'Einleitung zum Kommentar der Dogmatischen Konstitution über die göttliche Offenbarung des Zweiten Vatikanischen Konzils und Kommentar zu Kap. 1, 2 und 6 der Konstitution' *Lexikon für Theologie und Kirche.*

Supplementary Volume 2 (Freiburg 1967) pp 498–528; 571–581.

77. 'Gottlieb Söhngen' *Christ in der Gegenwart* 19 (1967) pp 182f.
78. 'Heilsgeschichte und Eschatologie. Zur Frage nach dem Ansatz des theologischen Denkens' in J. Neumann – J. Ratzinger (ed.) *Theologie im Wandel. Festschrift zum 150jährigen Bestehen der katholisch-theologischen Fakultät an der Universität Tübingen. 1817–1967* (Munich-Freiburg 1967) pp 68–89; *Theologisches Jahrbuch* 1970, pp 56–73; also as 'Heilsgeschichte, Metaphysik und Eschatologie' in *Theologische Prinzipienlehre* pp 180–199.
79. 'Ist die Eucharistie ein Opfer?' *Concilium* (German edition) 3 (1967) pp 299–304; *Theologisches Jahrbuch* (1969) pp 315–323.
80. 'Kardinal Frings. Zu seinem 80. Geburtstag' *Christ in der Gegenwart* 19 (1967) p 52.
81. 'Konzilsaussagen über die Mission außerhalb der Missionsdekrete' in J. Schütte (ed.) *Mission nach dem Konzil* (Mainz 1967) pp 21–47; also in *Das neue Volk Gottes* pp 376–403.
82. 'Das Menschenbild des Konzils in seiner Bedeutung für die Bildung' in *Christliche Erziehung nach dem Konzil. Berichte und Dokumentationen* 4, ed. Kulturbeirat beim Zentralkomitee der deutschen Katholiken (Cologne 1967) pp 33–65.
83. 'Das Problem der Absolutheit des christlichen Heilsweges' in W. Böld et al. *Kirche in der ausser christlichen Welt* (Regensburg 1967) pp 7–29; also in *Das neue Volk Gottes* pp 362–375. E.T. *Teaching all Nations* 4 (1967) pp 183–197.
84. 'Das Problem der Transsubstantiation und die Frage nach dem Sinn der Eucharistie' 147 (1967) *Theologische Quartalschrift* pp 129–158; *Theologisches Jahrbuch* 1969, pp 281–301.

1968
85. 'Die Bedeutung der Väter für die gegenwärtige Theologie'

Theologische Quartalschrift 148 (1968) pp 257–282; *Kleronomia* 1 (1969) pp 15–38; with discussion in T. Michels (ed.) *Geschichtlichkeit der Theologie* (Salzburg-Munich 1970) pp 63–95; also as 'Die Bedeutung der Väter im Aufbau des Glaubens' in *Theologische Prinzipienlehre* pp 139–159.

86. 'Kommentar zu Art. 11–22 der Pastoralkonstitution über die Kirche in der Welt von heute' *Lexikon für Theologie und Kirche. Supplementary Volume 3* (Freiburg 1968) pp 313–354.

87. 'Schwierigkeiten mit dem Apostolicum: Höllenfahrt – Himmelfahrt – Auferstehung des Fleisches' in P. Brunner et al., *Veraltetes Glaubensbekenntnis?* (Regensburg 1968) pp 97–123.

88. 'Tendenzen in der katholischen Theologie der Gegenwart' *Attempto* H. 29/30 (1968) pp 46–51.

89. ' "Vielleicht ist es aber wahr". Von der Unabweisbarkeit des Glaubens' *Orientierung* 32 (1968) pp 5–7.

90. ' "Von dannen er kommen wird, zu richten die Lebendigen und die Toten" ' *Hochland* 60 (1968) pp 493–498.

91. 'Zur Frage nach der Geschichtlichkeit der Dogmen,' *Martyria, Leiturgia, Diakonia. Festschrift für Hermann Volk zum 65. Geburtstag*, ed. O. Semmelroth with R. Haubst and K. Rahner (Mainz 1968) pp 59–70.

92. 'Zur Frage nach dem Sinn des priesterlichen Dienstes' *Geist und Leben* 41 (1968) pp 347–376. E.T. *Emmanuel* 76 (1970).

1969

93. 'Bemerkungen zur Frage der Charismen in der Kirche' *Korrespondenzblatt der Priestergemeinschaft des Collegium Canisianum zu Innsbruck* 104 (1969/70) pp 12–22; expanded version in *Die Zeit Jesu. Festschrift für Heinrich Schlier zum 70. Geburtstag*, ed. G. Bornkamm – K. Rahner (Freiburg 1970) pp 257–272.

94. 'De relatione inter conceptum historiae salutis et quaestionem eschatologicam' in D. Schönmetzer (ed.) *Acta*

congressus internationalis de theologica concilii Vaticani II (Rome 1969) pp 484–489.

95. 'Gibt es eine Zukunft – was kommt nach dem Tod?' in G. Rein (ed.) *Dialog mit den Zweifel* (Stuttgart 1969) pp 108–113; also as 'Für die Unsterblichkeit gerüstet? Die Bedeutung des christlichen Auferstehungsglaubens' in *Deutsche Zeitung. Christ und Welt* 47 (24.11.1972) Nr. 28; *Die Furche* 1973, Nr. 17, 8; W. Erk (ed.) *An die Hinterbliebenen. Gedanken über Leben und Weiterleben* (Stuttgart 1973) pp 206–211; also as 'Was kommt nach dem Tod?' in *Dogma und Verkündigung* pp 295–300.

96. 'Glaube, Geschichte und Philosophie. Zum Echo der "Einführung in das Christentum"' *Hochland* 61 (1969) pp 533–543.

97. 'Heil und Geschichte. Gesichtspunkte zur gegenwärtigen theologischen Diskussion des Problems der "Heilsgeschichte"' *Regensburger Universitätszeitung* 5 (1969), H. 11, 2–7; *Wort und Wahrheit* 25 (1970) pp 3–14; in revised form in *Theologische Prinzipienlehre* pp 159–179.

98. 'Kommentar zu Art. 26 der Kirchenkonstitution' in P. Foot et al., *Church* (New York 1969) p 57.

99. 'Nachwort des Theologen zu K. Hummel, Was Theologen nicht mehr sagen sollten. Überlegungen eines Naturwissenschaftlers' *Theologische Quartalschrift* 149 (1969) pp 343–349.

100. 'Der Priester im Umbruch der Zeit' *Klerusblatt* 49 (1969) pp 251–254; in revised form as 'Konturen der Kirche und des Priesters von morgen' in *Civitas* (Immensee) 25 (1969), pp 251–261.

101. 'Primat und Episkopat. Vortrag bei der Tagung des Institute of European Studies in Tübingen am 19.7.1964' in *Das neue Volk Gottes* pp 121–146. E.T. 'Primacy and episcopacy' in *Theological Digest* 19 (1971) pp 200–207 [résumé].

102. 'Schöpfungsglaube und Evolutionstheorie' in H. J. Schultz (ed.) *Wer ist das eigentlich – Gott?* (Munich 1969) pp 232–245; also in *Dogma und Verkündigung* pp 147–160.

103. 'Theologische Aufgaben und Fragen bei der Begegnung lutherischer und katholischer Theologie nach dem Konzil' in *Oecumenica* 1969 (ed.) F. W. Kantzenbach and V. Vatja, pp 251–270; also in *Das neue Volk Gottes* pp 225–245.

104. 'Der Verstand, der Geist und die Liebe. Eine Pfingstbetrachtung' *Die Rheinische Post* (24.5.1969), Nr. 119, n.p.; also in *Dogma und Verkündigung* pp 367–372.

105. 'Zur Theologie der Ehe' *Theologische Quartalschrift* 149 (1969) pp 53–74; G. Krems – R. Mumm (ed.) *Theologie der Ehe. Veröffentlichung des Ökumenischen Arbeitskreises evangelischer und katholischer Theologen. Mit einen Vorwort von L. Jäger und W. Stählin* (Regensburg 1969) pp 51–115; *Theologisches Jahrbüch* 1971, pp 881f; W. Ernst, *Moraltheologische Probleme in der Diskussion* (Leipzig 1971) pp 264f.

1970

106. 'Die anthropologischen Grundlagen der Bruderliebe' *Caritasdienst* 23 (1970) pp 45–49; *Pro Filia* 58 (1970) pp 109–118; *Dogma und Verkündigung* pp 239–253.

107. 'Der Holländische Katechismus. Versuch einer theologischen Würdigung' *Hochland* 62 (1970) 301–313; also as 'Theologie und Verkündigung im Holländischen Katechismus' in *Dogma und Verkündigung* pp 65–83. E.T. 'The Dutch Catechism: A Theological Appreciation' *The Furrow* 1971, pp 739–754.

108. 'Kirche – Dienst am Glauben' in E. Spath (ed.) *Offence Horizonte* (Freiburg 1970) pp 119–124; also as 'Kirche als Ort des Dienstes am Glauben' in *Dogma und Verkündigung* pp 255–262.

109. 'Il ministero sacerdotale.' *Osservatore Romano* 110

(28.5.1970), Nr. 121, pp 3; 8.

110. 'Schlusswort zu der Diskussion mit W. Kasper' *Hochland* 62 (1970) pp 157ff.

111. 'Vom Alpha zum Omega. Von der Vergöttlichung des Menschen im Opfer' *Die Presse* (Vienna) 28./29.3.1970, XV; also as 'Ostern heute' in *Dogma und Verkündigung* pp 353–359.

112. 'Der Weg der religiösen Erkenntnis nach dem heiligen Augustinus' *KYRIAKON Festschrift für Johannes Quasten zum 70. Geburtstag*, ed. P. Granfield – J. A. Jungmann (Münster 1970) II, pp 553–564.

113. 'Die Zeit der vierzig Tage. Predigt zum Aschermittwoch der Künstler in München' *Klerusblatt* 50 (1970) pp 75ff; also in *Dogma und Verkündigung* pp 323–330.

1971

114. 'Das Ganze im Fragment. Gottlieb Söhngen zum Gedächtnis' *Christ in der Gegenwart* 23 (1971) pp 398f; also as 'Von der Wissenschaft zur Weisheit' in *Catholica* 26 (1972) pp 2–6.

115. 'Interview für Redencion' in I. F. Görres – W. Lehmann – J. Ratzinger *Der gewandelte Thron. Bemerkungen zur Synode und anderes* (Freiburg 1971) pp 111–120.

116. 'Offenbarung und Transzendenzerfahrung' *Theologische Revue* 67 (1971) pp 11–14.

117. 'Widersprüche im Buch von Hans Küng' in K. Rahner (ed.) *Zum Problem der Unfehlbarkeit. Antworten auf die Anfrage von Hans Küng* Freiburg 1971) pp 97–116.

1972

118. Die Auferstehung Christi und die christliche Jenseitshoffnung' in G. Adler (ed.) *Christlich – was heißt das?* (Düsseldorf 1972) pp 34–37.

119. 'Die Bedeutung der Ökumene am Ort' *Osservatore romano* (German edition) 2 (8.12.1972) Nr. 49 pp 8–10; *Theologische*

Prinzipienlehre pp 314–327; expanded as 'Ökumene am Ort' in *Catholica* 27 (1973) pp 152–165.

120. 'Die Christologie im Spannungsfeld von altchristlicher Exegese und moderner Bibelauslegung' in *Urbild und Abglanz. Festgabe für Herbert Doms zum 80. Geburtstag*, ed. J. Tenzler (Regensburg 1972) pp 359–367.

121. 'Einheit der Kirche – Einheit der Menschheit. Ein Tagungsbericht' *Internationale Katholische Zeitschrift* 1 (1972) pp 78–83.

122. 'Das Geweissen in der Zeit' *Internationale Katholische Zeitschrift* 1 (1972) pp 432–442.

123. 'Jenseits des Todes' *Internationale Katholische Zeitschrift* 1 (1972) pp 231–244; also in A. Rosenberg (ed.) *Leben nach dem Sterben* (Munich 1974) pp 15–31.

124. 'Die Legitimität des christologischen Dogmas' *Estudios ecclesiásticos* 47 (1972) pp 487–503.

125. 'Metanoia als Grundbefindlichkeit christlicher Existenz' in E. C. Suttner (ed.) *Busse und Beichte. Drittes Regensburger Ökumenisches Symposion* (Regensburg 1972) pp 2–37; also as 'Glaube als Umkehr – Metanoia' in *Theologische Prinzipienlehre* pp 57–69.

126. 'Opfer, Sakrament und Priestertum in der Entwicklung der Kirche' *Catholica* 26 (1972) pp 108–125; *Theologische Prinzipienlehre* pp 263–281. E.T. *Theological Digest* 21 (1973) 100–105 [résume].

127. Der Priester als Mittler und Diener Christi' in P. Mai (ed.) *100 Jahre Priesterseminar in St. Jakob zu Regensburg. 1872–1972* (Regensburg 1972) pp 53–68; also as 'Der Priester als Mittler und Diener Jesu Christi im Licht der neutestamentlichen Botschaft' in *Theologische Prinzipienlehre* pp 281–299.

128. 'Taufe und Formulierung des Glaubens' *Didaskalia* 2 (1972) pp 23–34; *Ephemerides Theologicae Lovaniensis* 49 (1973) pp 76–86; also as 'Taufe and Formulierung des Glaubens – Traditionsbildung und Liturgie' in *Theologische*

Prinzipienlehre pp 106–116.

129. 'Was eint und was trennt die Konfessionen? Eine ökumenische Besinnung' *Internationale Katholische Zeitschrift* 1 (1972) pp 171–177.

130. 'Wozu noch Christentum?' *Lebendige Kirche. Mitteilungen des Diözesanrates im Erzbistum Köln* (Cologne 1972) pp 6–9; *Osservatore Romano* (German edition) 2 (1972), Nr. 23, 10; also in *Dogma und Verkundigung* pp 449–455.

131. 'Zur Frage nach der Unauflöslichkeit der Ehe. Bemerkungen zum dogmengeschichtlichen Befund und zu seiner gegenwärtigen Bedeutung' in F. Henrich – V. Eid (ed.) *Ehe und Ehescheidung. Diskussion unter Christen* (Munich 1972) pp 35–56.

1973

132. 'Abschied vom Teufel?' Diocesan Bulletins of:- Aachen (25.3.1973), Nr. 12 u. (1.4.1973), Nr. 13; Bamberg (11.3.1973), Nr. 10 u. (18.3.1973), Nr. 11; München (11.3.1973), Nr. 10 u. (18.3.1973), Nr. 11; Passau (11.3.1973), Nr. 10; Regensburg (11.3.1973), Nr. 10; Rottenburg (11.3.1973), Nr. 10, (18.3.1973), Nr. 11, (25.3.1973), Nr. 12 u. (1.4.1973), Nr. 13; Speyer (1.4.1973), Nr. 13; also in *Dogma und Verkündigung* pp 225–234.

133. 'Antwort [auf die Frage: Wer ist Jesus von Nazaret – für mich?] in H. Spaemann (ed.) *Wer ist Jesus von Nazaret – für mich? 100 zeitgenössische Antworten* (Munich 1973) pp 23–26; also as 'Was bedeutet Jesus Christus für mich?' in *Dogma und Verkündigung* pp 137–140.

134. 'Einleitung und Kommentar zu den Thesen I–VIII und X–XIL' *Internationale Theologenkommission* (ed.) *Die Einheit des Glaubens und der theologische Pluralismus* (Einsiedeln 1973) pp 11–51; 61–67.

135. 'Fragen zur Apostolischen Nachfolge. Zum Memorandum der sechs ökumenischen Universitätsinstitute' *Suchen und*

finden. Der katholische Glaube 22 (1973) pp 172–177.

136. 'Noch einmal: "Kurzformeln des Glaubens". Anmerkungen' *Internationale Katholische Zeitschrift* 2 (1973) pp 258–264; also as 'Kurzformeln des Glaubens? Über das Verhältnis von Formel und Auslegung' with an appendix 'Wandelbares und Unwandelbares in der Kirche' in *Theologische Prinzipienlehre* pp 127–139.

137. 'È partendo da Cristo che l'altro diventa prossimo' *Settimana del clero*, Nr. 40, Nov. 1973.

138. 'Les "Sources Chrétiennes" et la "source unique"' *Bulletin des amis de 'Sources chrétiennes'* Nr. 29 (May 1973) pp 28–32.

139. 'Verkündigung von Gott heute' *Internationale Katholische Zeitschrift* 2 (1973) pp 342–355; also in *Dogma und Verkündigung* pp 101–118; *Theologische Jahrbuch* 1975, pp 336–348. E.T. 'Preaching about God today' in *International Catholic Review* 1 (1974) pp 450–462; *Theological Digest* 22 (1974) pp 196–201.

140. 'Vom Sinn des Kirchbaus' *Kirchenbau in der Diskussion. Ausstellungskatalog* (Munich 1973); also in *Dogma und Verkündigung* pp 269–274.

141. 'Vorfragen zu einer Theologie der Erlösung' in L. Scheffczyk (ed.) *Erlösung und Emanzipation* (Freiburg 1973) pp 141–155.

1974

142. 'Dogma in Geschichte. Marginalien zu einem "Versuch einer Kritik des Dogmatismus"' *Theologische Revue* 70 (1974) pp 89–96.

143. 'Das Ende der Bannflüche von 1054. Folgen für Rom und die Ostkirchen' *Internationale Katholische Zeitschrift* 3 (1974) pp 289–303; also as 'Anathema – Schisma. Die ekklesiologischen Folgerungen der Aufhebung der Anathemata' in *Pro Oriente. Auf dem Weg zur Einheit des Glaubens* (Innsbruck Vienna-Munich 1976) pp 101–113;

Theologisches Jahrbuch 1976 pp 576–589; also as 'Rom und die Kirchen des Ostens nach der Aufhebung der Exkommunikation von 1054' in *Theologische Prinzipienlehre* pp 214–230.

144. 'Der Heilige Geist als communio. Zum Verhältnis von Pneumatologie und Spiritualität bei Augistinus' C. Heitmann – H. Mühlen (ed.) *Erfahrung und Theologie des Heiligen Geistes* (Hamburg-Munich 1974) pp 223–238.

145. 'Institución, Carisma, Sacramentos' Conferencia Episcopal de Colombia, *Cuestiones actuales de Teología* (Bogotá 1974) pp 55–118.

146. 'Magistero della chiesa, fede, morale' *Osservatore Romano* 114 (15.12.1974), Nr. 289, 3f; expanded in J. Ratzinger, M. J. Le Guillou, H. U. v. Balthasar *Problemi della chiesa, oggi* (Milan 1976) pp 1–15.

147. 'Ökumenisches Dilemma? Zur Diskussion um die Erklärung "Mysterium Ecclesiae" *Internationale Katholische Zeitschrift* 3 (1974) pp 56–63; *Osservatore Romano* (German edition) 4 (1974), Nr. 33 pp 6f; also as 'Ökumene in der Sackgasse? Anmerkungen zur Erklärung "Mysterium Ecclesiae"' in *Theologische Prinzipienlehre* pp 241–250.

148. (With S. Horn) 'The Structure of the Church' [in Japanese] in L. Elders – H. van Straelen (ed.) *Fides et theologia* (Tokyo 1974) pp 43–71.

149. 'Tradition und Fortschritt' *ibw-Journal* 12 (1974) pp 1–7; *Freiheit des Menschen* ed. A. Paus (Graz 1974) pp 9–30; *Theologisches Jahrbuch* 1979, pp 189–203; 'Anthropologische Grundelgung des Begriffs Uberlieferung' in *Theologische Prinzipienlehre* pp 88–106.

150. 'Zur theologischen Grundlegung der Kirchenmusik' in *Gloria Deo – Pax hominibus Festschrift zum 100 jährigen Bestehen der Kirchenmusikschule Regensburg* (Regensburg 1974) pp 39–62; Klerusblatt 55 (1975) pp 263–267; also in *Das Fest des Glaubens* pp 86–110.

317

1975

151. ' "Auferbaut aus lebendigen Steinen" ' in W. Seidel (ed.) *Kirche aus lebendigen Steinen* (Mainz 1975) pp 30–48.

152. 'Bedarf der Christ des Alten Testaments? Eine Anmerkung zu Meinrad Limbecks gleichnamigem Artikel' *Herder Korrespondenz* 29 (1975) 253f.

153. 'Bildung und Glaube in unserer Zeit. Drei Thesen zur christlichen Bildung' *ibw-Journal* 13 (1975) pp 113–116: 'Glaube und Bildung', in *Theologische Prinzipienlehre* pp 349–359.

154. 'Christ sein – plausibel gemacht' *Theologische Revue* 71 (1975) pp 353–364. (s.u. E 35) *Unsere Seelsorge* 26 (1976) pp 28–33. E.T. *Doctrine und Life* 27 (1977), Nr. 5, 3–17.

155. 'Gebet und Meditation' in W. Rupp (ed.) *Beten – leben – meditieren* (Würzburg 1975) pp 76–81.

156. ' "Ich glaube an Gott den allmächtigen Vater" '. *Internationale Katholische Zeitschrift* 4 (1975) pp 10–18; W. Sandfuchs (ed.) *Ich glaube* (Würzburg 1975) pp 13–24. Revised in W. Sandfuchs (ed.) *Brückenbau im Glauben* (Leipzig 1979) pp 17–29. 'Glaube als Erkenntnis und als Praxis – die Grundoption des christlichen Credo', in *Theologische Prinzipienlehre* pp 69–78.

157. 'Kirchliches Lehramt – Glaube – Moral' J. Ratzinger et al. *Prinzipien christlicher Moral* (Einsiedeln 1975) pp 41–66. E.T. 'Magisterium of the Church, Faith, Morality', in *Readings in Moral Theology Nr. 2: The Distinctiveness of Christian Ethics*, ed. E. Curran – R. A. McCormick (New York 1980) pp 174–189.

158. 'Theologie und Ethos'. K. Ulmer – H. Kohlenberger (ed.) *Die Verantwortung der Wissenschaft* (Bonn 1975) pp 46–61.

159. 'Theologische Fakultät und Seelsorge' *Klerusblatt* 55 (1975) p 39.

160. 'Vorwort' in S. Harkianakis, *Orthodoxe Kirche und Katholizismus. Ähnliches und Verschiedenes* (Munich 1975)

pp 7–10.

161. 'Was ist für den christlichen Glauben heute konstitutiv?' in *Mysterium der Gnade. Festschrift für Johann Auer zum 65. Geburtstag* ed. H. Roßmann – J. Ratzinger (Regensburg 1975) pp 11–19; also in *Theologische Prinzipienlehre* pp 15–27.

162. 'Der Weltdienst der Kirche. Auswirkungen von Gaudium et spes im letzten Jahrzehnt' *Internationale Katholische Zeitschrift* 4 (1975) pp 439–454; A. Bauch – A. Gläßer – M. Seybold (ed.) *Zehn Jahre Vaticanum II* (Regensburg 1976) pp 36–53; also as 'Kirche und Welt: Zur Frage nach der Rezeption des II. Vatikanischen Konzils' in *Theologische Prinzipienlehre* pp 395–411.

1976

163. 'A dieci anni dal Vaticano II' *Rivista del clero italiano* 57 (1976) pp 2–4.

164. 'Kirchenmusikberuf als liturgischer und pastoraler Dienst' in F. Fleckenstein (ed.) *Kirchenmusik im Gespräch. Ansparchen, Reden, Grussworte, Diskussionsbeiträge zur 100-Jahrfeier der Kirchenmusikschule Regensburg vom 21.–27.5.1975* (Bonn 1976) pp 24–27.

165. 'Die kirchliche Lehre vom sacramentum ordinis' in *Pluralisme et Oecuménisme en Recherches Théologiques. Mélanges offerts au R.P. Dockx O.P.* (Paris 1976) pp 155–166; *Internationale Katholische Zeitschrift* 10 (1981) 435–445; also as 'Das Weihesakrament (Ordo) als sakramentaler Ausdruck des Prinzips Überlieferung' in *Theologische Prinzipienlehre* pp 251–263.

166. 'Meditationen' *Pastoralblatt für d. Diözesen Aachen, Berlin, Essen, Köln, Osnabrück* 28 (1976) pp 1, 33, 65, 97, 129, 161, 193, 225, 257, 289, 321, 353.

167. 'Prognosen für die Zukunft des Ökumenismus' *Bausteine für die Einheit der Christen* 17 (1977) H. 65 pp 6–14; *Ökumenisches Forum. Grazer Hefte für konkrete Ökumene* 1

(1977) pp 31–41; *Pro Oriente. Ökumene – Konzil – Unfehlbarkeit* (Innsbruck 1979) pp 208–215; also as 'Die ökumenische Situation – Orthodoxie, Katholizismus und Reformation' in *Theologische Prinzipienlehre* pp 203–214; and as 'Die Zukunft der Ökumene' in *Regensburger Bistumsblatt* Nr. 8 (20.2.1977) p 6. E.T. 'The future of ecumenism' in *Theological Digest* 25 (1977) pp 200–205 [résumé].

168. 'Stimme des Vertrauens. Kardinal Frings auf dem Zweiten Vaticanum' in *Ortskirche im Dienst der Weltkirche. Festgabe für die Kölner Kardinäle Höffner und Frings* ed. N. Trippen – W. Mogge (Cologne 1976) pp 183–190.

169. 'Taufe, Glaube und Zugehörigkeit zur Kirche' *Internationale Katholische Zeitschrift* 5 (1976) pp 218–234; also in *Theologische Prinzipienlehre* pp 28–45. E.T. 'Baptism, Faith and Membership in the Church' in *Theological Digest* 25 (1977) pp 126–131 [résumé].

170. 'Wer verantwortet die Aussagen der Theologie? Zur Methodenfrage' in H. U. v. Balthasar et al. *Diskussion über Hans Küngs 'Christ sein'* (Mainz 1976) pp 7–18.

1977

171. 'Alcune forme bibliche ed ecclesiali di "presenza" dello Spirito nella storia' in L. Sartori (ed.) *Spirito santo e storia* (Rome 1977) pp 51–64.

172. 'Eschatologie und Utopie' *International Katholische Zeitschrift* 6 (1977) pp 97–110; O. Schatz (ed.) *Abschied von Utopia? Anspruch und Auftrag der Intellektuellen* (Graz 1977) pp 193–210. E.T. 'Eschatology and Utopia' in *International Catholic Review* 5 (1978) pp 211–227.

173. 'Die Gabe der Weisheit' in W. Sandfuchs (ed.) *Die Gaben des Geistes. Acht Betrachtungen* (Würzburg 1977) pp 35–48; also in *Theologische Prinzipienlehre* pp 372–382.

174. 'Gestalt und Gehalt der eucharistischen Feier' *Internationale Katholische Zeitschrift* 6 (1977) 385–396; also in *Das Fest des*

Glaubens pp 31–54. E.T. 'Form and content in the Eucharist' in *Theological Digest* 26 (1978) pp 117–121 [résumé].

175. 'Il sacerdozio dell'uomo: un'offesa ai diritti della donna?' *Osservatore Romano* 117 (26.3.1977) Nr. 70 pp 1f.

176. 'Ist der Glaube wirklich "Frohe Botschaft"?' in H. Boelaars – R. Tremblay (ed.) *In libertatem vocati estis. Miscellanea Bernhard Häring zum 65. Geburtstag* (Rome 1977) pp 523–533.

177. 'Kirche als Heilssakrament' in J. Reikerstorfer (ed.) *Zeit des Geistes. Zur heilsgeschichtlichen Herkunft der Kirche* (Vienna 1977) pp 59–70; also in *Theologische Prinzipienlehre* pp 45–47.

178. 'Liturgie – wandelbar oder unwandelbar? Fragen an J. Ratzinger' *Internationale Katholische Zeitschrift* 6 (1977) pp 416–427; *Musica Sacra* 98 (1978) pp 114–117.

179. 'Meditationen' *Pastoralblatt für die Diözesen Aachen, Berlin, Essen, Köln, Osnabrück* 29 (1977) pp 1, 33, 65, 97, 129, 161, 193, 225, 257, 289, 321, 353.

180. 'Der Stärkere und der Starke. Zum Problem der Mächte des Bösen in der Sicht des christlichen Glaubens in M. Adler et al. *Tod und Teufel in Klingenberg. Eine Dokumentation* (Aschaffenburg 1977) pp 84–101.

181. 'Wissenschaft – Glaube – Wunder' in L. Reinisch (ed.) *Jenseits der Erkenntnis* (Frankfurt 1977) pp 28–44.

182. 'Zum Zölibat der katholischen Priester' *Stimme der Zeit* 195 (1977) pp 781–783.

1978

183. 'Anmerkungen zur Frage einer "Anerkennung" der Confessio Augustana durch die katholische Kirche' *Münchener Theologische Zeitschrift* 29 (1978) pp 225–237; also as 'Klarstellugen zur Frage einer "Anerkennung" der Confessio Augustana durch die katholische Kirche' in *Theologische Prinzipienlehre* pp 230–240.

184. 'Aus meinem Leben' in K. Wagner – A. H. Ruf (ed.) *Kardinal Ratzinger. Der Erzbischof von München und Freising in*

Wort und Bild (Munich 1978) pp 54–67.

185. 'Intervenciones' Congreso Mariano Nacional, *Memorias.* T. II (Guayaquil 1978) pp 21–44.

186. 'Kirche und wissenschaftliche Theologie' in W. Sandfuchs (ed.) *Die Kirche* (Würzburg 1978) pp 83–95; also in *Theologische Prinzipienlehre* pp 339–348. E.T. 'The Church and Scientific Theology' in *International Catholic Review* (1980) pp 332–342.

187. 'Der Primat des Papstes und die Einheit des Gottesvolkes' in J. Ratzinger (ed.) *Dienst an der Einheit. Zum Wesen und Anfang des Petrusamtes* (Düsseldorf 1978) pp 165–179.

188. 'Theologische Probleme der Kirchenmusik' *Theologische Probleme der Kirchenmusik* ed. R. Walter in collaboration with the directors of church music in the diocese of Rottenburg-Stuttgart (Rottenburg 1978); also as 'Die künstlerische Transposition des Glaubens. Theologische Probleme der Kirchenmusik' in *Musica Sacra* 99 (1979) pp 129–135; *Internationale Katholische Zeitschrift* 9 (1980) pp 148–157. E.T. in R. A. Skeris (ed.) *Crux et cithara* (Altötting 1983) pp 214–222.

189. 'Vom Verstehen des Glaubens. Anmerkungen zu K. Rahners Grundkurs des Glaubens; *Theologische Revue* 74 (1978) pp 177–186.

190. 'Wandelbares und Unwandelbares in der Kirche' *Internationale Katholische Zeitschrift* 7 (1978) pp 182–184.

191. 'Zum Geleit' in R. Graber *Stärke deine Brüder. Predigten, Ansprachen, Vorträge* (Regensburg 1978) pp 17f.

192. 'Zur Frage nach der Struktur der liturgischen Feier' *Internationale Katholische Zeitschrift* 7 (1978) pp 488–497; also in *Das Fest des Glaubens* pp 55–67.

1979

193. 'Erwägungen zur Stellung von Mariologie und Marienfrömmigkeit im Ganzen von Glaube und Theologie'

Die deutschen Bischöfe (ed.) *Maria die Mutter des Herrn* (Bonn 1979) pp 13–27; also in J. Ratzinger – H. U. v. Balthasar *Maria – Kirche im Ursprung* (Freiburg 1980) pp 15–40. *Theologisches Jahrbuch* 1983 pp 137–166.

194. 'Europa – verpflichtendes Erbe für die Christen. Tagung der katholischen Akademie in Bayern: "Europa und die Christen" v. 28./29.4.1979' *Zur debatte* 9 (1979) pp 1–4; in F. König – K. Rahner (ed.) *Europa. Horizonte der Hoffnung* (Graz 1983) pp 61–74.

195. 'Kleine Korrektur. Zur Frage der Eucharistie' *Internationale Katholische Zeitschrift* 8 (1979) pp 381f; expanded as 'Anmerkung zur Frage der Zelebrationsrichtung' in *Das Fest des Glaubens* pp 121–126.

196. 'Préface' in Commission théologique internationale: Ph. Delhaye et al., *Problèmes doctrinaux du mariage chrétien* (Louvain-la-Neuve 1979) pp 7–12.

197. 'Sparsam sein mit Bühnenauftritten. Gespräch mit Joseph Kardinal Ratzinger' *Lutherische Monatschifte* 18 (1979) pp 732–736.

198. 'Was ist Theologie? Rede zum 75. Geburtstag von Hermann Kardinal Volk' *Internationale Katholische Zeitschrift* 8 (1979) pp 121–128; also in *Theologische Prinzipienlehre* pp 331–339.

1980

199. 'Dorothea von Montau' in W. Herbstrith (ed.) *Zeugen der Wahrheit* (Munich 1980) pp 63–66.

200. 'Erfahrung und Glaube. Theologische Bemerkungen zur katechetischen Dimension des Themas' *Internationale Katholische Zeitschrift* 9 (1980) pp 58–70; also as 'Glaube und Erfahrung' in *Theologische Prinzipienlehre* pp 359–370.

201. 'Europa: Erstanden aus dem christlichen Glauben' in R. Hammerschmid (ed.) *Eine Pilgerreise durch Polen* (Kevelaer 1980) pp 55–64.

202. 'Geleitwort' in H. Schlier *Der Geist und die Kirche* (Freiburg 1980) pp VII–X.

203. 'Gemeinde aus der Eucharistie' in W. Hülsbusch (ed.) *800 Jahre St Martini Münster* (Münster 1980) pp 32–34.

204. 'La sinfonia della Croce: "La conoscenza di Dio che rifulge sul volto di Cristo"' *Antonianum* 55 (1980) pp 280–286.

205. (With International Theological Commission) 'Quaestiones selectae de Christologia. Sessio plenaria 1979, relatio conclusiva' *Gregorianum* 61 (1980) pp 609–632.

206. 'Theologie und Kirchenpolitik' *Internationale Katholische Zeitschrift* 9 (1980) pp 425–434; L. S. Schulz (ed.) *Wem nützt die Wissenschaft?* (Munich 1981) pp 106–117.

207. 'Das "Vater unser" sagen dürfen' in R. Walter (ed.) *Sich auf Gott verlassen. Erfahrungen mit Gebeten* (Freiburg 1980) pp 64–69; and A. L. Balling (ed.) *Mit tausend Flügeln trägst du mich. Gebete, die froh machen* (Freiburg 1986) pp 15–22.

208. 'Wort bei der Schlußversammlung der Augsburger CA-Festtage (29.6.1980)' *Unam Sanctam* 35 (1980) pp 199.

209. 'Worte der Widmung' *Gottesherrschaft – Weltherrschaft. Festschrift für Bischof Rudolf Graber* ed. J. Auer – F. Mussner – G. Schweizer (Regensburg 1980) pp 7–9.

210. 'Zwischen Tod und Auferstehung' *Internationale Katholische Zeitschrift* 9 (1980) pp 209–223; *Theologisches Jahrbuch* 1984, pp 274–287.

1981

211. 'Das I Konzil von Konstantinopel 381. Seine Voraussetzungen und seine bleibende Bedeutung' *Internationale Katholische Zeitschrift* 10 (1981) pp 555–563; also as 'Das Credo von Nikaia und Konstantinopel: Geschichte, Struktur und Gehalt' in *Theologische Prinzipienlehre* pp 116–127.

212. 'L'essentiel del propositions élaborées par le Synode' J. Potin (ed.) *Aujourd'hui la famille* (Paris 1981) pp 281–303. See

also Rapport d'introduction, *ibid.* pp 25–43; Deuxième rapport, *ibid.* pp 221–232; also as 'Le message du Synode 1980. Présenté par le Cardinal J. Ratzinger' in *Esprit et Vie* 91 (1981) pp 241–252. Abbreviated as:- 'Le lendemain du Synode 1980', in: *Louvain* 1 (1981) pp 8–23.

213. 'Freiheit und Bindung in der Kirche. Vortrag auf dem IV. Internationalen Kongreß für Kirchenrecht, Fribourg (Suisse) 6–11.10.1980' E. Corecco et al. (ed.) *Die Grundrechte des Christen in Liebe und Gesellschaft* (Fribourg/Freiburg/Milan 1981) pp 37–52; see also *Verein der Freunde der Universität Regensburg* H. 7 (Regensburg 1981) pp 5–21.

214. 'Geleitwort' in L. Weimer *Die Lust an Gott und seiner Sache oder Lassen sich Gnade und Freiheit, Glaube und Vernunft, Erlösung und Befreiung vereinbaren?* (Freiburg 1981) p 5f.

215. 'Hort des Glaubens und der Hoffnung' *Benedikt 480–1980. Ettal 1330–1980. Festschrift zum Ettaler Doppeljubiläum 1980* ed. A. Kalff with L. Koch (Ettal 1981) pp 50–53.

216. 'Sicherheit im Aspekt der Sozialethik' in P. C. Compes (ed.) *Sicherheit – verwirklichbar, vergleichbar, tragbar?* (Wuppertal 1981) pp 17–27; also as 'Technische Sicherheit als sozialethisches Problem' in *Internationale Katholische Zeitschrift* 11 (1982) pp 51–57; *Theologisches Jahrbuch* 1984 pp 245–251; M. Spangenberger (ed.) *Technik und Ökonomie im Lichte sozialethischer Fragestellungen* (Cologne 1985) pp 24–34. E.T. 'Technological Security as a Problem of Social Ethics' in *International Catholic Review* 9 (1982) pp 238–246.

217. 'Theologische Grundlagen der Kirchenmusik' in B. Moser (ed.) *Das christliche Universum* (Munich 1981) p 362.

1982

218. 'Geleitwort' in Ph. Delhaye – L. Elders (ed.) *Episcopale munus. Recueil d'études sur le ministère épiscopal offertes en hommage à Son Excellence Msgr. J. M. Gijsen* (Assen 1982)

pp XI–XVI.

219. 'Interpretation – Kontemplation – Aktion. Überlegungen zum Auftrag einer Katholischen Akademie in *25 Jahre Katholische Akademie in Bayern* (Munich 1982); *Internationale Katholische Zeitschrift* 12 (1983) pp 167–179.

220. 'Matrimonio e famiglia nel piano di Dio' *Familaris consortio* (Vatican City 1982) pp 77–88; also in *Osservatore Romano* (German edition) 12 (1982) Nr. 25 pp 8f.

221. 'Misterio Pascual y culto al Corazón de Jesus' *Tierra nueva* 11 (1982) pp 77–86. E.T. 'The Paschal Mystery as Core and Foundation of Devotion to the Sacred Heart' in *Towards a Civilization of Love. A Symposium on the Scriptural and Theological Foundations of the Devotion to the Heart of Jesus* (San Francisco 1985).

222. 'Stellungnahme zum offiziellen orthodox-katholischen Dialog' *Ut omnes unum* 45 (1982) pp 154–158.

223. 'Über die Wurzeln des Terrors in Deutschland' in D. Froitzheim – A. Wienand (ed.) *Almanach für das Erzbistum Köln* (*Zweite Folge*) (Cologne 1982) pp 99–103.

224. '"Wähle das Leben." Eine Firmhomilie' *Internationale Katholische Zeitschrift* 11 (1982) pp 444–449.

225. 'Was feiern wir am Sonntag' *Internationale Katholische Zeitschrift* 11 (1982) pp 226–231.

1983

226. 'Anglican-Catholic Dialogue: Its problems and hopes' *Insight. A Journal for church and community* I (1983) pp 2–11.

227. ' "Auf Dein Wort hin". Eine Meditation zur priesterlichen Spiritualität' in J. Ratzinger – H. Volk – B. Henrichs *Auf Dein Wort him* (Cologne 1983) pp 15–36.

228. 'L'eucaristià al centro della communità e della sua misisone' (Collevalenza 1983).

229. 'Luther und die Einheit der Kirchen. Fragen an Joseph Kardinal Ratzinger' *Internationale Katholische Zeitschrift* 12

(1983) pp 568–582. E.T. 'Luther and the Unity of the Churches: An interview with Joseph Cardinal Ratzinger' in *International Catholic Review* 11 (1984) pp 210–226.

230. 'Orientaciones Cristológicas' Consejo Episcopal Latinoamericano – CELAM, *Cristo el Señor. Ensayos Teológicos* (1983) pp 5–22; also as [in revised form] 'Christologische Orientierungspunkte' in *Schauen auf den Durchbohrten* pp 13–40.

231. 'Schwierigkeiten mit der Glaubensunterweisung heute. Fragen an Joseph Kardinal Ratzinger' *Internationale Katholische Zeitschrift* 12 (1983) pp 259–267; Pastoralblatt für die Diözesen Aachen, Berlin, Essen, Hildesheim, Köln, Osnabrück 35 (1983) 196–203. E.T. 'Problems in Catechesis Today: An Interview with Joseph Cardinal Ratzinger' in *International Catholic Review* 11 (1984) pp 145–156.

232. 'La speranza elemento fondamentale che definisce l'esistenza del cristiano' *Osservatore Romano* 123 (10.6.1983) p 5.

233. 'Transmission de la foi et sources de la foi' in D. J. Ryan – J. Ratzinger – G. Daniels – F. Marcharski *Transmettre de la foi aujourd'hui* (Paris 1983) pp 41–61. E.T. 'Sources and Transmission of the Faith' in *International Catholic Review* 10 (1983) pp 17–34.

1984

234. 'Christliche Orientierung in der pluralistischen Demokratie? Über die Unverzichtbarkeit des Christentums in der modernen Gesellschaft' in *Pro fide et justitia. Festschrift für Kardinal Casaroli zum 70. Geburtstag* (ed.) H. Schambeck (Berlin 1984) pp 747–761; N. Lobkowicz (ed.) *Das europäische Erbe und seine christliche Zukunft* (Cologne 1985) pp 20–35.

235. 'Gesicht und Aufgabe einer Glaubensbehörde. Ein Gespräch mit Joseph Kardinal Ratzinger über die römische

THE THEOLOGY OF JOSEPH RATZINGER

Glaubenskongregation' *Herder-Koresspondenz* 38 (1984) pp 360–368.

236. 'Instrução sobre a Teologia da libertação (apresentação)' *Revista eclesiástica brasileira* 44 (1984) pp 691–695.

237. 'Kirchenverfassung und Umkehr. Fragen an Joseph Kardinal Ratzinger' *Internationale Katholische Zeitschrift* 13 (1984) pp 444–457.

238. 'Obispos, Teólogos y Moralidad' in J. L. Baragan (ed.) *Teología moral hoy* (Mexico 1984) pp 23–52.

239. 'Problemas principales de la teología contemporánea' *La Revista Católica* 84 (1984) Nr. 1063/64 pp 13–23.

240. 'Der Streit um die Moral: Fragen der Grundlegung ethischer Werte. Festvortrag am 31.5.1984 in Regensburg anläßlich der 72. Fortbildungstagung für Ärtze, Regensburg 1984' ibw-journal 10 (1985) pp 1–11.

241. 'Sulla speranza' *La speranza II* (ed. B. Giordani) (Brescia-Rome 1984). E.T. 'On hope' in *International Catholic Review* 12 (1985) pp 71–84.

242. (In collaboration) *Teología de la liberación: Documentos sobre una polémica* (San Jose, Costa Rica 1984).

243. 'Die Theologie der Befreiung' *Neue Ordnung* 38 (1984) pp 285–295.

244. 'Vi spiego la teologia della liberazione' 30 giorni. Mensile internazionale II (März 1984) pp 48–55.

1985

245. 'La celebrazione del sacramento con assoluzione generale' in La '*reconciliatio et paenitentia*' (Rome 1985) pp 136–145.

246. 'A Cristologia nasce de oração' *Questões actuais de Cristologia* ed. J. E. M. Terra (São Paulo 1985) pp 52–65.

247. 'L'ecclesiologia del Vaticano II' in J. Ratzinger et. al. *La Chiesa del Concilio* (Milan 1985) pp 9–24.

248. 'Glaube, Philosophie und Theologie' *Internationale Katholische Zeitschrift* 14 (1985) pp 56–66. E.T. 'Faith,

Philosophy and Theology' in *International Catholic Review* II (1984) 350–363; Pope John Paul II Lecture Series, College of St Thomas 1985, pp 10–14.

249. 'Guardinis theologischer Ansatz' in *zur debatte. Themen der Katholischen Akademie in Bayern* 15 (1985) pp 9f.

250. 'Liturgy and church music' *Sacred Music* 12 (1985) pp 13–22; and *Homiletic and Pastoral Review* 86 (1986) pp 10–22.

251. 'Neues Zueinander von Ethik und Wirtschaft. Einführungsvortrag zum Symposion "Kirche und Wirtschaft in der Verantwortung für die Zukunft der Weltwirtschaft" in der Päpstlichen Universität Urbaniana am 21.11.1985' *Osservatore Romano* (German edition) 15 (1985) Nr. 48 p 8.

252. 'Pourquoi la foi est en crise' *La Pensée Catholique* 1985 Nr. 214 pp 22–38.

253. 'Scopi e metodi del Sinodo dei vescovi' in J. Tomko (ed.) *Il Sinodo dei vescovi. Natura – metodi – prospettiva* (Vatican City 1985) pp 45–58.

254. 'Unità e pluralismo nella Chiesa dal Concilio al post-Concilio' *Bollettino diocesano per gli ufficiali e attività pastorali dell'arcidiocesi di Bari* 61 (1985) Nr. 1 *Orientamenti pastorali* 12 (1985) pp 125–144.

255. 'Von der Liturgie zur Christologie. Romano Guardinis theologischer Grundansatz und seine Aussagekraft' in J. Ratzinger (ed.) *Wege zur Wahrheit. Die bleibende Bedeutung von Romano Guardini* (Düsseldorf 1985) pp 121–144.

256. 'Vorwort' in J. Ratzinger (ed.) *Wege zur Wahrheit. Die bleibende Bedeutung von Romano Guardini* p 7.

257. 'Zum Sinn des Sonntags' *Pastoralblatt für d. Diözesen Aachen, Berlin, Essen, Hildesheim, Köln, Osnabrück* 37 (1985) pp 258–269; Forum katholische Theologie 1 (1985) pp 161–175; *Klerusblatt* 65 (1985) pp 209–214.

258. 'Vorwort' in J.-H. Nicolas *Synthése dogmatique. De la*

Trinité à la Trinité (Fribourg–Paris 1985) pp V–Vi.
259. 'Zuversicht für ein Leben in Freiheit. Das Ende des Krieges im Mai 1945' *Osservatore Romano* (German edition) 15 (1985) Nr. 18 p 11.

1986
260. 'Le baptême et la foi' *Al-Liqâ: Communio* 1 (1986) pp 15–24.
261. 'Geleitwort' in R. Spaemann – R. Löw – P. Koslowski *Evolutionismus und Christentum* (Weinheim 1986) pp VII–IX.
262. 'Freiheit und Befreiung. Die anthropologische Vision der Instruktion "Libertatis conscientia"' *Internationale Katholische Zeitschrift* 15 (1986) pp 409–424; *Osservatore Romano* (German edition) 15 (1985) Nr. 35 p 8f [résumé].
263. 'Kirche und Wirtschaft in der Verantwortung für die Zukunft der Weltwirtschaft' *Technik und Mensch* 1 (1986) pp 7–9.
264. 'Marktwirtschaft und Ethik' in L. Roos (ed.) *Stimmen der Kirche zur Wirtschaft* (Cologne 1986) pp 50–58.
265. 'Teses de Cristologia' in J. E. M. Terra (ed.) *Novo Testamento e Cristo* (São Paulo 1986) pp 3–5.
266. 'Theologie und Kirche' *Internationale Katholische Zeitschrift* E.T. *The Church as an Essential Dimension of Theology* (University of St Michaels College, Toronto 1986).
267. 'Zum Fortgang der Ökumene' *Theologische Quartalschrift* 166 (1986) pp 243–248.
268. 'Le pluralisme: problème posé à l'Eglise et à la théologie' *Studia Moralia* 24 (1986) pp 299–318.

C. Contributions to works of reference

Lexikon für Theologie und Kirche (ed.) J. Höfer – K. Rahner
(Freiburg 1957ff).

1. 'Auferstehung des Fleisches: I. Lehre der Kirche, VI. Dogmengeschichte, VII. Systematik' I (1957) pp 1042, 1048–1052.
2. 'Auferstehungsleib I (1957) pp 1052f.
3. 'Benedictus Deus' II (1958) pp 171ff.
4. 'Donatismus als Lehre' III (1959) pp 504f.
5. 'Ewigkeit: II. Theologisch' III (1959) pp 1268ff.
6. 'Gerhard von Borgo San Donnino' IV (1960) pp 719f.
7. 'Haus, Haus Gottes' V (1960) pp 32f.
8. 'Heil: II. Theologisch' V (1960) pp 78ff.
9. 'Himmel: III. Systematisch' V (1960) pp 355–358.
10. 'Himmelfahrt Christi: II. Systematisch' V (1960) pp 360ff.
11. 'Hölle' V (1960) pp 446–449.
12. 'Joachim von Fiore' V (1960) pp 975f.
13. 'Kirche: II. Die Lehre des kirchlichen Lehramtes, III. Systematisch' VI (1961) pp 172–183.
14. 'Leib Christi: II. Dogmatisch' VI (1961) pp 910ff.
15. 'Leichnam' VI (1961) pp 917ff.
16. 'Leibe: III. Geschichte der Theologie der L' VI (1961) pp 1032–1036.
17. 'Mittler: II. Dogmatisch' VII (1962) pp 499–502.
18. 'Neuheidentum' VII (1962) pp 907–909.
19. 'Primat' VIII (1963) pp 761–763.
20. 'Schöpfung' IX (1964) pp 460–466.
21. 'Sterben' IX (1964) p 1055.
22. 'Sühne: V. Systematisch' IX (1964) pp 1056ff.
23. 'Ticonius' X (1965) pp 180f.
24. 'Tradition: III. Systematisch' X (1965) pp 293–299.

Reallexikon für Antike und Christentum, founded by F. J. Dölger
ed. Th. Klauser (Stuttgart 1959ff).
25. 'Emanation' IV (1959) pp 1219–1228.

Die Religion in Geschichte und Gegenwart ed. K. Galling with H.
Frhr. v. Campenhausen, E. Dinkler, G. Gloege and K. E.
Logstrup (Tübingen 1957ff).
26. 'Protestantismus: III. Beurteilung von Standpunkt des
Katholizismus' V (1961) pp 663–666.
27. 'Katholische Theologie' VI (1962) pp 775–779.

Der Große Herder (Freiburg 1956ff).
28. 'Gottesbegriff und Gottesbild' XII (1962) (Supplementary
volume 2) pp 1087–1090.

Handbuch theologischer Grundbegriffe ed. H. Fries (Munich
1962ff).
29. 'Licht' II (1963) pp 44–54.
30. 'Stellvertretung' II (1963) pp 566–575.

Dictionnaire de spiritualité, ascétique et mystique, doctrine et histoire
ed. M. Viller with F. Cavallera and J. de Guibert (Paris
1937ff).
31. 'Fraternite' V (1964) pp 1141–1167.

Sacramentum mundi ed. K. Rahner and A. Darlap (Freiburg
1967ff).
32. 'Auferstehung des Fleisches: II. Theologie' I (1967)
pp 397–402.
33. 'Himmelfahrt Christ' II (1968) pp 693–696.

Meyers enzyklopädisches Lexikon. 9. (Mannheim-Vienna-Zürich
1971ff).
34. 'Christentum' 5 (1972) 669–671, 678–681.

INDEX OF NAMES

Tyconius, 133

Valentinus, 176, 177
Vanzan, P., 5
Varro, 48
Vaughan Williams, R., 217
Vaussard, M., 198
Vico, G. B., 107, 108
Vincent of Lérins, 226
Volk, L., 17
Vorgrimler, H., 76, 81, 114

Wagner, R., 5
Waldstein, M., 155
Webern, A, von, 218
Weigl, E., 199
Weiss, J., 160

Weiszäcker, C. F. von, 118
Wendel, J., 25
Werner, M., 156, 228
Wessenberg, I. H. von, 198
Wiederkehr, D., 157
William IV, 8, 20
William V, 8
William of St Amour, 135
William of St Thierry, 194
Wilpert, P., 61
Wiseman, N., 41

Zechariah, 103, 223
Zimmermann, H., 113
Zizioulas, J., 246
Zoepfl, F., 20
Zotto, C. B. del, 64